PAY

Billions of people throughout the world are paid for their work. This book was written to explain why they earn what they earn and, in doing so, to help readers understand how they can earn more in both the short and long run. It describes wages, wage differences across groups, wage inequality, how organizations set pay and why, executive and "superstar" pay, the difference between pay and "total rewards" (including benefits, opportunities for growth, colleagues, and working conditions), compensation in nonprofits, and the differences between the cost of compensation to organizations and the value employees place on that compensation. It also offers tips on what an individual can do to earn more.

Kevin F. Hallock is the Donald C. Opatrny '74 Chair of the Department of Economics and Joseph R. Rich '80 Professor and Professor of Economics and of Human Resource Studies at Cornell University in Ithaca, New York. He is also the Director of the Institute for Compensation Studies at Cornell. He previously served as Chair of Cornell's Financial Policy Committee. Professor Hallock is also a Research Associate at the National Bureau of Economic Research in Cambridge, Massachusetts, and Distinguished Principal Researcher on Executive Compensation at The Conference Board. He serves on the compensation committee of Guthrie Health and is a member of the WorldatWork Society of Certified Professionals Board. He has published in numerous academic journals including *The American Economic Review*, the *Journal of Economic Perspectives*, the *Journal of Corporate Finance*, *Labour Economics*, the *Journal of Public Economics*, and the *Industrial and Labor Relations Review*. His work has been discussed in the *Wall Street Journal*, *The New York Times*, *Barron's*, *Business Week*, *Time*, and *Newsweek*. He has authored, edited, or co-edited ten volumes and holds a PhD in economics from Princeton University.

To Tina, Emily, and Ty

Pay

*Why People Earn What They Earn
and What You Can Do Now to Make More*

KEVIN F. HALLOCK

Cornell University

CAMBRIDGE
UNIVERSITY PRESS

CAMBRIDGE UNIVERSITY PRESS
Cambridge, New York, Melbourne, Madrid, Cape Town,
Singapore, São Paulo, Delhi, Mexico City

Cambridge University Press
32 Avenue of the Americas, New York, NY 10013-2473, USA

www.cambridge.org
Information on this title: www.cambridge.org/9781107014985

First published 2012

Printed in the United States of America

A catalog record for this publication is available from the British Library.

Library of Congress Cataloging in Publication Data
Hallock, Kevin F., 1969–
Pay : why people earn what they earn and what you can do now to make more / Kevin F. Hallock.
p. cm.
Includes bibliographical references and index.
ISBN 978-1-107-01498-5
1. Wage payment systems. 2. Wages. I. Title.
HD4926.H33 2013
658.3′2–dc23 2012012296

ISBN 978-1-107-01498-5 Hardback

Contents

Figures

Tables

Acknowledgments

I have always been fascinated by how people are paid. I remember being a paperboy in western Massachusetts and being paid by the paper and with tips. Is this the right way to pay paper delivery people? Later I picked cucumbers and corn at a local farm. We were paid by the hour. In high school I worked at a lumberyard. There I was also paid by the hour. Why? From an early age my parents, Bob and Norma, encouraged me to ask questions – of any type – and encouraged me to work hard and study. They and my brother Bob were my first and most vital teachers. I then ran into some extraordinary teachers, including Kathy Masalski (at Hopkins Academy – the public high school in Hadley, Massachusetts), who helped me think critically and carefully and really helped me focus on the future. Starting in high school, both Mike and Carla Grabiec were an extraordinarily positive influence in my life and their impact is still felt today. Mike Podgursky, Dale Ballou, and Leonard Rapping taught me a lot of economics at the University of Massachusetts at Amherst and they and Deb Barbezat advised my undergraduate thesis – on compensation. David Card and Orley Ashenfelter were my PhD dissertation advisors in economics at Princeton University. Both are off-the-charts brilliant, extraordinarily funny, have been great role models, and taught me tons. I really lucked out when I ran into those two.

I also owe a great debt to my many colleagues at the University of Illinois in Urbana-Champaign where I taught for the first decade of my career. Wally Hendricks, Roger Koenker, Craig Olson, and Larry DeBrock were patient with a young colleague and spent many, many hours of their valuable time with me. They also treated my family like their own. Another friend and colleague from Illinois, Darren Lubotsky, read this entire manuscript and made his usual excellent comments. Todd Elder and I overlapped for several years at Illinois and I learned a lot from him. At Cornell, where I have been since, I am also blessed with many great colleagues. Ron Ehrenberg has motivated my interest in compensation since I first met him when, as a college sophomore, I saw him present a paper in Amherst on compensation "tournaments." I am very lucky to now be his colleague. I also have learned a great deal from my colleagues in the Department of Economics at Cornell. I am also in the Department of HR Studies at Cornell where Lee Dyer, Chris Collins, and Pat Wright in particular have taught me a lot about what really happens inside companies. George Milkovich, whose retirement opened the door for a new guy to come to Cornell to teach compensation, co-authored the classic textbook on compensation, and I have learned a great deal from him and his work. Darrie O'Connell, Theresa Woodhouse, and Jo Hagin have been incredibly kind and helpful to me in my time at Cornell. Bob Frank encouraged me to write this and gave me helpful advice along the way. Sam Bacharach, a constant source of energy and enthusiasm, motivated me to write this book, and suggested the title: "Just call it 'Pay'." My dean at Cornell, Harry Katz, has been extremely supportive of my research on compensation. He and Joe Grasso, Associate Dean at the ILR School, have been supportive of my work and supportive of the Institute for Compensation Studies at Cornell. I am grateful to them both. Chris Crooker, head of Alumni Affairs and Development at the ILR School, has been a constant supporter and an extremely helpful colleague. I am really lucky he is my friend. I also owe a great debt to my many students who have listened to and sometimes been critical of my ideas on compensation. They have helped me think more clearly about this work. Special thanks go to Sherrilyn Billger, Jamie Boderck, Joshua Rosenberg-Daneri, Amy Jordan, Felice Klein, Michael Strain, Doug Webber, and Ken Whelan. My editor at Cambridge University Press, Scott Parris, and his colleagues Frances Bajet, Adam Levine, and Kristin Purdy, have been important contributors to this work.

I have also learned a great deal about compensation and am grateful to my friends and colleagues in the real world, including Jim Abolt, Trevor Blackman, Bob Bluestein, Doug Braunstein, Jeff Chambers, Maggie Gagliardi, Anne Hatcher, Pam Kimmet, Don Opatrny, Anne Ruddy, Leslie Thornton, and especially Beth Florin. Beth is extraordinary and has supported my work in many ways. Selfishly, I would have loved to have asked my friend Joe Rich to discuss the final ideas in this book. Sadly, he passed away way too young. Linda Barrington is Managing Director of the Institute for Compensation Studies at Cornell. She is supersmart and organized and is an extraordinary colleague who understands the academic and practical worlds and has helped me immensely improve my work. Katherine Solis, Yeong Joon

(YJ) Yoon, Leo Ding, Lee Sager, and Victor Lei did an excellent job helping proofread the manuscript.

I am most grateful to my wonderful family. I met my wife Tina when we were four years old. I am so lucky she is part of my life. She also has been an invaluable resource for and critic of my ideas on compensation for decades and, more importantly, the glue that keeps our family together and happy. Emily and Ty are kind, compassionate, smart kids who, along with their mother, remind me of what is important. And finally Maggie, who sat with me while I wrote nearly every word in this book. Good dog, Maggie.

PART I

HOW HARD CAN THIS BE?

ONE

Common Sense, Economics, and HR

How to Pay

Billions of people throughout the world are paid for their work. This book was written to demonstrate why they earn what they earn and, in doing so, to help them understand how they can earn more in the short run and even more in the longer run. There are many ways pay is determined across a wide variety of organizations, from for-profit firms, to nonprofit organizations, to government agencies. By the time you finish reading this book, you will know how a well-run organization takes its overall strategy and converts that into a system for properly paying people. Then you can apply the lessons in the book to your own organization and take actions that can lead you to earn more.

But how difficult can this be? All we are trying to do is consider how and why people are paid the way they are paid. It turns out that this *is* difficult, but I will try to show you why firms and other organizations do what they do, and with this help, you will hopefully understand how you may be able to better navigate work and consider some things you can do to earn more. Many firms set pay on an ad hoc basis and, frankly, they don't really know what they are doing. Many others have sophisticated systems in place for how to set pay within their organizations. There are many variants to this latter approach, and I highlight these as we go through a basic system that is essentially used by most organizations.

Still other firms have unionized workplaces where wages, benefits, and working conditions are negotiated with labor unions. In addition, some people work for the government and have a set of pay scales that are determined in yet another way. The bulk of this book focuses on what many large employers do. What these companies do is important because it trickles down to many of the rest of the organizations that follow the lead. It is also the case that many of the lessons learned from the "standard" case are applied in unionized, nonprofit, and government settings. In any event, I stress the "standard" case but also point out these other special cases as we go along.

Consider two jobs and how you might best design a pay system for them: professional cucumber (pickle) picker and chief executive officer (CEO). What is the "right" *level* of pay for these occupations? Separately, *how* should each of these occupations be paid? Consider the simple example I first use every time I teach compensation to students, both undergraduate and graduate, as well as compensation practitioners and executives. I picked cucumbers on a small farm for four years when I was growing up. You probably don't know many professional cucumber pickers, but think for a minute about how much they should be paid. Ten dollars an hour? More? Less? Perhaps they should be paid a "market" wage – but what market? How is this determined? We will get to this as we go along.

A much more interesting question is *how* (relative to how much) to pay the pickers? Should they be paid by the pound? This makes sense on the surface, but "big" cucumbers are really not worth very much at all, especially relative to smaller cucumbers that can be made into pickles. Further, counting how many of each type each person picks is a demanding and expensive process that may not be worth the trouble. Another problem with paying by the pound is that workers might suffer too much risk from this. For example, when there is no rain for a period of time, the cucumber vines dry up and produce very few cucumbers, and if workers are paid by the pound then they don't earn much money. We will discuss later why it might be better for the company, rather than individual workers, to take on this risk.

It turns out that cucumber picking is much more complicated than it sounds: *institutions* matter and how the cucumbers are picked matters. Designing an effective compensation plan for cucumber pickers requires careful and clear knowledge of how cucumbers are picked. This is true when considering pay in *all* occupations. We will go into this in more depth later, but it turns out that professional cucumber pickers are largely paid by the hour.

Consider CEOs next. Some people think CEOs are paid too much. Why? They are paid way more than most of us, but is it too much? How is their pay determined? Is it a "real" labor market or, as some have suggested, is this a market that is not efficient and CEOs gain at the expense of others? Should CEOs be paid by the hour? Would it be better to motivate them and pay them by some sort of "piece rate" (similar to paying by the cucumber)? The piece rate for CEOs could be a measure of profitability, sales, or stock price. It turns out that these objective metrics are easier to measure than cucumbers but they may not always be the things you want CEOs to respond to. In the end, CEOs are typically paid partly for their time (salary) and partly for certain other measures of performance. This is not to say that they are paid correctly, and we will cover more of this as we go along.

One problem with the way firms pay is that it isn't always clear that they know the way they are paying is the right way to pay. Consider one set of companies (A) that pays its employees only in cash (salaries). Consider another set (B) that pays only in equity (stock and stock options). Further suppose that the companies in set A are less profitable than those in set B. Does this mean that it is better for the shareholders or owners of a given company to pay in stock and stock options? Maybe, but there is no way to know with the information I have provided you. Just because a particular Human Resource (HR) practice (e.g., paying mostly in salary) is associated with one set of firms and another practice (e.g., paying mostly in equity) is associated with another set of firms doesn't mean that either HR practice had an effect on profits. Maybe more profitable firms can afford to pay a certain way and the causality actually goes in reverse. It turns out that we could test this by having firms switch from one HR practice (e.g., switching from one form of pay to another) and observing what happens. But this is very hard to do in practice. Most managers don't have the time, energy, or resources to see what works best. They typically have to make a decision and move on. In many cases they pick a practice, declare "victory," and move on to the next issue, but they never *really* know if the practice "worked." Organizations can do more to learn about how to make themselves and their employees better off.

Another big issue is organization strategy and the difficulties it imposes. Imagine having to think about how to pay the CEOs of Bristol Meyers Squibb (BMS) and of Tupperware. Tupperware, among other things, designs and manufactures plastic products. These products can go from concept to consumer relatively quickly. Paying a CEO of Tupperware in a relatively short-term way (e.g., in part in an annual bonus) might make some sense. On the other hand, the time lag from concept to consumer in a company like BMS can be many, many years. Therefore, heavily relying on short-term bonuses may not make much sense. To make this even more complicated, certain BMS rivals – Astra-Zeneca (the British pharmaceutical company), for example – may also want to pay its CEO and other employees differently for competitive reasons of their own.

The rest of the book discusses some details about pay levels and differences in society and then discusses how organizations start with an organizational strategy, translate that into a compensation strategy, and, in turn, translate that into a pay system. It then goes on to discuss some suggestions for earning more in the short term and others that will lead to financial payoffs in the future.

Chapter 2 is about wages, the wage distribution, and wage inequality. This begins with a simple discussion of compensation differences. There have been dramatic differences in levels of pay between men and women, African Americans and others, the young and others, and many other groups. I discuss whether and why this is changing. This chapter goes on to discuss the extraordinarily wide distribution of income in the world and in the United States in particular. I discuss reasons for this dramatic level of income inequality and whether it is likely to change in the near future.

Chapter 3 discusses who makes what and their characteristics. This includes a list of occupations and a discussion of the level of compensation and benefits in those jobs, as well as the characteristics of people holding those jobs, including, among others, age, education, gender, levels of experience, and average seniority on the job.

Chapter 4 asks a simple but very rarely considered question: Is there a difference between the cost of compensation to organizations and the value of that compensation to employees? This idea is introduced by showing the wide disparity between cash compensation and the variety of benefits that employees earn. There is also wide diversity in the kinds of benefits employees receive. In fact, only about 70 cents for every dollar paid by organizations goes directly into the pockets of workers.

Part II of the book is mostly focused on how and why firms set their pay structure. This includes a discussion of the mechanics of how most large companies set pay. Chapter 5 discusses why where you work matters a lot. This includes a discussion of why it is important that an organization's business strategy and compensation strategy are linked and what the implications of that are for workers. Chapter 6 tackles job analysis, job evaluation, and internal comparisons. Job analysis is, in some sense, a description of jobs – even breaking jobs down into their most mundane and simple tasks. Jobs are then rated across a number of features to come up with "scores" across a variety of characteristics. In a second step, jobs are "evaluated" and scored by essentially rating them in a variety of dimensions along what are known as "compensable" factors. I was skeptical of this when I first learned about it, but this makes sense – rather than making subjective judgments about jobs, this type of system requires people to be explicit about what matters and how jobs are in some sense "ranked." Note that neither Chapter 5 nor Chapter 6 examines compensation at all. They simply discuss what was done in each occupation and the relative value of those jobs to *the organization in question.*

Chapter 6 continues with a discussion of internal comparisons. Internal comparisons of compensation are extremely difficult, but it is essential for organizations to consider carefully the relative value of each position in the company. If an organization does not make these kinds of difficult decisions early, then it will lead to arbitrary and capricious compensation decisions later. This can also lead to employee dissatisfaction and lawsuits. Having managers and employees truly understand how they are paid is very important.

In Chapter 7, I discuss the importance of collecting the right comparison data and matching the internal structure to external market data. If organizations do not make comparisons to the appropriate competitor firms, then much of the rest of the work discussed here is for naught. In this chapter, I show how we can take the internal structure developed in Chapters 5 and 6 and match that with data external to the firm (typically purchased from compensation consulting firms). In this step, the "benchmark" jobs that we focused on in Chapters 5 and 6 are individually matched with "benchmark jobs" from the consultants' data. This combination of internal work and data on jobs and external data on compensation levels for similar kinds of jobs forms the basis for the internal pay structure of the company. In this, we will see how companies with different strategies (e.g., BMS and Astra-Zeneca) may both optimally pay similar workers (e.g., salespeople) in different ways, even though both companies are in the same industry.

Paying people at the very high end of the compensation scale has a unique set of issues and problems. Chapter 8 focuses on the highly paid. Although there is discussion of athletes, entertainers, and other "superstars," the primary focus in this chapter is on executives, with particular emphasis on CEOs of publicly traded for-profit companies. This is not just a "trendy" issue that has come out of the recent financial crises; there has been scrutiny of the pay packages of CEOs for decades.

As I noted earlier, trying to determine *how* people are paid can be as (or more) important as *how much* they are paid. Part III is devoted to these and other issues. It begins with Chapter 9, which outlines the problems and difficulties of evaluating performance, as well as circumstances where incentive pay can be very useful and helpful, and others where providing incentives to workers can lead to unintended consequences and negative outcomes.

A large number of people, not just executives, are being paid in equity (stock and stock options). Chapter 10 describes stock and stock options and offers a guide to where they are and are not useful as a way to pay people. Equity compensation can have important incentive and retention value. But there are problems with equity pay, including the fact that some forms of equity are difficult for employees to understand and value, and there are important and changing accounting and tax consequences of equity compensation.

Although I don't really think of "pay" and "benefits" as separate subjects, the "mix" of pay and the interesting question of why employers offer any benefits rather than just pay workers cash are the subject of Chapter 11. Why not just pay cash and let the workers choose which benefits they want to purchase with their money? In addition to the obvious tax reasons for offering certain benefits (e.g., health insurance in the United States), many employers offer unique benefits. For example, Cornell University pays one-half of Cornell's tuition for each of my children if they attend Cornell and 30 percent of tuition if they attend some other college or university. Would I be better off with the cash equivalent to do what I want? What about my colleagues who don't have kids? They are essentially being paid less.

Surprisingly little is known about international compensation. In a recent meeting I had with a group of international compensation executives, we were all surprised at how much variability there was in answers with respect to basic "factual" questions about international pay. Based on some recent research and discussions with scores of multinational firms, Chapter 12 attempts to begin to remedy the situation. As companies are becoming more global, this is becoming increasingly important and is an area where managers could do small things well and increase their firms' profitability with much less effort than many other possibilities. Chapter 13 explores compensation in the nonprofit sector and suggests the similarities (of which there are many) and differences in pay in it, relative to the for-profit sector.

By Chapter 14 you will likely understand quite a bit about how organizations set pay. Then you can apply that to your own organization and think about what you can do to make more. This includes simple and obvious things like "do your work," "work hard," "be respectful of those who evaluate you and set your pay" and less obvious ones like being sure you understand the mission of the organization and what *you* do to meet that objective so that you may be able to increase your earnings while you help the organization. I also discuss what you can do in the long run to make more money, including training, continuous learning, not being afraid to change jobs or try something new, and even having a willingness to change occupations or move.

In Chapter 15, I offer a summary and some concluding thoughts. Again, designing pay plans and considering what you can do now (and later) is not rocket science. But it isn't easy either. I hope this book helps you learn more about how and why people are paid what they are paid, as well as how to earn more yourself.

TWO

Wages, the Wage Distribution, and Wage Inequality

This chapter focuses on four main areas. First, how much are people paid in the United States today – how are wages distributed? If you earn $25 per hour, is that relatively highly paid or not? Second, we will consider the issue of wage inequality. Given the obvious news about CEO pay levels, clearly *some* people are paid extremely high wages, but how many? Do a large fraction of people earn less than $10 per hour? Do a large fraction earn more than $50 per hour? After we establish the "spread" in wages across different kinds of workers, we will turn to the question of whether wage patterns and wage inequality have changed over time. Using data from the U.S. Census Bureau over a thirty-year period, I document that the "spread" in wages in the United States has, in fact, changed quite dramatically in the last generation. Next, I document the difference between CEO pay and that of "other" workers. As has been documented, the difference between CEO pay and most other workers' pay has increased greatly in the last generation. In this chapter, we explore what this means and foreshadow a deeper discussion of executive compensation, which we pick up again in Chapter 8. Finally, I discuss the intergenerational correlation and transmission of wages. That is, if you have a wage that is particularly high or low, how likely are your children to have the same kind of wage?

What do Wages Look Like in the United States?

The "median" wage in the United States was $16.83 per hour in 2010.[1] This means that just as many people earned more than $16.83 per hour that year as earned less than that. It was the "middle" wage. Is this number big or small? Your answer to that question may depend on whether you or your friends or family or people you know make more or less than that amount (more on this later). A few years ago, I took a group of (roughly

Table 2.1. *Hourly wage distribution in the United States in 2010*

| | Percentile of the wage distribution | | | | | | |
	5th	10th	25th	50th	75th	90th	95th
All	7.28	8.25	11.00	16.83	25.83	38.46	48.08
Women	7.25	8.00	10.03	15.00	23.07	34.00	42.95
Men	7.50	8.75	12.00	18.75	28.85	42.85	52.45
High School Graduate							
Female	7.00	7.70	9.36	12.35	16.97	23.00	27.88
Male	7.50	8.50	11.00	15.55	22.50	30.00	36.25
College Graduate							
Female	8.65	10.25	14.42	20.19	29.72	40.85	50.00
Male	10.00	12.02	17.79	26.43	38.46	52.45	60.08

Source: Author calculations from Outgoing Rotation Group Files of Current Population Survey (CPS) from the National Bureau of Economic Research (NBER).

eighteen year-old) Cornell University freshman undergraduate students to a local manufacturing facility as part of a class project. When we were talking with the head of HR for the plant, one of the students asked what the "starting hourly wage" was for the plant. We were told that it was about $13.50 per hour. It was interesting to see that some students thought that $13.50 was so *much* money and others thought it was so *little* money. On average, those students who came from families that had lower wages thought that was a lot and those students who came from higher-earning families thought it was little.

Assuming that a full-time worker works 52 weeks in a year and 40 hours per week, then he or she is working 2,080 hours a year. Therefore, at the median wage in the United States, this person would be earning $16.83 × 2,080 = $35,006 per year.

The median hourly wage is just a single simple statistic and, obviously, there is much more to be learned about wages in the United States. Table 2.1 shows a few other statistics on the distribution of hourly wages in the United States. For example, if one earned $11 per hour, he or she would be at the 25th percentile. That is to say, he or she would be earning more than one-quarter of those working but less than three-quarters of those working. If one earned $8.25 per hour, he or she would be earning more than only one in ten people (10 percent) and would be earning less than 90 percent of those working. For a worker working 2,080 hours a year (52 weeks times 40 hours per week), this amounts to $17,160 in annual income. At the other end of the spectrum, the top row of Table 2.1 also shows that if one were earning $38.46 per hour, then he or she would be earning more per hour than 90 percent of those working and less than only 10 percent of those working. Earning $48.08 would put one at the 95th percentile of the wage distribution. That is, only 5 percent (one in twenty) of workers earn more. Again, for someone working 2,080 hours (52 weeks times 40 hours per week), this amounts to $48.08 × 2080 = $100,006 per year.

As is well known, on average, men and women earn considerably different levels of wages. There is even a reference to the "gender gap" in the bible! Chapter 27 of Leviticus states " . . . for persons between the ages of 20 and 60, the fixed sum, in sanctuary shekels, shall be 50 silver shekels for a man, and thirty shekels for a woman." This "ratio" of 60 percent (30/50) is actually wider than the current estimated gap, but for some time in the United States women did earn about 60 cents for every dollar men earned.

Of course, just cutting the wage distribution data by percentiles also masks a great deal of interesting heterogeneity by different kinds of workers. As an example, the second and third rows of Table 2.1 split the data by gender. Men earn more per hour than women. Several potential explanations for this are covered in Chapter 3. At the median, women earn $15.00 per hour and men earn $18.75. Just as many women earn more than $15.00 per hour than women who earn less than $15.00 per hour. And just as many men earn more than $18.75 per hour as earn less than $18.75 per hour. Within the male and female samples, there is quite a bit of variation in wages. At the 5th percentile (95 percent earn more and only 5 percent earn less), women earn $7.25 per hour.[2] Women at the 10th percentile earn $8.00 per hour, at the 25th percentile $10.03, the 75th percentile $23.07, the 90th percentile $34.00, and the 95th percentile $42.95. As was the case at the median, men also earn more at all points in their wage distribution than women. At the 5th percentile, men earn $7.50 per hour, at the 10th percentile $8.75, the 25th percentile $12.00, the 75th percentile $28.85, the 90th percentile $42.85, and the 95th percentile $52.45. Figure 2.1 plots the entire distribution of male hourly wages in the left-hand panel and the entire distribution of female hourly wages in the right-hand panel.[3] The horizontal axis in each panel displays the hourly wage. The vertical axis reports the fraction of the data that are in each "bin" of data. The curved line in each figure is a "normal distribution" overlaid over each figure. The vertical line represents the median of the entire distribution ($18.75 for men and $15.00 for women). The figure plainly shows that men's wages are higher (to the right) of women's at all points in the distributions.

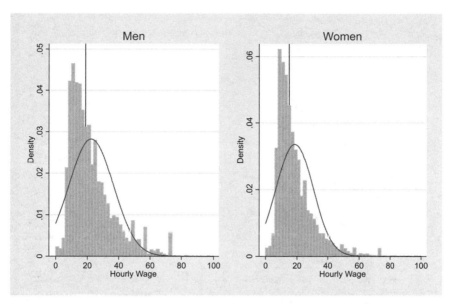

Figure 2.1. Hourly Wage Distribution by Gender, United States 2010. *Source:* Author calculations from Outgoing Rotation Group Files of Current Population Survey (CPS) from the National Bureau of Economic Research (NBER).

Has Wage Inequality Changed Over Time?

As is plainly clear from the preceding discussion, not all wages are the same. In fact, there is a great deal of dispersion in wages. Some have very high wages and some have very low wages. But has this always been the case? Figure 2.2 is the start of an attempt to investigate this issue using data from thirty-two years, from 1979 through 2010. As the figure plainly shows, over this entire time period, there has been wage dispersion. However, wages have become progressively more disperse over the time period. The left-hand panel of Figure 2.2 plots the 5th, 25th, 50th, 75th, and 95th percentiles of the wage distribution each year from 1979 through 2010. Take 2010, for example. The figure shows that wages at the 95th percentile are $48.08, at the 75th percentile they are $25.83, and so on. The figure also shows that as we go back to previous years of data, the percentiles get closer together, so the wages are less disperse. In fact, it is plain to see that the lower percentiles of the wage distribution have increased little over time, especially relative to the upper percentiles of the wage distribution. For example, the 95th percentile of the wage distribution was about $12 per hour in 1979 and rose to more than $48 per hour in 2010. At the other end of the spectrum, the

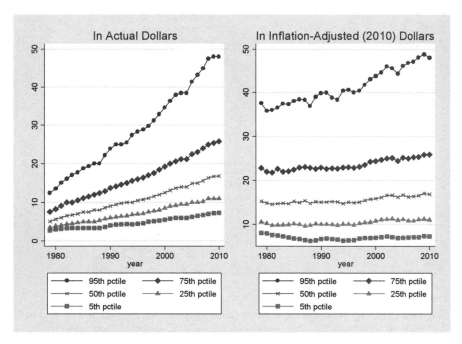

Figure 2.2. Wage Percentiles by Year, United States 1979–2010. *Source:* Author calculations from Outgoing Rotation Group Files of Current Population Survey (CPS) from the National Bureau of Economic Research (NBER).

5th percentile of the wage distribution was less than $4 per hour in 1979 and rose to only slightly higher than $7.28 per hour in 2010. The right-hand panel of Figure 2.2 plots the same data but "adjusts" for inflation. That is, it recalculates the figure so that all numbers are in inflation-adjusted (to 2010) dollars.

Another (common) way to think about wage inequality is to take the ratio of some of the numbers from Figure 2.2 by year. Figure 2.3 displays information from four different measures of inequality that are each interesting. Consider the left-hand panel of Figure 2.3 first. This figure plots what is called the 90-to-50 ratio (90th percentile's hourly wage/50th percentile's hourly wage), which is a measure of inequality, by year. The figure shows that in 1979, the 90th percentile's wage was slightly more than two times the 50th percentile's wage. This grew steadily over time to about 2.25 times in 2010. The 50-to-10 ratio (50th percentile's hourly wage/10th percentile's hourly wage) also rose over this time period. The 50-to-10 ratio was about 1.75 in 1979 and rose quickly by the mid-1990s and then flattened out and is now about 2.0. So those at the 50th percentile of hourly wage earn a

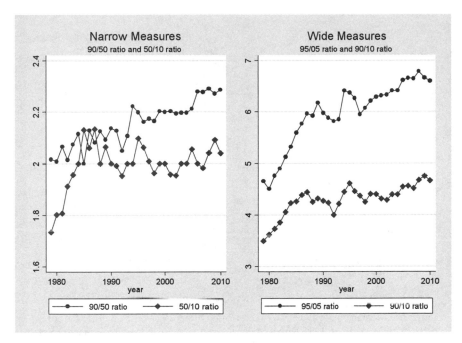

Figure 2.3. Wage Inequality by Year, United States 1979–2010. *Source:* Author calculations from Outgoing Rotation Group Files of Current Population Survey (CPS) from the National Bureau of Economic Research (NBER).

little bit more than twice as much as those at the 10th percentile of hourly wages.

The right-hand panel of Figure 2.3 displays two other measures of wage inequality.[4] These are "wider" measures of inequality in that they are comparing percentiles that are farther apart. The 90-to-10 ratio was about 3.5 in 1979. That is, those at the 90th percentile of the wage distribution earned 3.5 times that of those who earned at the 10th percentile. This number has grown rather steadily over the past three decades to around 4.75 in 2010. The 95-to-5 ratio is obviously even larger. This was about 4.8 in 1979 and has grown to about 6.6 in 2010. So those that are at the 95th percentile of wages earn about 6.6 times more than those at the 5th percentile of earnings.

Why has this happened? Why are the rich getting richer and the poor getting (relatively) poorer? There is actually a great deal of debate (and academic writing) about this by economists and other social scientists. There are a number of interesting explanations, some of which we will get into later in this book. The explanations include a change in the "rate of

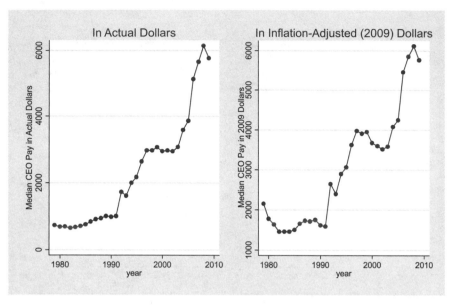

Figure 2.4. Median Total CEO Pay by Year, United States 1979–2009. *Source:* Author calculations from (a) 1979–1991 *Forbes Magazine* annual compensation issues from Kevin Murphy, (b) 1992–2006 Standard and Poor's ExecuComp, (c) 2007–2009 Salary.com. Data are based on the 800 largest firms for which data were available each year.

return" to education over time. That is, investing in education has had an increasingly higher payoff over time. Another reason for the change in wage inequality that has been suggested is the change in certain labor market institutions, such as the minimum wage and labor unions. Labor unions have been associated with relatively high wages, and because labor unions have been in decline, some have argued that this has lead to increased wage inequality. An additional argument is called skill-biased technological change, whereby there have been increasing "returns" to certain sets of skills and those who have them have experienced wage growth whereas those who do not have not. We will discuss several of these in other parts of the book.

CEO Pay Compared to the Rest
In any discussion of pay inequality, it doesn't take long for someone to bring up the issue of chief executive officers (CEOs). Chapter 8 is devoted entirely to the issue of CEO pay and the pay of other very highly compensated people. In this section, however, the issue of levels of CEO pay and CEO pay relative to the general population of workers is discussed. In Figure 2.4,

I have used data from three different sources to plot the level of CEO compensation over the past three decades. One data source, for the years between 1979 and 1991, is the Annual Compensation Issues of *Forbes* Magazine. The second data source, covering the years between 1992 and 2006, is Standard & Poor's ExecuComp. The third data source, for the 2007–2009 period, is Salary.com/Kenexa. The samples are adjusted so that they capture roughly the 800 largest firms (as measured by market value) in the United States each year. The left-hand panel of Figure 2.4 shows that CEO pay was relatively stable for the first few years of the period and then increased sharply.[5] In any event, CEO pay has increased sharply over the last three decades. This is plainly seen if we consider actual dollars (in the left-hand panel of Figure 2.4) or inflation-adjusted dollars (in the right-hand panel of Figure 2.4). The median CEO in the sample earned slightly less than $6 million in 2009. This pay includes salary, bonus, non-equity incentive pay, stock, stock options, pension, and other pay. These types of pay are discussed in much more detail in Chapter 8. It is also interesting to note that total compensation actually fell for CEOs from 2008 to 2009 as a result, in part, of the financial crisis.

We all know that CEOs are paid large amounts of money. But how are they paid *relative* to "regular" workers? The panels of Figure 2.5 are an attempt to consider this. The top left figure plots the ratio of the median CEO's pay to the 5th percentile of annual compensation for workers in the United States.[6] So this is essentially the ratio of CEO pay to "typical" low-wage worker pay in the United States each year.[7] In 1979, this ratio was about 140. Therefore, the "typical" CEO earned about 140 times the pay of a "typical" low-wage worker. It is easy to see in the top left panel of Figure 2.5 that this ratio remained relatively flat during the 1980s. This ratio stayed flat because both the CEO pay and the pay of the worker at the 5th percentile were both relatively "flat" over the decade.

However, starting in the early 1990s, CEO pay increased dramatically. This is the result, in part, of the increasing use of "equity" (stock and stock options) and the fact that the stock market took off at this time. However, low-wage workers' pay remained relatively stagnant, so the ratio of CEO pay to low-wage worker pay increased dramatically to about 400 by 2009. This means that the "typical" CEO earned on the order of 400 times the pay of the "typical" low-wage worker. Many have argued that this is inappropriate. Again, there is a much deeper discussion of CEO compensation in Chapter 8.

When most groups show figures like that in the upper left panel of Figure 2.5, they compare CEO pay to low-wage worker pay, just as I have

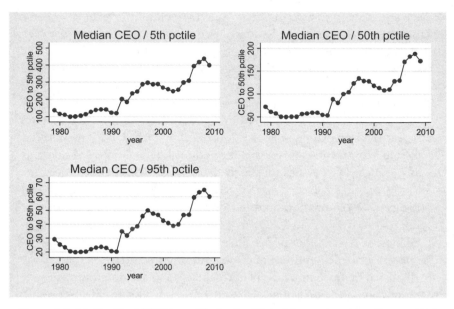

Figure 2.5. Median Total CEO Pay to Worker Pay, United States 1979–2009. *Sources:* CEO compensation data based on author calculations from (a) 1979–1991 *Forbes Magazine* annual compensation issues, (b) 1992–2006 Standard and Poor's ExecuComp, (c) 2007–2009 Salary.com. CEO data based on the 800 largest firms for which data were available each year. Worker data from author calculations from Outgoing Rotation Group Files of Current Population Survey (CEO) from the National Bureau of Economic Research (NBER).

done. However, that is only one comparison. Why not compare the pay of the median CEO in the sample to the median worker in the sample (not the "typical" low-wage worker – or worker at the 5th percentile of the wage distribution as I have done in the top left panel of Figure 2.5)? The top right panel of Figure 2.5 compares the pay of the median CEO to the pay of the median worker in the United States. This ratio starts out much lower and increases at a much slower rate. This is not at all surprising, because we saw earlier that wages of the median worker increased relatively quicker than those of low-wage workers. So the "typical" CEO earned about 75 times the annual wages of the "median" worker in 1979. This gap increased to about 175 times by 2009.

The final panel of Figure 2.5 compares the pay of the "typical" CEO to the annual earnings of the person at the 95th percentile of the wage distribution. In 2009, this is essentially comparing CEO pay to someone who earns about $100,000 per year. Remember: this roughly represents those who earn more than 19 out of 20 people. These kinds of employees may be (in terms of perhaps education), on average, more comparable to CEOs. In any event, as the bottom left panel in Figure 2.5 shows, in 1979, CEOs earned about 30 times the pay of people at the 95th percentile of the wage distribution. This ratio remained relatively flat until the 1990s, when it increased quite sharply. Now, the "typical" CEO earns about 60 times the pay of people at the 95th percentile of the wage distribution. None of this is to say that these levels are "reasonable" or "appropriate." Rather, ratios and comparisons that are made can sometimes be misleading. It is important to always keep in mind exactly what is being compared to what. There is more on this throughout the book, including when we get back to CEO pay in Chapter 8.

If Your Parents Make a Lot of Money, Will You Too? What If They Don't?

Now that diversity in the wage distribution has been documented, we turn to the question of whether wages are "sticky" across generations. That is, if you have high wages, is it likely that your children will also have high wages? Or, if you have low wages, is it likely that your children will have low wages? If one were to prefer to live in a society where one can "pull herself up by her bootstraps" or that "anything is possible," then she would like to live in a place where the relationship between one's wages and those of her parents (or children) is low. This means that even if your wages are low, this does not sentence your child to a life of low wages.

Early work in this area by Becker and Tomes (1979 and 1986) suggested that the "intergenerational correlation" between wages in the United States was about 0.2, which is relatively low and implies a relatively high level of wage mobility from one generation to another. A practical way to think about this is to ask how many generations it would take for a particular wage disadvantage between two families to go away? These early estimates by Becker and Tomes suggest that any earnings disadvantage would disappear after three generations.

Later work by Zimmerman (1992) and Solon (1992), after taking into account a number of technical issues, has suggested that earnings mobility in the United States is considerably lower (that is, a higher correlation between the incomes of generations in the same family) than previously estimated. More recently, Mazumder (2005), using higher-quality data, has suggested that even those estimates are "too small." The bottom line is that the most recent estimates in this area of research suggest that earnings mobility in the United States is much lower than originally thought. That is to say, if your parents have high earnings, you are quite likely to as well. Unfortunately, if your parents have low earnings, you are more likely to have the same. Of course, there are many exceptions.

A related question about the correlation in earnings between generations is why? Is it "nature" or "nurture"? That is, can this be something that an individual can change? Is the correlation stemming from the fact that some parents are able to (or choose to) invest more in their children than others? If, for example, parents with low earnings have trouble borrowing to invest in the education of their children, then there could be a link between parent's earnings and wealth and children's education and then earnings.[8]

This chapter has tried to carefully demonstrate that people earn wildly different wages in the United States and that this has been changing over the past three decades. Why do people earn different wages? This is, in part, because of differences in education and training and to changes in institutions and technology. The next chapter explores in more detail who makes what and begins to explore why.

THREE

The Facts

Who Makes What And What Are Their
Characteristics?

As was discussed in the previous chapter, there is a wide diversity in the wages of workers in the United States. This chapter is a closer investigation of wage differences. This includes a discussion of specific occupations. It is important to consider wages *within* occupations. Next, it is important to think about why wages differ. This includes a discussion of the variation in wages by gender, race, age and education. Some characteristics are measurable and easily seen by employers (e.g., age, education) and others are more difficult for employers to observe (e.g., motivation, organizational ability, leadership). Additionally, some of these are alterable by the worker (e.g., education) and some are clearly not (e.g., age). This chapter also confronts the issue of dramatic pay differences (for the same levels of measurable characteristics) by different regions of the country (variation by country around the world is explored in Chapter 12). The chapter concludes by showing how you can find the pay of people who do your job in your region of the country. This is very easy to do on the Internet using freely available government data sources.

Wage Differences by Occupation

In May 2010, there were more than 127 million people working for pay in the United States alone. We know this by examining the U.S. Department of Labor Occupational Employment Statistics (OES). From this same data source we can also see that, for example, in May 2010, approximately 3.2 million people worked in "protective service occupations" (see Table 3.1 for the kinds of occupations included in this grouping). The occupations are simply chosen as an example and as a way to begin the broader discussion of occupations generally. Take, as an example, detectives and criminal investigators, of which, according to Table 3.1, there were 110,640 in May 2010.

Table 3.1. *Hourly wages nationally for protective service occupations*

Occupation	Employment	Hourly wage, mean and percentiles					
		Mean	10th	25th	50th	75th	90th
All Occupations	127,097,160	21.35	8.51	10.65	16.27	26.08	39.97
Protective Service Occupations	3,187,810	20.43	9.05	11.80	17.63	26.53	35.69
First-Line Supervisors of Correctional Officers	39,920	28.02	16.69	19.95	26.88	34.44	43.29
First-Line Supervisors of Police and Detectives	102,200	38.83	22.42	29.04	37.62	46.37	59.44
First-Line Supervisors of Fire Fighting and Prevention Workers	58,800	34.56	19.93	25.65	32.81	42.43	53.42
First-Line Supervisors of Protective Service Workers, All Other	55,190	23.40	12.60	16.44	22.17	28.32	36.05
Firefighters	302,400	22.95	11.08	15.38	21.76	28.80	36.25
Fire Inspectors and Investigators	13,050	27.00	16.45	20.25	25.11	33.04	40.99
Forest Fire Inspectors and Prevention Specialists	1,530	19.33	10.04	12.81	16.78	24.41	32.91
Bailiffs	17,310	19.67	9.12	13.01	18.54	26.34	31.93
Correctional Officers and Jailers	457,550	20.57	12.52	14.97	18.77	25.25	32.33
Detectives and Criminal Investigators	**110,640**	**35.10**	**18.68**	**24.05**	**33.08**	**43.63**	**57.37**
Fish and Game Wardens	7,240	26.75	14.97	18.16	23.91	29.85	39.06

Table 3.1 *(continued)*

Occupation	Employment	Hourly wage, mean and percentiles					
		Mean	10th	25th	50th	75th	90th
Parking Enforcement Workers	9,430	17.37	9.69	12.89	17.01	21.43	25.29
Police and Sheriff's Patrol Officers	644,300	26.74	15.24	19.63	25.74	33.21	40.15
Transit and Railroad Police	3,540	26.89	17.57	21.07	26.12	32.43	38.70
Animal Control Workers	15,040	16.35	9.48	12.25	15.41	19.78	24.93
Private Detectives and Investigators	28,210	22.99	12.38	15.69	20.61	27.95	36.05
Gaming Surveillance Officers and Gaming Investigators	6,620	15.87	9.85	11.80	14.75	19.09	23.87
Security Guards	1,006,880	12.92	8.23	9.39	11.50	14.92	19.83
Crossing Guards	68,740	12.43	8.13	9.19	11.35	14.58	17.94
Lifeguards, Ski Patrol, Recreational Protective Service Workers	117,540	9.98	7.64	8.21	9.06	10.82	13.74
Transportation Security Screeners (federal only)	42,430	18.10	15.11	16.39	17.82	19.22	21.56

Source: U.S. Department of Labor's Occupations Employment Statistics (OES) as of May 2010, www.bls.gov/oes/current/oes_nat.htm

This is a very specific occupation with very specific sets of knowledge, skills, and abilities expected and certain professional expectations and procedures required. Even though there is a common set of knowledge, skills, abilities, standards, and expectations in this very specific occupation, there is a wide diversity on how people working in the occupation are paid.

Table 3.1 shows that the average (mean) hourly wage for detectives and criminal investigators in 2010 was $35.10. However, even though this is a very specific occupation, that one number masks a large set of differences in pay for people who work in this occupation. Detectives and criminal investigators at the "low end" of the distribution of pay for the occupation earn an hourly wage of $18.68. That is, those at the 10th percentile (90 percent of detectives and criminal investigators earn more) earn $18.68. At the median (half earn more and half earn less), detectives and criminal investigators earn $33.08. At the 90th percentile (only 10 percent earn more), detectives and criminal investigators earn $57.37. But why are there such differences? There is a wide variety of reasons including region of the country, age, experience, training, education, and a host of less easily measured characteristics (e.g., motivation, work ethic) that can also factor into pay. We will focus on some of these in this chapter and throughout the rest of the book. Elementary school teachers and health care support occupations will also get some special attention in the chapter – again, just as examples. There are a host of other specific examples of protective service occupations in Table 3.1, including fire inspectors and investigators (median hourly wage $25.11), correctional officers and jailers (median hourly wage $18.77), bailiffs (median hourly wage $18.54), parking enforcement workers (median hourly wage $17.01), animal control workers (median hourly wage $15.41), and crossing guards (median hourly wage $11.35). So even within the protective service occupations, there is significant heterogeneity in wages across occupations.

The problem with just statistics on wages from certain occupations is that people cannot just pick any occupation they want, nor can we switch (without cost) from one occupation to another. When I was in college, my (future) father-in-law (then a police detective) drove me back to my dorm late one night after I had dinner with him, his wife, and his daughter (now my wife). On the way back to the dorm he had on his police radio and we heard that a "grand theft auto" chase was in progress! This is not the kind of "grand theft auto" that my son plays on his video game console; this was a *real* chase. My father-in-law (armed with his radio and a flashlight) sped in his personal pickup truck in the direction of the chase. He cut off the perpetrators *with me in the truck*. I was exhilarated and terrified. He eventually got them off the road and out of the stolen car and on the ground until uniformed officers cuffed them and took them away. In retrospect, this was a lot of fun – especially since "we" got the bad guys.

But if I decided tomorrow that I wanted to switch from being an economist to being a detective (like my father-in law, who sadly passed

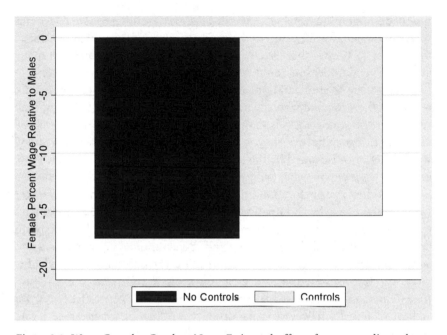

Figure 3.1. Wage Gaps by Gender. *Notes:* Estimated effects from an ordinary least-squares regression of the natural logarithm of the hourly wage on the characteristic. The controls include race (white, black, and other), age (age and its square), schooling (less than high school, high school, some college, college, and more than college), union coverage (indicator variable), industry controls (21 of them), occupation controls (22 of them), and state indicator variables. *Source:* Author calculations from Outgoing Rotation Group Files of the Current Population Survey (CPS) 2010 from the National Bureau of Economic Research.

away too young in 2001), I could surely apply for jobs as a detective, but given that I have no training at all in the area, I would have no hope of landing a job. I just don't have the right credentials and experience. In the next section, we will examine a set of easily measured characteristics of workers, such as education, age, gender, and race, in terms of their relation to different levels of wages. Of course, these are not the only characteristics that are related to wages. But they are some, and economists and other social scientists are often interested in them.

Wage Differences by Age, Gender, Race, and Education

Figure 3.1 considers the "gender wage gap" in the United States. This shows that, on average, the female hourly wage is a little more than 18 percent lower than the male hourly wage. Keep in mind that this doesn't "control" for any type of demographic variable(s); it is just the average difference between the wages of men and women, arrived at using the same data source I outlined in Chapter 2. Why is there such a large difference in wages between men and women? One reason could be discrimination against women. This is a difficult issue to study and one that I do not specifically focus on in this book, but there are many excellent references for those interested.[1] Another reason for this average gap is that men and women have different levels of experience. If men have more years of work experience than women and if work experience is valued by the labor market, then part of the "raw" (no controls) wage gap may be owing to experience.

Yet another reason for the difference could be that men, on average, work in higher-paying occupations than women. For example, if elementary school teachers are relatively more likely to be women and accountants are relatively more likely to be men, and if accountants are paid, on average, more than women, then not controlling for occupation will yield a larger gap between the wages of men and women, relative to the gap estimated that controls for occupation. In the right-hand bar of Figure 3.1 the "adjusted" female-male wage gap is displayed. Adjusting for age, race, levels of schooling, union coverage, occupation and industry controls, and state of residence (e.g., on average, people in Connecticut are paid more than people in Nebraska), women earn about 15 percent less than men.[2] So the "adjusted" wage gap is smaller but still exists.

Why isn't it zero? Why, after these controls are applied, aren't men and women paid the same? First, I have only controlled for a certain set of characteristics. For example, I have not controlled for actual work experience (in part because it is notoriously difficult to collect), city of residence, or very detailed occupation and industry codes (I only controlled for broad industry and occupation). Nor have I controlled for other issues that may be present, including nepotism, discrimination, motivation, organizational ability, and so forth. So, in fact, there are potentially many "unmeasureables" (or at least not measured in this case) in this analysis. Again, this is meant to illustrate differences in wages among groups, not to develop a definitive estimate of wage gaps of any particular type.[3]

Figure 3.2 also shows wage gaps, but this time by race. In the left-hand side of the figure, the first bar shows that the "raw" (no controls) hourly wage of those identified as "black" is 15 percent less than that of those identified as "white." However, as with the discussion of gender previously, this comparison has no "controls" for the fact that people also differ by gender, occupation, the region in which they live, their age, and so on. Once a set of controls is used (that is holding age, gender, schooling levels, occupation,

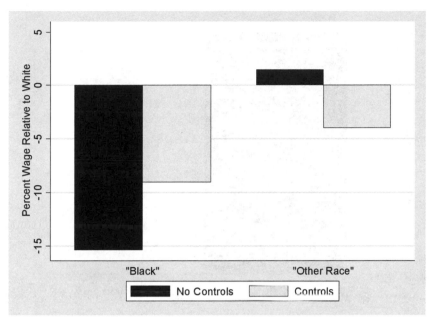

Figure 3.2. Wage Gaps by Race, Relative to "White" Workers. *Notes:* Estimated effects from an ordinary least-squares regression of the natural logarithm of the hourly wage on the characteristic. The controls include gender, age (age and its square), schooling (less than high school, high school, some college, college, and more than college), union coverage (indicator variable), industry controls (21 of them), occupation controls (22 of them), and state indicator variables. *Source:* Author calculations from Outgoing Rotation Group Files of the Current Population Survey (CPS) 2010 from the National Bureau of Economic Research.

and industry constant), those identified as "black" earn 9 percent less than those identified as "white."

The same can be done for the group identified as "other race" relative to those identified as "white." The "raw" (no controls) gaps is 1 percent *positive* – that is, those identified as "other race" earn, on average, 1 percent more per hour than those identified as "white." However, once other characteristics (the same ones used as controls in Figure 3.1) are controlled for, the wage gap goes the other way – those identified as "other race" earn 4 percent less than those identified as "white." Note that exactly the same discussion about the interpretation of these numbers as was put on those of gender can be done here. The hourly wage differences by race after controlling for all of the other characteristics does not control for all of them, and the remaining gap could be as a result of discrimination, nepotism, and a host of other reasons. Once again, this is meant to illustrate differences in wages among

Figure 3.3. Wage Bonus for Additional Year of Age. *Notes:* Estimated effects from an ordinary least-squares regression of the natural logarithm of the hourly wage on the characteristic. The controls include gender, race (white, black, and other), age-squared, schooling (less than high school, high school, some college, college, and more than college), union coverage (indicator variable), industry controls (21 of them), occupation controls (22 of them), and state indicator variables. *Source:* Author calculations from Outgoing Rotation Group Files of the Current Population Survey (CPS) 2010 from the National Bureau of Economic Research.

groups, not to develop a definitive estimate of wage gaps for any particular group.

Age is the next easily measured characteristic by which wages vary. In fact, there is quite a bit of history of the study of age and experience on wages. As displayed in Figure 3.3, on average, for each additional year of age, people are paid about 8 percent higher wages. In fact, it is a little bit more complicated than this. The "rate of return" (percentage extra pay for each additional year) to age is "steeper" at younger ages but then flattens out over time. In other words, for each additional year of age in the early stages of one's career, one can expect to have faster increases in wages per year than later in life. But, on average, and controlling for nothing else, for each additional year of age, one earns about 8 percent more.

However, just as in the case of gender and race, age surely is not the only determining factor. Age is essentially a "proxy" for both what we first think of – experience – and other things such as different kinds of jobs. Among lawyers, new associates are relatively young and relatively low paid. However, judges are relatively highly paid and they are relatively older. So if we just consider age when examining the wages of lawyers, we will overestimate the "effect" of age. In fact, once we "hold constant" our set of control variables (including, again, gender, race, industry, occupation, schooling, union coverage, and state of residence), the "effect" of age is cut to about 5 percent. That is, after controlling for other characteristics, the wage bonus is only about 5 percent per extra year of age (and a reasonable fraction of that is likely a result of labor market experience – older workers are more experienced and could, as a result and in some circumstances, be more valuable to their employers).

The final characteristic we will consider closely in this section is education. In a landmark study, Gary Becker (1964), of the University of Chicago, suggested that "human capital" factors can be considered just as physical capital. Just as we can invest in machines or companies and expect an economic return to these investments, we can invest in education or "human capital." These investments could be training (on or off the job) or formal education. Becker won the Nobel Prize in economics in 1992 for this, among other contributions to social science.

Figure 3.4 shows four levels of schooling and the "returns" to those levels of schooling, relative to someone with exactly a high school education. The four comparison groups are: (1) less than high school, (2) greater than high school but less than college, (3) exactly college, and (4) more than college. Figure 3.4 shows the "raw" (no controls) differences, on average, between someone with exactly a high school education and the other groups. Those with less than high school earn, on average, 27 percent less than those with exactly a high school degree. Those with some college earn 9 percent more than those with exactly high school degree, those with a college degree earn 62 percent more than those with a high school degree, and those with more than a college degree earn 109 percent more than those with exactly a high school degree.[4]

With education, as with race, age, and gender, the results are generally more tempered, once occupation, industry, state, gender, race, and other characteristics are controlled for. One of the reasons that attorneys are paid more than administrative assistants is that for most jobs, the level of education required for attorneys is higher than that for administrative assistants. So once we control for occupation and other measurable characteristics of the jobs and those in the jobs (a distinction that will be made more explicit in Part II of this book), the "returns" to education are smaller but still

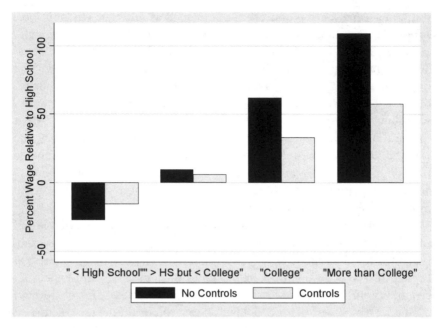

Figure 3.4. Wage Gaps by Education Level, Relative to High School Education. *Notes:*
Estimated effects from an ordinary least-squares regression of the natural logarithm of
the hourly wage on the characteristic. The controls include gender, race (white, black, and
other), age (age and its square), union coverage (indicator variable), industry controls
(21 of them), occupation controls (22 of them), and state indicator variables. *Source:*
Author calculations from Outgoing Rotation Group Files of the Current Population
Survey (CPS) 2010 from the National Bureau of Economic Research.

substantial. For example, after controls, those without a high school degree
earn, on average, about 15 percent less than those with a high school degree.
Also, after controlling for the common set of characteristics that have been
controlled for in this chapter, those with some college earn 6 percent more
than those with exactly a high school degree, those with a college degree
earn, on average, 33 percent more than those with exactly a high school
degree, and those with more than a college degree earn, on average, 57
percent more than those with exactly a high school degree.

Does Education Cause Higher Wages?

Considering that there are differences in average wages by levels of education is one thing. Trying to disentangle whether the differences are *causal* is
altogether more difficult. Do we really know, for example, that people with

college degrees earn more than people with high school degrees because the education caused them to be more productive? Or could it, among other reasons, just be that the kinds of people who do relatively well in school (and therefore found it easier to get through college) would have earned higher wages, even in the absence of schooling? This is an extremely complicated question. One way we would study this would be to "randomly" assign people to levels of schooling – just the way a biologist would randomly assign some patients to a "treatment" group for a drug trial and others to a "control" group with a sugar pill and not the real drug. Later we could observe the outcomes for the two groups to see if the drug worked. We obviously can't manipulate schooling levels in a similar way because of ethical considerations. But some economists have come close by studying twins in a clever way. Orley Ashenfelter and Alan Krueger (1994) among others, have shown that schooling, in fact, does have a *causal* economic payoff.[5] However, the "returns" estimates they come up with are considerably more complicated than those discussed in this chapter.

This is not to say that some people with relatively lower levels of education cannot earn relatively larger amounts of money. No doubt, you can think of many examples of people with high levels of education and low wages and people with low levels of education and high wages. This is just meant to say that *on average*, education pays. But education is obviously only one piece, albeit an extraordinarily important one, of the compensation puzzle.

It is again worth mentioning that some of the characteristics that have been discussed here are measureable. For example, it is quite easy to measure someone's age, gender, race, and level of education. It is considerably more difficult to measure their trustworthiness, motivation, discipline, and organization – all of which (and many other characteristics) may also matter to one's wage and could reveal themselves over time. Note also that some of these measures can be "improved." One can work harder, get more schooling, or on-the-job training. Other characteristics are much more difficult to alter. Again, we will discuss these and other things that can be done to earn more in the short run and longer run in Chapter 14.

Regional Differences in Pay

Another issue to think about when considering who makes what is *where* the work is being done. This section does not focus on offshoring or outsourcing jobs to other countries (the related topic of International Compensation is the subject of Chapter 12). Rather, we will consider similar jobs in different parts of the United States. When I took my first academic job as an Assistant Professor of Economics at the University of Illinois at Urbana-Champaign, a very good friend of mine took a job as an Assistant Professor of Economics at the University of California, Los Angeles (UCLA). We were doing essentially the same job but in two entirely different cities. The costs of living and standard of living in Los Angeles and Champaign are dramatically different. But we were paid essentially identical wages. This is *extremely* unusual and was a strange artifact of the standardized labor market for new PhDs in economics at the time.

In most occupations, however, wages differ dramatically by region of the country. Table 3.2 provides "pay relatives" for large occupational groupings in metropolitan areas in the United States as of July 2010. The data are from the National Compensation Survey (NCS) of the U.S. Department of Labor. Consider the first column of Table 3.2, labeled "all occupations." Consider first "Hartford-West Hartford-Willimantic, CT" with a score of 125. This means that across all occupations, those in this region near Hartford, Connecticut are paid 25 percent more than the nation as a whole.[6] On the other hand, "Lincoln, NE" has a score of 97. This means that across all occupations, those in this region are paid about 3 percent less than the nation as a whole. The panels of Table 3.2 make similar comparisons across seventy-five different regions in the United States.

A similar sort of analysis can also be done in the remaining columns of Table 3.2 within occupations. For example, management, business, and financial occupations pay about 15 percent less in Corpus Christi, Texas, than they do nationally. Similarly, management, business, and financial occupations pay 15 percent more in the Salinas, California area. As another example, in Springfield, Massachusetts, transportation and material-moving workers earn about 15 percent more than the national average, whereas workers in similar occupations in Johnstown, Pennsylvania, earn about 7 percent less than the national average. Table 3.2 makes similar comparisons for nine major occupational categories.

How You Can Find Out if Your Pay Stacks Up to Others in Your Occupation and Region

An additional issue to consider in thinking about who makes what is how you can figure out how your individual pay stacks up relative to similar workers in similar areas. Although many think this is a difficult question to handle, especially given how secretive most people are about how much

Table 3.2. *Relative pay for major occupational groups by metropolitan area*

Metropolitan area	All Occupations	Management, business, and financial	Professional and related	Service	Sales and related	Office and administrative support	Construction and extraction	Installation, maintenance, and repair	Production	Transportation and material moving
National Average	100	100	100	100	100	100	100	100	100	100
Amarillo, TX	98	101	94	100	104	102	106	112	91	100
Atlanta-Sandy Springs-Gainesville, GA-AL	110	108	119	106	104	114	104	109	101	114
Austin-Round Rock-San Marcos, TX	105	99	108	102	111	107	102	125	93	105
Birmingham-Hoover, AL	105	99	116	110	97	110	96	113	97	108
Bloomington, IN	101	101	103	96	93	104	100	108	108	108
Bloomington-Normal, IL	112	97	121	111	112	110	142	100	120	108
Boston-Worcester-Manchester, MA-NH	124	110	130	126	117	129	138	131	112	120
Brownsville-Harlingen, TX	90	90	104	99	77	91	82	92	83	83
Buffalo-Niagara-Cattaraugus, NY	109	102	106	113	100	106	129	113	114	110
Charleston-North Charleston-Summerville, SC	105	97	115	98	114	104	100	111	112	106
Charlotte-Gastonia-Rock Hill, NC-SC	111	108	114	109	112	114	105	121	104	103
Chicago-Naperville-Michigan City, IL-IN-WI	119	112	126	118	112	121	155	127	106	113
Cincinnati-Middletown-Wilmington, OH-KY-IN	112	111	114	111	120	114	96	116	106	114
Cleveland-Akron-Elyria, OH	112	109	116	111	107	116	131	130	104	110
Columbus-Marion-Chillicothe, OH	112	102	113	114	113	116	129	119	107	107
Corpus Christi, TX	101	85	107	98	98	99	116	126	100	99

(*continued*)

Table 3.2 (continued)

Metropolitan area	All Occupations	Management, business, and financial	Professional and related	Service	Sales and related	Office and administrative support	Construction and extraction	Installation, maintenance, and repair	Production	Transportation and material moving
Dallas-Fort Worth, TX	110	105	118	104	111	113	108	114	97	109
Dayton-Springfield-Greenville, OH	107	107	109	113	104	104	111	114	103	108
Denver-Aurora-Boulder, CO	114	104	118	118	115	118	113	129	104	109
Detroit-Warren-Flint, MI	114	105	123	107	107	113	124	114	122	112
Elkhart-Goshen, IN	104	104	105	112	103	107	124	100	96	109
Fort Collins-Loveland, CO	113	103	115	114	107	110	120	154	111	116
Grand Rapids-Wyoming, MI	111	96	116	113	124	114	126	106	105	104
Great Falls, MT	102	103	91	115	100	94	116	111	86	108
Greenville-Mauldin-Easley, SC	106	106	109	108	101	108	93	95	114	106
Hartford-West Hartford-Willimantic, CT	125	115	129	133	116	129	135	131	113	116
Hickory-Lenoir-Morganton, NC	106	100	99	105	99	103	114	109	107	110
Honolulu, HI	117	111	119	128	113	110	139	127	116	103
Houston-Baytown-Huntsville, TX	111	108	124	103	111	114	108	113	101	103
Huntsville-Decatur, AL	110	112	120	104	108	107	109	109	102	104
Indianapolis-Anderson-Columbus, IN	106	92	113	105	89	110	117	119	108	105
Iowa City, IA	109	105	110	111	106	116	142	108	101	114
Johnstown, PA	99	93	100	105	99	102	114	91	91	93
Kansas City, MO-KS	110	100	118	107	110	109	115	117	110	120
Kennewick-Pasco-Richland, WA	118	110	116	123	116	118	129	118	99	117
Knoxville, TN	101	104	116	88	102	102	104	107	94	102

Lincoln, NE	97	84	99	102	89	102	99	102	95	101
Los Angeles-Long Beach-Riverside, CA	120	116	126	125	117	121	131	127	103	113
Louisville/Jefferson County-Elizabethtown-Scottsburg, KY-IN	107	95	113	111	109	111	120	107	107	96
Memphis, TN-MS-AR	106	103	112	98	108	110	110	111	96	100
Miami-Fort Lauderdale-Pompano Beach, FL	108	111	105	110	108	112	116	114	100	108
Milwaukee-Racine-Waukesha, WI	114	107	114	111	118	114	139	116	111	113
Minneapolis-St Paul-St Cloud, MN-WI	120	109	120	129	116	119	134	126	113	123
Mobile, AL	101	105	107	100	94	105	123	96	99	112
New Orleans-Metairie-Kenner, LA	109	100	121	100	110	113	109	123	115	113
New York-Newark-Bridgeport, NY-NJ-CT-PA	127	129	134	128	118	130	155	128	110	112
Ocala, FL	98	90	100	99	97	107	97	106	88	101
Oklahoma City, OK	103	103	106	106	107	99	139	98	84	113
Orlando-Kissimmee-Sanford, FL	101	95	99	104	102	104	115	110	104	114
Palm Bay-Melbourne-Titusville, FL	102	87	103	105	105	101	117	110	101	110
Philadelphia-Camden-Vineland, PA-NJ-DE-MD	117	111	123	113	106	123	129	125	102	114
Phoenix-Mesa-Glendale, AZ	110	113	122	110	110	112	104	114	98	108
Pittsburgh-New Castle, PA	106	95	112	105	103	108	115	111	104	105
Portland-Vancouver-Hillsboro, OR-WA	118	108	121	124	115	120	127	132	108	109
Providence-New Bedford-Fall River, RI-MA	116	101	124	118	112	121	137	128	117	112
Reading, PA	113	111	125	108	111	115	121	112	106	108
Reno-Sparks, NV	112	116	116	111	112	116	117	121	105	109

(continued)

Table 3.2 (continued)

Metropolitan area	All Occupations	Management, business, and financial	Professional and related	Service	Sales and related	Office and administrative support	Construction and extraction	Installation, maintenance, and repair	Production	Transportation and material moving
Richmond, VA	109	103	113	105	106	115	108	119	103	107
Rochester, NY	113	110	119	115	114	113	122	112	110	116
Rockford, IL	109	94	110	113	109	110	139	111	102	113
Sacramento-Arden-Arcade-Truckee, CA-NV	121	112	129	124	118	116	141	128	121	117
Salinas, CA	126	115	136	138	135	121	140	139	96	118
San Antonio-New Braunfels, TX	103	97	113	103	98	106	117	113	93	99
San Diego-Carlsbad-San Marcos, CA	120	113	125	129	118	117	128	124	104	110
San Jose-San Francisco-Oakland, CA	134	116	142	141	135	136	154	144	113	119
Seattle-Tacoma-Olympia, WA	125	113	128	137	118	122	139	120	119	127
Springfield, MA	120	104	129	125	107	120	138	113	109	115
St Louis, MO-IL	112	103	119	109	108	115	128	129	101	106
Tallahassee, FL	98	83	96	103	100	102	116	104	88	99
Tampa-St Petersburg-Clearwater, FL	104	102	104	108	101	109	112	105	93	101
Virginia Beach-Norfolk-Newport News,VA-NC	103	94	109	101	101	107	105	113	94	96
Visalia-Porterville, CA	111	93	124	120	111	105	114	115	107	107
Washington-Baltimore-Northern Virginia,DC-MD-VA-WV	122	113	131	118	119	126	127	130	111	114
York-Hanover, PA	109	108	118	108	106	107	122	108	106	111
Youngstown-Warren-Boardman, OH-PA	102	105	105	101	100	104	109	111	104	95

Source: The National Compensation Survey (NCS) of the U.S. Department of Labor, USDL: 09–0843, July, 2010.

36

they are paid, it is surprisingly simple to find specific information about wages in very specific occupations in very specific areas, and here I will show you how.

The first place one can go to find out about wages in a particular occupation is O*NET Online (http://onetcenter.org). O*NET is the successor to the U.S. Department of Labor "Dictionary of Occupational Titles." This source will prove very useful in Part II of this book – specifically in Chapter 6 on job analysis, job evaluation, and internal comparisons. For any given occupation, O*NET provides details about tasks required in the job, tools and technology used in the job, knowledge, skills, and abilities necessary in the job, work activities, work context, work styles, and work values. In the occupation "Elementary School Teachers, Except Special Education,"[7] examples of tasks include "observe and evaluate students' performance, behavior, social development, and physical health" and "establish clear objectives for all lessons, units, and projects and communicate those objectives to students." For the purposes of this occupation, "knowledge" is defined to include such things as mathematics, geography, and psychology. O*NET also provides median wages for each occupation, and includes estimates of employment and projected employment growth over the next decade. It is a very useful source for those looking for wage information, specifics about what is actually done in occupations, and an estimate for the future demand for the work.

An alternate route for one to look up specific details on occupational wages within very specific regions is Occupational Employment Statistics (OES) from the U.S. Department of Labor. This source can be accessed from www.bls.gov/oes/data.htm. I compiled the data in Table 3.3 using this source. I was interested in what health care support occupations were paid in and around Barnstable, Massachusetts (note: very specific occupations, very specific region). It is very easy to recover these data. From www.bls.gov/oes/data.htm, a series of multiple-choice options are given, such as: (1) multiple occupations for one geographic area (say, you are living in one place and are considering different occupations) or (2) one occupation for multiple geographic areas (say, you have a chosen occupation but are considering different places in which to live). I chose health care support occupations for multiple geographic areas. In the next step, one is prompted to choose one or more geographic areas. I chose just one: Barnstable, Massachusetts. Finally, one is prompted to choose the types of data he or she may find of interest. I chose employment levels, hourly wages and percentiles, and annual earnings and percentiles.

Table 3.3. *Finding pay for people who do what you do where you do it: Hourly wages by specific occupation and specific region (healthcare support occupations, Barnstable, MA, May 2010)*

		Hourly wage, mean and percentiles					
	# people	Mean	10th	25th	50th	75th	90th
Health Care Support Occupations	3740	15.32	10.23	11.79	14.12	17.68	22.81
Home Health Aides	960	12.72	9.6	10.77	12.57	14.71	16.32
Nursing Aides Orderlies and Attendants	1680	14.1	10.28	11.58	13.52	15.93	19.04
Occupational Therapy Assistants	30	26.3	14.44	23.9	27.25	30.84	34.01
Occupational Therapy Aides	60	17.04	12.54	13.93	16.24	18.26	22.61
Physical Therapist Assistants	80	27.5	20.3	22.31	26.04	31.03	34.89
Physical Therapist Aides	30	12.72	9.38	10.61	13.04	14.54	15.61
Massage Therapists	50	20.74	9.15	13.53	18.9	22.98	39.14
Dental Assistants	280	21.43	16.61	19.22	21.74	24.22	26.05
Medical Assistants	300	18.94	12.51	14.52	17.89	23.24	26.99
Medical Transcriptionists	30	18.14	12.26	13.34	17.56	23.14	25.77
Pharmacy Aides	N/A	11.13	8.89	9.55	10.74	12.37	14.03
Vet Assist and Lab Animal Caretakers	60	15.38	9.93	13.36	15.71	17.56	20.09
Health Care Support Workers All Other	60	17.56	12.84	14.53	17.38	20.39	22.85

Source: U.S. Bureau of Labor Statistics Occupational Employment Statistics (OES), May 2010. Extracted October 2011 from www.bls.gov/oes/data.htm

The results of the data gathered from the OES are summarized in Table 3.3 (for hourly wages). This table shows, for example, that dental assistants in Barnstable, Massachusetts, earn, on average, $21.43 per hour and the median wage is $21.74. The 10th percentile wage for this occupation in this region is $16.61 and the 90th percentile is $26.05. Similar statistics can be seen from the table for other health care support occupations in Barnstable, Massachusetts. Tables like this can be easily made for any occupation by following the simple steps in this section.

In this chapter, we looked within the large variation in wages. To do this we considered gender, race, education, age, region of the country, occupation, and other characteristics of jobs. We also began to consider what people can do about earning more by examining some things we can alter (such as how much training we have or our level of education) and some we, sadly, can't do anything about (such as our age). We also considered ways to use the Internet to look up wages and salaries for nearly any occupation in nearly any region in the United States.

The next chapter outlines the difference between "wages and salaries" and total compensation. Although many people are fixated on the former, I show that a significant fraction of total compensation (for many people) comes in the form of non-wage and non-salary benefits such as health insurance, vacation time, and holidays.

FOUR

The Difference Between Wages and Total Compensation

Is There a Difference Between Employee Value of Compensation and the Cost to Organizations?

Given my work with companies and with practitioners who set compensation for their employees, I don't think there is enough communication between employers and employees regarding costs of compensation versus value to employees. Employees often know what they are "paid" or, at least, what they "take home" or even their taxable income. But most people don't truly understand how much their total compensation *costs* their employer. This chapter first discusses the fact that employers pay for many things that employees don't directly see in their paychecks. What are employer costs of employee compensation? The chapter also suggests that employers that pay relatively more in non-direct-paid compensation should communicate they do this so as to gain an advantage over their competitors. Third, the chapter suggests that employees should spend time trying to figure out what their employers pay in terms of *total* compensation, relative to competitor firms. Finally, the chapter discusses that employers could better elicit the *value* employees place on certain forms of compensation and explicitly suggests specific examples where the cost of compensation to the firm varies from the value employees place on compensation and what the implications of these issues may be.[1] Later in the book (in Chapter 11) we will cover more detail on why firms provide certain forms of pay (e.g. bonus) over other forms (e.g. salaries) and why firms offer certain benefits.

Employer Costs of Employee Compensation (It's a Lot More Than Wages)

How much does it cost employers to have certain workers on hand? This sounds a little bit like what we were exploring in Chapter 2, but it is distinctly different. Previously we were studying the *hourly wages* of workers in the United States. In this section, the focus is on the *cost to employers* for each hour worked. The cost per hour for each hour worked is considerably higher. The data for this analysis come from a Federal Government Survey called "Employer Costs of Employee Compensation." This survey covers roughly 62,700 occupations from a sample of 13,200 establishments in private industry and roughly 11,700 occupations from a sample of about 1,900 establishments in state and local governments.[2] These data are much different than the data used in Chapter 2 and part of Chapter 3. Those data were asked of individuals about their earnings. These data come from questions that are asked of employers about some of the occupations within their organizations. The surveys are incredibly detailed and complicated and can take up to three hours to complete.

The beauty of the "Employer Costs of Employee Compensation" data is that they provide a rich view of the costs employers face for employing workers. Table 4.1 is an example of the kinds of data that are collected. According to the September 2011 survey, the total cost of employing an average worker in the United States was $30.11 per hour. This is the first row, labeled "total compensation," in Table 4.1. Of this, the table shows that $20.91 per hour is in wages and salaries and $9.21 *per hour* is in "benefits." So the average worker is paid more in benefits per hour than more than 10 percent of the U.S. working population earns in wages per hour (see Table 2.1).

So we know that the average worker costs firms $30.11 per hour and of that $20.91 (69.4 percent) is in wages and salaries and $9.21 (30.6 percent!) is in other forms of compensation. This is a striking figure that, I feel, is underappreciated by many workers. These numbers are just averages and many workers don't enjoy any decent benefits.

What are these benefits that make up a cost of $9.21 to employers? A related question that we will get to later is whether employees even know these are costs to the firm and whether employees perceive (some of) them as benefits to themselves as individuals. Of the $9.21 per hour, $2.07 (on average) is for paid leave time. So 6.9 percent ($2.07/$30.11) of the costs to employers for each hour worked can be traced to paid leave. Again, this is obviously zero for those who have no paid leave and higher than 6.9 percent for many who do have paid leave. This paid leave consists of vacation (3.3 percent), holiday (2.1 percent), sick time (1.1 percent), and personal time (0.4 percent).

Some workers are paid cash in addition to their normal wages or salaries. For the overwhelming majority of workers who are paid extra, this money comes in the form of overtime and "other premium pay" such as shift differentials and nonproduction bonuses. Overall, on average, supplemental

Table 4.1. *Employer costs per hour worked*

	All workers		Management, professional, and related		Service	
	Cost	Pct.	Cost	Pct.	Cost	Pct.
Total Compensation	30.11	100.0	50.11	100.0	16.48	100.0
Wages and Salaries	20.91	69.4	35.01	69.9	11.71	71.0
Total Benefits	9.21	30.6	15.10	30.1	4.77	29.0
Paid Leave	2.07	6.9	3.96	7.9	0.91	5.5
Vacation	1.00	3.3	1.87	3.7	0.43	2.6
Holiday	0.64	2.1	1.19	2.4	0.29	1.7
Sick	0.32	1.1	0.68	1.4	0.15	0.9
Personal	0.11	0.4	0.23	0.5	0.04	0.3
Supplemental Pay	0.73	2.4	1.20	2.4	0.30	1.8
Overtime and Premium	0.25	0.8	0.15	0.3	0.17	1.0
Shift Differentials	0.06	0.2	0.11	0.2	0.05	0.3
Nonproduction Bonuses	0.42	1.4	0.95	1.9	0.08	0.5
Insurance	2.67	8.9	4.03	8.0	1.39	8.5
Life	0.05	0.2	0.10	0.2	0.02	0.1
Health	2.54	8.4	3.78	7.5	1.35	8.2
Short-Term Disability	0.05	0.2	0.07	0.1	<0.01	<0.05
Long-Term Disability	0.04	0.1	0.08	0.2	<0.01	<0.05
Retirement and Savings	1.38	4.6	2.59	5.2	0.64	3.9
Defined Benefit	0.85	2.8	1.55	3.1	0.50	3.1
Defined Contribution	0.53	1.8	1.04	2.1	0.14	0.8
Legally Required Benefits	2.36	7.8	3.31	6.6	1.54	9.3
Social Security and Medicare	1.69	5.6	2.73	5.4	0.98	5.9
Social Security	1.35	4.5	2.15	4.3	0.79	4.8
Medicare	0.34	1.1	0.58	1.2	0.19	1.2
Federal Unemp. Insurance	0.02	0.1	0.02	<0.05	0.02	0.1
State Unemp. Insurance	0.20	0.7	0.19	0.4	0.17	1.0
Workers' Compensation	0.45	1.5	0.38	0.8	0.36	2.2

Source: National Compensation Survey, September 2011.

pay accounts for 2.4 percent of the total hourly costs of workers. This breaks down into 0.8 percent for overtime and premium pay, 0.2 percent for shift differentials, and 1.4 percent for nonproduction bonuses. Note that each of these types of supplemental pay end up in the workers' paychecks. This money comes as actual income.

The next major cost – and it is significant – is insurance. Different types of insurance cost employers an average of $2.67 per hour, or 8.9 percent of the total cost of employing each worker per hour. This is almost entirely attributable to health insurance, which makes up 8.4 percent of the hourly total costs of employing the average worker. The rest is made up by life insurance (0.2 percent), short-term disability insurance (0.2 percent), and long-term disability insurance (0.1 percent).

The next substantial category is retirement and savings. All of these numbers are independent of any retirement saving an employee may save on his or her own. The average cost to employers for retirement savings is $1.38 per hour (or 4.6 percent) of total hourly employee costs. Of this, 2.8 percent of the total compensation costs goes toward defined benefit pension plans and 1.8 percent goes toward defined contribution pension plans. There has been a dramatic shift away from defined benefit and toward defined contribution plans in the past two decades. In defined benefit plans, the employer agrees to pay a preset amount per month upon retirement, usually based on a function of years of service and highest earnings while working. On the other hand, defined contribution plan money is put into an account and invested and that money can be withdrawn at retirement. In contrast to defined benefit plans, defined contribution plan payouts depend on how much money is contributed and how the money is invested.

The last major category of employer costs includes those legally required. Employers are required to pay for a set of benefits (including social security, Medicare, unemployment insurance, and workers compensation insurance) that amount to an average of $2.36 per hour per worker (7.8 percent of total hourly employee costs). Of this, 4.5 percent of total hourly costs is for Social Security, 1.1 percent of hourly costs is for Medicare, 0.1 percent is for federal unemployment insurance, 0.7 percent is for state unemployment insurance, and 1.5 percent is for workers' compensation insurance. Please note that only some of these benefits are required of firms to pay; others are not. But remember, on average, roughly 30 percent of the cost of an average worker does not go directly into the pocket of the worker – these are simply costs firms face.

What is Your Total Compensation?

When I teach executives or other practitioners, I show them the numbers just noted here and then I have them think about whether they communicate these kinds of things to their employees. And should they? If you were an employer and had very high costs of employee compensation that were not paid out directly in cash to the employees – say, you have very generous health insurance, life insurance, vacation time, and personal time – wouldn't you want to tell this to your employees? Yes, you would. Why? You want to do this to let the workers know they are actually being "paid" much more than their hourly wage. One important point I hope to impress upon my audience regularly is that pay is a lot more than the basic hourly wage or salary. And if you owned a company or were a supervisor in some organization, wouldn't you want to tell your employees about all of these additional "benefits" that actually have value and should be considered? But many companies for some reason don't do a very good job of this. It would be easy to do better. Employers who pay more should use that to their advantage, relative to their competitors – given that they are essentially paying more – and could, on average, attract better workers.

On the other hand, imagine that you are an employer and you have relatively poor benefits (e.g., you don't have good health insurance, you don't offer vacation or sick time, there are no bonuses). If you are an employer in this sort of an organization, you probably want to be pretty quiet about the "total compensation" package. Why? Because if you have almost no non-wage and non-salary benefits, your total compensation = wage and salary + 0 = wage and salary. Why would you want to publicize that you have lousy benefits? That would not be smart.

But what if you are not a compensation practitioner or an HR professional setting pay or designing compensation systems? Should you care about this? Yes, absolutely. The reason that employees should be aware of this is so that they can be better informed when they shop for jobs. If you are considering two new jobs and one offers an hourly wage of $17.00 and the other offers an hourly wage of $18.00, which one should you take? You don't have enough information? True. Let's suppose the working conditions, coworkers, hours, and general culture of the organizations are similar and that you expect to work 2,000 hours per year in either job. This means you would earn $34,000 in the first one and $36,000 in the second one. Which should you take? I still don't think you have enough information. What if I told you all of the benefits were the same except that the first one offered you health insurance for free (that you decide you need) and that the second one offered the same insurance (that you still need) that would cost you $500 per month. This essentially means that the first job will "pay" you $34,000 and give you insurance and the second one will "pay" you $30,000 = ($36,000–12 × $500) = ($36,000–$6,000).[3] Therefore, the job that has a higher hourly wage actually has substantially lower total compensation.

It is also interesting to consider differences in wages and salaries versus benefit levels for different kinds of workers. For example, Table 4.1 not only displays the breakdowns for all workers, but also the fraction of total compensation that comes from non-wage and salary components for two subgroups of workers: management, professional, and related occupations ("management") and service occupations.[4] As is clear from Table 4.1, the fraction of total compensation costs from firms that are attributable to benefits is 30.6 percent for all occupations. For management occupations, the fraction attributable to benefits is 30.1 percent, whereas for service occupations, the fraction attributable to benefits is 29.0 percent. So, these are really not that different from one another. On the other hand, if we look more closely into the kinds of benefits that make up these numbers, we do see substantial differences. For example, paid leave is 6.9 percent of total compensation cost for all occupations, 7.9 percent of total compensation costs for management occupations, and only 5.5 for service occupations. On average, service-related jobs have much less paid leave as a fraction of the total compensation cost. Management occupations also have higher fractions of benefits costs than service occupations for the categories of supplemental pay (2.4 versus 1.8 percent) and retirement and savings (5.2 versus 3.9 percent). However, management occupations have a lower fraction of total compensation than service occupations for legally required benefits (6.6 versus 9.3 percent) and insurance (8.0 versus 8.5 percent). Health insurance is particularly interesting. In that category, management occupations have employer costs of $3.78 per hour (7.5 percent of total compensation costs for those occupations) versus service occupations that have health insurance costs of $1.35 per hour (8.2 percent of total compensation costs for those occupations). So even though employers of managers pay much more per hour for health insurance for those workers (presumably it is "better" insurance) relative to service workers, because service workers are paid so much less per hour, the fraction of total compensation costs attributable to health insurance is actually higher in service occupations.

I provide these examples to try to highlight that I think it is extremely important for employees to truly understand what and how they are being paid. There are two other examples that I'd like to include here. Both are very specific and don't apply to very many workers, but they are relevant in that they are examples that folks can use in other situations. Firms pay in all sorts of strange ways. Think of the particulars of your own organization and think about the value of certain types of pay to you. The first example is stock options. Some workers in some organizations receive stock options as part of their compensation (and I am not just talking about rich executives), but in some companies *all employees* are given stock options. I think that some employees who receive stock options may consider them as "gravy" or "extra" and don't really appreciate that they have some value or even think about what that value may be. I think this is too bad, and we will spend more time later (in this chapter) and especially in Chapter 10 exploring stock options.

The second is the benefit that employees at Cornell University get for their children's education. Every single person who works for Cornell University and who has worked at the university for at least four years has an educational benefit for their children. The deal for current employees is that the university will pay half of Cornell's tuition for each of employee's children to attend Cornell and thirty percent of Cornell's tuition if the child goes to another college or university. That amounts to a lot of money, and a very large relative amount for employees with relatively low earnings. As of the time of this writing, Cornell tuition is more than $43,000 per year (fees and room-and-board adds more than $14,000 per year to that figure).

How Employers Can Think About How Employees Value Compensation

One thing that employers don't do enough of is to try to consider how employees value certain forms of compensation.[5] Would employees rather have more insurance? Would they rather have less insurance and more cash? Does this differ depending on the types of workers we are talking about? How do young people care about retirement contributions on behalf of their employer relative to how older employees feel? Is the same true for health insurance, or stock options, or paid time off? These kinds of questions are important, and few employers take the time to consider the kinds of compensation their employees might prefer, even though it would benefit the companies (or nonprofit organizations) to find the answers to these questions. But how would an employer know? Would the employer just ask employees? Imagine if your employer asked you if you would prefer more time off? You would probably answer that, of course, you would prefer more time off. But at what cost? Would you prefer unpaid time off? Would you be willing to trade 5 percent of your annual earnings for an extra week of paid vacation?

Part of the reason employers don't ask these kinds of questions enough is that it is very hard to ask the questions and, furthermore, it is extremely difficult to get honest answers to the questions. An alternative that some employers have done is to change compensation systems and *observe how employees behave*. I have worked with a few companies that have done this. This kind of exercise works well because it provides actual data on actual behavior of employees. Employers can see what decisions employees make and from that elicit the true values employees place on certain types of compensation relative to other types. This is vastly better than asking employees because their responses on surveys may be very different from their actual behavior when confronted with actual, real-life economic decisions.

If this was a book created solely for compensation practitioners, I would go into this in much more detail. But given that this is a book for a more general audience (and for practitioners), I will not dwell on these points. Nevertheless, I would like to remind the reader that all employees would better serve themselves if they (1) thought more clearly and carefully about what certain parts of their compensation "total package" meant to them and (2) how they would be willing to trade off each of those components for another. A specific example of this came to me recently when a friend asked her small-business employer (a medical office) if they would pay her more if they dropped her medical insurance coverage. Why would she drop her coverage? It turns out that her husband, a state employee, had very comprehensive and generous medical coverage that served his entire family. He also was employed in a position that was extremely stable. That is, it would be very unlikely, given his seniority and other characteristics, that he would lose his job before he decided to retire. The small medical practice where my friend worked said that they would give her *no more* wage and salary compensation if she gave up her medical insurance, even though it was costing them more than (say) $10,000 per year to provide her coverage. Surely they would be willing to pay her, say $5,000 more and drop the insurance than pay the $10,000 insurance. She would be better off by $5,000 and they would be better off by $5,000. But this never occurred to them. I think it is important for employees to consider these kinds of issues.

There are two other examples I'd like to share before ending this section of the book and turning to Part II on how firms set pay structure and why. In the first example, my friend Craig Olson, from the University of Illinois, and I worked with a company that wanted to determine the value employees placed on stock options. They wanted to do this without explicitly asking employees how they value them but by observing employee behavior. One reason you would imagine the company wanted to do this was, in case they were planning to switch compensation, they might know how much cash to replace the options with (if they decided to take the options away). The estimates we came up with showed that the types of employees the firms were interested in valued options differently than some standard economic models would have suggested.

In another example (Hallock and Olson, 2009), a firm with which we worked actually told employees that in the next year, they could take fewer stock options or less performance-based bonus in exchange for higher guaranteed salaries. In essence, they gave the workers a choice over the way they could be paid. It turns out that it is extraordinarily rare to give employees so much choice. In the end, at this one company, women made much different choices than men. In particular, men preferred more "risky" types of pay (such as stock options and performance-based bonus), whereas women preferred guaranteed compensation. This is consistent with a large body of research in economics and psychology.

In many cases, employing organizations (companies, governments, nonprofit organizations) and employees value compensation exactly the same. One hundred dollars in cash costs the firm exactly as the employee values it. However, many forms of pay are valued differently by different people. A child care benefit means nothing to an employee with no children. Dependent medical insurance means nothing to a single person. But organizations don't think about this enough, and neither do employees. You will serve yourself well to think about how you value different forms of pay. And it would be a good idea to do this in advance of having to make a quick decision about your compensation or employment, such as in the case where you are suddenly facing competing job offers. Now that we have covered some of the basic facts and underlying issues that employees and employers need to think about related to compensation, it is time to turn to how organizations design pay structures.

PART II

HOW ORGANIZATIONS SET PAY
STRUCTURE AND WHY

FIVE

Business Strategy and Compensation Strategy

Where You Work Matters

This part of the book is intended to give the reader a feel for how many organizations design their compensation systems. Even if your organization doesn't do it this way, it is helpful to understand how this is done because many organizations follow suit, either directly or by comparing compensation with others through consultants and other intermediaries. The basic structure is important to understand if you want to make your own compensation system more effective and if you want to understand how to make more yourself. This part of the book starts with a discussion of business strategy and compensation strategy. It then goes on to present the "guts" of how most compensation systems are organized. It also includes a discussion of internal and external comparisons and how to collect the right data. We start with strategy.

Starting With a Basic Framework

My PhD is in economics, so when I started making the transition from purely academic work in economics to interdisciplinary academic work on compensation to the more practical world, I must admit that I was more than a little skeptical when I first started hearing about and reading about compensation "strategy." Therefore, I don't blame you if you are a bit suspicious too. Don't markets work and aren't people just paid what they are worth? And if this is so, why should we waste time and resources thinking about how to pay people and why we would ever even think about "strategy?" If the "market" acts appropriately, won't things just sort themselves out? Finally, isn't thinking about compensation "strategy" just a total waste of time? No: compensation "strategy" isn't a waste of time and this chapter is intended to highlight a few reasons why it is important to consider strategy when paying workers.

To really understand pay plans, it is helpful to start with thinking about what the objective of the organization really is. Many for-profit organizations claim a responsibility to shareholders, customers, employees, the government, and society. But many people think that most for-profit organizations are interested in some combination of profitability, share-price increases, and dividend payments to the shareholders (owners). In fact, many executive compensation plans are quite explicit about this and suggest that there should be a strong "link" between the pay of the CEO and "performance" of the company (see a lot more on this in Chapter 8).

In my mind, when an organization is considering its strategy, it doesn't really matter what the end-of-the-day or bottom-line objective actually is, so long as people in the organization actually understand what it is. So the objective for a for-profit firm could be profitability or share price. The objective for certain nonprofits may be the eradication of a particular type of disease, or to help reduce poverty in a certain region, or to provide shelter and food in a region (see Chapter 13 for a lot more detail on compensation in nonprofit organizations).[1] So in the end, much of what is to follow in this book applies to publicly held for-profit companies, privately held for-profit companies, governmental institutions, the military, and nonprofit organizations of any kind. This framework and what appears in this book can be applied to any type of organization. Even if one finds him- or herself in a very unusual type of employment relationship, understanding the way most people are paid can help better understand how he or she is paid.

When I teach or talk with groups about compensation design, I try to discuss "organizations" and not "companies" (unless, of course, I am speaking with folks from a specific *company*), because the fundamental framework and discussion of pay can work for for-profits and nonprofits equally well. In fact, in the past year I have had discussions with three nonprofit organizations about how they compensate their employees (and I serve on the boards of two nonprofits and we regularly discuss compensation) and, in the end, I have very similar (sometimes identical) conversations – at the outset – with people from for-profit and nonprofit organizations in that regard.

It is fundamental to consider the end-of-the day objective of an organization before designing a compensation plan, because, in essence, the ideal compensation systems should help the organization reach its goals. For example, if it is important for an organization to have outstanding customer service, it is important for everyone in the organization to understand that. This is not to say that the organization should *only* pay its employees based on customer service outcomes or, for that matter, that the organization necessarily needs to pay employees based on a specific customer service

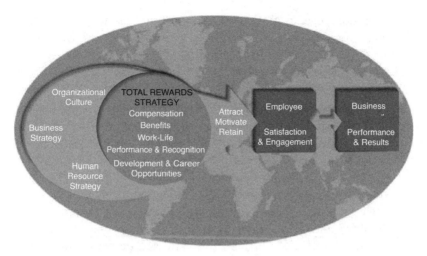

Figure 5.1. The WorldatWork Total Rewards Model. *Source:* WorldatWork: The Total Rewards Association. Available at http://www.worldatwork.org/waw/aboutus/html/aboutus-whatis.html#model.

measure at all – perhaps the costs of doing so (e.g., difficulty in measurement) would outweigh the benefits. There will be many examples in the chapters that follow that will make this clearer.

WorldatWork: The Total Rewards Association is the largest professional association of compensation (broadly defined) and benefits (broadly defined) professionals in the world and has more than 20,000 members.[2] WorldatWork offers extensive basic training on compensation and benefits and provides certifications such as Certified Compensation Professional (CCP) and Global Remuneration Professional (GRP). WorldatWork also provides many resources to those in compensation through its Web site (www.wordatwork.org), including the WorldatWork "Total Rewards Model," reproduced in Figure 5.1.

This is simply one among many depictions that exist of how compensation (broadly defined) fits in organizations. The model suggests precursors that exist, which underpin compensation strategy, including the organization's culture, business strategy, and human resource strategy. These lead to a "total rewards strategy" that includes a lot more than cash pay (as I suggest in Chapters 4 and 11), including compensation, benefits, work-life issues, performance and recognition (would one rather have an award, a higher title, or more pay?), and development and career options (what are the trade-offs between lower pay today in exchange for a higher probability for a promotion – and possibly higher compensation – tomorrow)?

As this model suggests, this compensation strategy is designed to attract employees, motivate them, and retain them. Attracting, motivating, and retaining (the right) employees can lead to what the WorldatWork model suggests are "performance and results." I would suggest that this is just the end-of-the-day objective as I have been discussing. I do like the "double arrow" at the end of Figure 5.1. This suggests that attracting, motivating, and retaining the right employees leads to better results (fulfillment of objectives), and better fulfillment of objectives also leads to more successful attraction, motivation, and retention of employees. This is actually very important in relation to some issues discussed elsewhere in the book. It is often very difficult to test whether a specific HR practice leads to a particular outcome. For example, if one observes that companies paying with stock options are more profitable, it doesn't necessarily mean that the options *caused* the higher profits. In fact, perhaps firms that are more profitable find it easier to pay options. Chapter 9 on evaluating performance, incentives, and incentive pay focuses on this more carefully and aims to suggest ways to tell whether certain practices lead to better outcomes.

I often start new courses on compensation or sessions with managers by focusing on the fact that specific *circumstances* matter. But this is really just to highlight that it matters that those designing compensation plans must *really* understand how the organization does what it wants to do (e.g., reduce disease, make profits, help children to read, etc.). And it is very important that the organization's strategy for getting done whatever it wants to get done be aligned with the compensation strategy and compensation system that is designed.

An Example to Help Justify the Importance of Having a System: When Salaries Aren't Secret

One of my favorite hypothetical teaching cases is about a disgruntled employee who sends compensation information on every employee to every employee in her company (Case, 2001). In the case, a young employee, on her last day at the company, sends a spreadsheet with the compensation information for every single employee to every single person at the company. The company, like most American companies, kept compensation information pretty quiet and few employees discussed their compensation with others. So the information was quickly read, discussed, and disseminated. Needless to say, the e-mail revealing the compensation levels created chaos in the company.

Not all organizations keep their compensation secret, and it is interesting to consider organizations that do relative to those that do not. In my first academic job, at the University of Illinois at Urbana-Champaign, compensation was public, and to this day salaries of all faculty are public information.[3] At Illinois, I was often part of a committee that helped determine faculty salaries in my two departments. It was always interesting to see my colleagues' reactions when they were told their raises and then, later, when they heard what everyone else got. (We will encounter this again in Chapter 6, which includes a discussion of internal comparisons). At Cornell, compensation information is much more closely guarded. It is not immediately obvious whether a confidential system is generally a "better" system. One thing is for sure: there is a lot less discussion each year when the raises come out. Many other organizations have compensation systems that are entirely public (e.g., unionized teachers, police officers, and firefighters, where compensation is often a direct function of seniority and education).

There were several reasons why the e-mail reporting the compensation level of everyone in the organization created such turmoil. On the one hand, there was a set of people who were very angry that they were making so little relative to their colleagues. On the other hand, there were also some people who were embarrassed that they were making so much and didn't want their colleagues to know.

In the case (Case, 2001), one of the senior executives, Vice President of Human Resources Charlie Herald, suggested that the company take advantage of the situation and continue to make compensation public. He suggested this for at least two reasons. First, he thought that it would force the company to be fairer in compensation decisions, given potentially added scrutiny. The second reason was that it might force the employees to better understand the compensation and lead them to higher performance. In fact, Herald said that keeping the system public "forces people to understand our business. We've always said we wanted employees to understand our costs and learn to think like businesspeople. Well, here in headquarters our biggest cost is payroll" (Case, 2001).

Another senior executive, Chief Financial Officer Harriet Duval suggested the company apologize for the mistake, fix the compensation system, and keep salaries secret going forward. Duval countered Herald's proposal with the following: "All of those differences in pay – they're the result of stuff you could never talk about out loud. They reflect a hundred judgment calls that every manager makes about every employee every day. Pay like the Postal Service – people won't stand for it and our best people will leave" (Case, 2001).

Whether a compensation system should be public depends on many factors including the industry, life cycle of the company, type of workers, region of the world, and many others. But both Herald and Duval make important points worthy of consideration. I completely agree with Herald in that it is a shame (and a waste!) if employees don't understand the compensation system in operation where they work (the scary part is that many *managers* don't understand the compensation system either, even if there is one in place!). Understanding the organization's overall strategy to meet its objectives is a necessary condition for developing an appropriate compensation system. I agree with Duval in that some people may leave if the organization pays like the Postal Service (a fixed seniority-based system). I only partially agree with the point about the "judgment calls." Yes, judgments calls are important, but a compensation system can't be based on managerial judgment calls alone. Managers have many things to worry about and compensation cannot be the only one. The "judgment call" argument often masks some other agenda, and there is no reason these issues can't be written down and formalized. There are many reasons to want to do this, as detailed in Chapters 6 and 7.

What is Strategy?

Consider a set of for-profit organizations (the same could be done for non-profits but, for now, let's just focus on for-profit firms). What if all of the firms in a given industry did exactly the same thing? "A firm that follows the same best practices as other firms can only achieve parity. To go beyond that, it would need to develop unique alignments between elements of its pay strategy and between the pay strategy, other HR practices, and the business strategy" (Gerhart, 2000). The most famous source on strategy is Porter (1996). Simple, straightforward operational effectiveness and strategy are different. Operational effectiveness means actually performing the same activities as other organizations in a better way. On the other hand, acting strategically means taking different actions, or performing different activities from those with whom you compete, or performing similar activities in different ways. However, it must be the case that performing actions in better ways better match your organization's objectives. In fact, merely doing something different from a rival (and successful) organization may be a very bad idea. It is quite likely that the rival is doing what it is doing in this particular way for a good reason. On the other hand, doing something different that also melds well with your overall activities may prove a great idea. Porter (1996) notes that "few companies have competed successfully on the basis of operational effectiveness over an extended period" because "competitors can quickly imitate management techniques, new technologies, input improvements, and superior ways of meeting customer needs." Precisely because these are easy to copy, they are not valuable for sustaining competitive advantage. Instead, strategy can be helpful.

With strategy, it is important to be different. There are a series of options for strategic positioning, including variety-base positioning and needs-based positioning. Milkovich and Newman (2008) describe variety-based positioning, based on a product or service (such as Jiffy Lube for automobile oil changes), needs-based positioning, such as a focus on a particular type of customers (such as Ikea in furniture), and access-based positioning, such as certain movie outlet chains that are only located in rural areas. In summary, Porter (1996) notes, "The success of a strategy depends on doing many things well – not just a few – and integrating among them. If there is no fit among activities, there is no distinctive strategy and little sustainability. Management reverts to the simpler tasks of overseeing independent functions, and operational effectiveness determines an organization's relative performance."

Some Factors That Matter in Influencing Strategy

There are a wide variety of issues that can influence strategy, including national culture, organizational culture, and organizational and product life cycle (each mentioned by Martocchio, 2001). There is also a wider variety including understanding the industry and specific company history, regulation, mergers and acquisitions, and institutions.

National culture is fundamental to really understanding compensation systems. Often, however, compensation plan designers can become overwhelmed by national culture and forget about other important aspects of culture (see Chapter 12 for more discussion on this point). National culture is a set of shared norms or beliefs held in one nation. Hofstede (1980) mentions four important parts of national culture: power distance, individualism versus collectivism, masculinity versus femininity, and uncertainty avoidance. These ideas can be considered as broadly as across countries or as narrowly as within an industry in a specific country.

The idea of power distance is very interesting. It is essentially the issue of whether people feel comfortable in a more rigid hierarchical system or one that is more consultative and democratic. This is not necessarily the true way things are but reflects how people perceive the power distance. Some nations are much more likely to be known as low in power distance (such as New Zealand, Sweden, Finland, and Norway). Malaysia is considered very high on power distance metrics.

Individualism and collectivism are related ideas. The issue here is whether people are more comfortable being on their own or as part of a group. The United States is known to be extraordinarily individualistic and would, therefore, be a more likely location to implement an individual-based pay-for-performance system. On the other hand, Japan is a much more collectivist society. Stock options were not even legal in Japan until the mid-1990s.

Masculinity and femininity are two other important parts of national culture according to Hofstede (1980) and others. In more masculine cultures, people of both genders are more likely to tend toward traits such as aggressiveness, competition, ambition, and money. In more feminine cultures, people of both genders are more likely to value issues such as quality of life and work-life balance. This is not to suggest that those in more feminine cultures do not seek higher *compensation*; rather, that they seek compensation in different forms. For example, those in Scandinavian countries may be more likely to favor balance traded off against cash compensation.

Just as individuals may vary by level of risk aversion, some countries are known to want to avoid risk more than others. In those cultures that are more risk averse, it would make relatively more sense to favor forms of compensation that tend toward fixed components, such as salary and fixed benefits. In cultures that feel less cost in the face of risk, more emphasis could be put on variable aspects of pay (e.g., stock options, bonuses).

As noted, it can be easy to get lost in issues of national culture and there are many other aspects of strategy that should not be overlooked. Some organizations are particularly hierarchical. These organizations have many layers including a CEO, senior vice presidents, vice presidents, directors, managers, and so on. They are very formalized and structured. Others are much "flatter," have fewer organizational levels, and are less formal. It is interesting when organizations spread internationally (or merge). In these cases, leaders have to manage the company and national cultures simultaneously.

It is particularly interesting when two firms with much different cultures and strategies merge. Imagine one organization that is competitive and aggressive and offers many bonuses, stock options, and incentives. Imagine another that is focused on steady results, formalized systems, and pays high base salary and benefits but little incentive compensation. Merging these two kinds of organizations can be tricky. And if Human Resources is left out of the equation at the time of the merger, the value of the merger is often overestimated, because these costs are ignored.

It is very interesting to see that some of my students go to more hierarchical organizations and others go to flatter ones, some go to more aggressive and competitive organizations and others do not. There are very stark examples. And it is rare when a student of a particular extreme personality (e.g., aggressive) takes a job in an organization that does not welcome that sort of behavior.

Martocchio (2001) also mentions organization and product life cycle as factors that could influence strategy. He suggests growth, maturity, and decline as three parts of the organization life cycle. It would be natural to have different kinds of strategies early in the growth stages of an organization, relative to a more mature time in the history of the organization. This would naturally lead to potentially different ways to pay. For example, early on it may make more sense for a company to pay with more stock and stock options (relative to cash) because the company may not have much cash on hand.

As mentioned earlier, industry can dramatically influence strategy as can regulation and institutions. Minimum wage laws, labor unions, and state and international laws on hiring and firing workers can all have extraordinary consequences for how workers are paid.

Strategy Matters

Strategy and understanding the "business" (for-profit or nonprofit) and industry are essential to a well-designed and well-functioning compensation system. This chapter concludes with a story of an organization that hadn't carefully considered strategy and, as a result, faced significant difficulty. Nicoson (1996) describes a hypothetical case study of "Waterway Industries" and its CEO, Cyrus Maher. The company was in the business of making canoes and had a relaxed culture of balance; it was not unusual for employees to leave work early on a particularly nice day.

In the case (Nicoson, 1996), the company hires Lee Carter and her well-known "high-powered" sales ability to dramatically increase sales. The CEO, Maher, soon overhears Carter on a phone call considering a job with another company and discussing stock in the new firm, and he is worried that she might leave.

Although the company originally had a relaxed working culture, more and more employees who were initially satisfied with the way they were being paid have begun to change their minds. And some of them suggested wanting more of the profits, in some fashion.

In the end, the problem in the case is that the organization (and the CEO) never really had a plan for how they were going to transform the small canoe company into something new. When, out of the blue, the CEO (Maher) discovered that Carter might leave, he didn't know what to do because he never had really thought about the longer-term business strategy or the compensation strategy to match it. If you don't understand how and why your organization pays the way it pays, you should be concerned because the organization may not know either.

SIX

What's in a Job?

Job Analysis, Job Evaluation, and
Internal Comparisons

Imagine that we want to figure out how to pay a set of administrative assistants in an organization. Should we just let the "market" tell us what to do? That certainly is one way to go, but it turns out that most organizations do not do that entirely. Consider Figure 6.1. In this figure, the vertical axis is dollars and the horizontal axis is "stuff that people do at work." It seems perfectly natural to have an upward-sloping relationship between stuff the person does and how much he gets paid. But how do we measure the "stuff that people do at work?" And why is Assistant I paid so much less than Assistant III? And why is the difference in pay between Assistant II and Assistant III smaller than the difference in pay between Assistant III and Assistant IV? The next few chapters begin to show us the answers to these kinds of questions. And if you think that we are going to immediately see how pay fits into this, you are wrong. It turns out that most organizations do tons of work thinking about internal comparisons and the contributions of specific jobs before thinking at all about pay.

This is the first of two chapters that present the basic technical details of how many organizations throughout the world design compensation systems for their employees. In this chapter, we begin with discussing what is known as job analysis and job evaluation and a discussion of internal comparisons, the market and the right data, and matching the two together to form the basis of a system in Chapter 7. Let's get started with job analysis.

An interesting thing about job analysis is that, as far as I can tell, nothing is really being analyzed. In fact, job analysis often goes hand in hand with job evaluation, which we tackle next. But job evaluation is where the analysis comes in. Harvey (1991) notes that "[j]ob analysis has grown far beyond its previous emphasis on task analysis; instead, compliance with external regulations, the avoidance of discrimination lawsuits, and the need to closely link job analysis data with specific personnel functions have become major

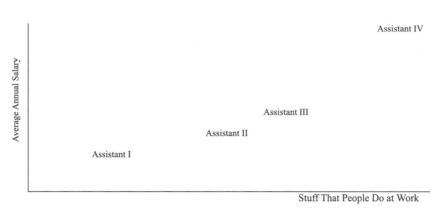

Figure 6.1. Pay versus "Stuff That One Does"

concerns to organizations." So, in fact, job analysis is useful far beyond compensation. Harvey (1991) continues to suggest (as I noted earlier) that there is confusion about job analysis, for three reasons. First, some ways for gathering data for job analysis have often had little formal basis. Second, "the term job analysis should only be applied to procedures that collect information describing verifiable job behaviors and activities; it should not be used to denote the wide assortment of procedures that make inferences about people or otherwise apply job analysis data (e.g., to infer personal traits that might be necessary for successful job performance)." Third, Harvey (1991) notes that job analysis has an "image" problem. According to Prien (1977), "although job analysis is an essential feature of almost every activity engaged in by industrial-organizational psychologists, the subject is treated in textbooks in a manner which suggests that any fool can do it and thus it is a task which can be delegated to the lowest level technician. This is quite contradictory to the position taken ... in the EEOC selection guidelines." In fact, I think one reason that it is often relegated is not because it is not important or a respected activity for HR practitioners, but because it is pretty monotonous and boring. In what follows, I show you why job analysis is boring, but also why it is so important.

Defining Job Analysis

Job analysis is "the systematic process of collecting information that identifies similarities and differences in work" (Milkovich and Newman, 2008). Harvey (1991) adds that job analysis data must describe "observable (or otherwise verifiable) job behaviors performed by workers, including both what is accomplished as well as what techniques are employed to accomplish the end result" and "verifiable characteristics of the job environment with which workers interact, including physical, mechanical, social, and informational elements." So it should be clear here that this technique can be useful in designing the understructure of a compensation system but may also be good general Human Resource practice so as to make sure that employees are treated fairly and appropriately.

Harvey (1991) goes on to make two important points. First, job analysis techniques should be able to describe "observable" characteristics of jobs. Second, and very important, the individual characteristics of those in the job should be kept separate from job analysis. The point is that the system should be describing the job and not the person in it. This became even clearer to me when I was leading a group to reorganize two work units. There was one person – let's call her "Matilda" – who was an extraordinary employee and was in one job but was temporarily also doing the job of another on an interim basis. If one did a job analysis of her job, they would need to keep *her* out of it and simply study the jobs, the reason being that she was an unusually productive employee and actually *could* do the job of two people. Failing to keep Matilda out of the equation would have lead to problems later, especially if she ever moved on to another position.

Organizing Job Analysis: What are the Units?

Martocchio (2001) suggests that when doing job analysis, it is useful to consider the "units" of analysis. He points out six of them: element, task, position, job, job family, and occupation. I think this is important to discuss for two reasons. First, it highlights just how painful and tedious doing an appropriate job analysis can be. Second, it introduces the important concept of "job family," which will be useful in the coming chapters.

A job element is the most minor function in a job. An example would be putting a piece of paper in a scanner to scan a document. A separate element would be attaching the resulting digital image to an e-mail message and sending it to someone. So keep in mind that job analysis can include the business of describing the very most basic parts of a job. The rest of the list from Martocchio (2001) just aggregates up to higher and higher levels. A task is the next level up. A position is a group of tasks that make up the activities for one employee. A junior administrative assistant may get the mail and distribute it, arrange meetings and schedule rooms for meetings, make flight reservations, and so on. The job is next up the line. A job is a set of positions. There may be multiple junior administrative assistants who are all doing a very similar job.

The job family is really fundamental to what we will be considering in the next chapters. The roles described in Figure 6.1 all represent the administrative job family. It is clear that there are many different jobs in the family (and perhaps thousands of workers in positions performing many elements in those positions with the same organization). An occupation is an even higher level. Examples of occupations include legal occupations, sales and related, and the like.[1]

Data: How and What to Collect

We next have to consider how to collect information for an appropriate job analysis and from whom to collect it. It is important to consider both the job and the employee when doing this. In fact, as suggested by Milkovich and Newman (2008), one could consider the job content (e.g., tasks, activities, conflicting demands, working conditions), employee characteristics (e.g., manual skills, verbal skills, quantitative skills, leaderships skills, interpersonal skills), internal relationships (e.g., supervisors, subordinates, peers), and external relationships (e.g., customers, suppliers, regulators, community, labor unions).

There are multiple ways to actually collect the data and each has costs and benefits. For example, one could ask employees about their job content, responsibilities, and relationships. The main problem with this is that it takes a very, very long time and it is relatively difficult to be formal and have consistent information, because many people will be doing the questioning. The main rival method is to use a questionnaire (and there are many, many possible questions, as we will see shortly). The problem with the questionnaire method is that it may be somewhat restrictive. That is to say, it is set up and formal in advance. This way, if any new interesting and subjective information comes out in the process of administering the questionnaire, it would be lost. On the other hand, this method is objective and easily administered, tabulated, and comparable across organizations. These are among the reasons it is so popular.

There is a very wide variety of these questionnaires. The questionnaires can be incredibly long and detailed and literally include hundreds of questions. There is a wide variety of specific job analysis methods (see Henderson, 2006). These include O*NET from the U.S. Department of Labor (and a revision of dictionary of Occupational Titles), Functional Job Analysis (FJA), the Job Information Matrix System (JIMS), Position Analysis Questionnaire (PAQ), Professional and Managerial Position Questionnaire

(PMPQ), Occupational Analysis Inventory (OAI), Comprehensive Occupation Data Analysis Program (CODAP), and Job Analysis Questionnaire (JAQ). Acronyms are obviously popular in this line of work.

O*NET is interesting and focuses on seven "O*NET descriptors": knowledge, skills, abilities, work activities, interests, work context, and work values.[2] See Table 6.1 for a description of the kinds of details O*NET provides for one occupation: dental assistants.

Each of these methods is similar but has a different pitch or focus. For example, FJA is a variant of Labor Department methods and includes items to measure discretion and development (Henderson, 2006). JIMS focuses on what the worker does, what the worker uses, the knowledge the worker must have, worker's responsibilities, and working conditions (Henderson, 2006). PAQ is a 194-element system that has six parts including information input, mental process, work input, relationships with others, job context, and other job characteristics (Henderson, 2006). PMPQ is like PAQ but focuses on managers. The others are related in similar kinds of ways. An example of a question from one of the questionnaires would be "communicates with customers:" almost never, occasionally, sometimes, frequently, almost all of the time.

An Additional Job Analysis Note

Before turning to job evaluation, it is worth raising the point mentioned earlier: is this really worth it? It seems like an awful lot of work. Why don't we just pay people according to "market rates?" As explained in a few case studies elsewhere (one where an employee leaks all of the compensation data to all members of the company and another when a CEO has to decide [quickly] whether to raise someone's wage or lose her), without this sort of detail, many pay decisions may end up being made on "gut" feelings and may introduce all sorts of bias. Also, it is difficult to compare to "market rates" without knowing what employees in each organization are actually doing. So if you are still skeptical, bear with me. We are getting there.

Job Evaluation: The Basics

The main point in doing "job evaluation" is to value work. Going back to Figure 6.1, notice that the horizontal axis is "stuff that people do at work." This isn't particularly satisfactory or clear. In most basic economics textbooks, there is a discussion of "the value of the marginal product" of worker's output. And in a simple, perfectly competitive market, the idea is that the worker's output should be just equal to her wage. The idea in

Table 6.1. *Some O* NET details for dental assistant occupation*

Knowledge

Medicine and Dentistry – Knowledge of the information and techniques needed to diagnose and treat human injuries, diseases, and deformities. This includes symptoms, treatment alternatives, drug properties and interactions, and preventive health care measures.

Customer and Personal Service – Knowledge of principles and processes for providing customer and personal services. This includes customer needs assessment, meeting quality standards for services, and evaluation of customer satisfaction.

English Language – Knowledge of the structure and content of the English language, including the meaning and spelling of words, rules of composition, and grammar.

Skills

Speaking – Talking to others to convey information effectively.

Active Listening – Giving full attention to what other people are saying, taking time to understand the points being made, asking questions as appropriate, and not interrupting at inappropriate times.

Reading Comprehension – Understanding written sentences and paragraphs in work related documents.

Service Orientation – Actively looking for ways to help people.

Critical Thinking – Using logic and reasoning to identify the strengths and weaknesses of alternative solutions, conclusions, or approaches to problems.

Monitoring – Monitoring/Assessing performance of yourself, other individuals, or organizations to make improvements or take corrective action.

Coordination – Adjusting actions in relation to others' actions.

Social Perceptiveness – Being aware of others' reactions and understanding why they react as they do.

Abilities

Oral Comprehension – The ability to listen to and understand information and ideas presented through spoken words and sentences.

Oral Expression – The ability to communicate information and ideas in speaking so others will understand.

Speech Recognition – The ability to identify and understand the speech of another person.

Near Vision – The ability to see details at close range (within a few feet of the observer).

Arm-Hand Steadiness – The ability to keep your hand and arm steady while moving your arm or while holding your arm and hand in one position.

Speech Clarity – The ability to speak clearly so others can understand you.

Finger Dexterity – The ability to make precisely coordinated movements of the fingers of one or both hands to grasp, manipulate, or assemble very small objects.

Written Comprehension – The ability to read and understand information and ideas presented in writing.

Category Flexibility – The ability to generate or use different sets of rules for combining or grouping things in different ways.

Control Precision – The ability to quickly and repeatedly adjust the controls of a machine or a vehicle to exact positions.

Table 6.1 *(continued)*

Work Activities

Assisting and Caring for Others – Providing personal assistance, medical attention, emotional support, or other personal care to others such as coworkers, customers, or patients.

Communicating with Supervisors, Peers, or Subordinates – Providing information to supervisors, coworkers, and subordinates by telephone, in written form, e-mail, or in person.

Performing for or Working Directly with the Public – Performing for people or dealing directly with the public. This includes serving customers in restaurants and stores and receiving clients or guests.

Getting Information – Observing, receiving, and otherwise obtaining information from all relevant sources.

Organizing, Planning, and Prioritizing Work – Developing specific goals and plans to prioritize, organize, and accomplish your work.

Establishing and Maintaining Interpersonal Relationships – Developing constructive and cooperative working relationships with others and maintaining them over time.

Inspecting Equipment, Structures, or Material – Inspecting equipment, structures, or materials to identify the cause of errors or other problems or defects.

Interpreting the Meaning of Information for Others – Translating or explaining what information means and how it can be used.

Identifying Objects, Actions, and Events – Identifying information by categorizing, estimating, recognizing differences or similarities, and detecting changes in circumstances or events.

Making Decisions and Solving Problems – Analyzing information and evaluating results to choose the best solution and solve problems.

Source: O*NET: http://online.onetonline.org/link/summary/31-9091.00

the remainder of this chapter is to define more formally the "value" that employees add. Or, to say it another way, the point here is to assign each position and job a number of "points" (defined in more detail later) that the job is "worth." We also want to be sure that the system is internally consistent. If Engineer II gets assigned 1,350 points and Marketing Manager III is assigned 1,200 points, it must make sense that the Marketing Manager III position is worth "less" to the firm than the Engineer II position. But it is noteworthy that we are *still* not yet considering compensation – only the relative value of given jobs. Note also that the value or worth of a given job in an organization can be *different* in one company than in another. Hopefully this will become clear in the coming chapters. But, given an organization's strategy, a given job description and worker in a job could be worth considerably more (or less) in one organization than another, depending on the business and compensation strategy of the organizations (e.g., salespeople may be more fundamental in one organization and engineers in another). An analogous idea comes up in professional sports. Some athletes are actually worth more on one team than another precisely because they "fit" better in one organization than another (e.g., the team needs a specific player in a particular position, who can work well in a particular team structure).

The Point System

There are many ways to consider doing job evaluation, including ranking (order jobs from highest to lowest "value"), classification systems, and the point system (Milkovich and Newman, 2008). The U.S. government uses a classification system as outlined in Table 6.2. There are fifteen grades and ten steps within each grade. There are still other systems that are based on "persons" and not on jobs. These methods are sometimes used but not as frequently as the point system. But the most common and the one on which this chapter focuses is the point system.

In going through the point system, there are a few issues that we need to keep in mind. First, we need to find a set of "benchmark jobs." Then for each of those jobs we need to define "compensable factors," set "factor degrees," set the points for each factor, and then set the weight for each factor (Milkovich and Newman, 2008). In the end, remember that all this is assigning "points" to jobs so that they can have actual rankings relative to one another. Keep in mind, however, that there are no dollars or levels of compensation yet.

Benchmark jobs are important because they are the ones that will help a given organization link itself with the outside world. Note that benchmark jobs are not necessarily the most important ones in the organization. Rather, they are jobs that are relatively easily defined and actually exist in other organizations. If your organization has unique or unusual jobs, they cannot be used as benchmarks, because the ideal "benchmark" matches to similar jobs in other organizations. So benchmark jobs have to be ones that are clearly defined, the content of which probably does not change too much over time, and that many other organizations have as well. It is also useful to have a set of benchmark jobs that run from "lower" value to "higher value," for reasons that will become clear in later sections.

The next step is to set a series of what are known as "compensable factors." These are factors for which the company sees value. Examples could be responsibility, leadership, technical ability, communication, and working conditions. These compensable factors should be ones that employees actually agree with and ones that match the strategy of the organization (Chapter 5).

Table 6.2. *U.S. government's GS system pay scales salary table 2011-DCB. Incorporating a locality payment of 24.22%, rates frozen at 2010 levels. For the locality pay area of washington-baltimore-northern virginia, DC-MD-VA-WV-PA effective january 2011, annual rates by grade and step*

Grade	Step 1	Step 2	Step 3	Step 4	Step 5	Step 6	Step 7	Step 8	Step 9	Step 10
1	22,115	22,854	23,589	24,321	25,056	25,489	25,215	26,948	26,977	27,663
2	24,865	25,456	26,279	26,977	27,280	28,082	28,885	29,687	30,490	31,292
3	27,130	28,034	28,938	29,843	30,747	31,651	32,556	33,460	34,364	35,269
4	30,456	31,471	32,486	33,501	34,516	35,531	36,546	37,560	38,575	39,590
5	34,075	35,210	36,346	37,481	38,616	39,752	40,887	42,022	43,158	44,293
6	37,983	39,249	40,514	41,780	43,046	44,312	45,578	46,843	48,109	49,375
7	42,209	43,616	45,024	46,431	47,338	49,246	50,653	52,061	53,468	54,875
8	46,745	48,303	49,861	51,418	52,976	54,534	56,092	57,649	59,207	60,765
9	51,630	53,350	55,070	56,791	58,511	60,232	61,952	63,673	65,393	67,114
10	56,857	58,752	60,648	62,544	64,439	66,335	68,230	70,126	72,022	73,917
11	62,467	64,548	66,630	68,712	70,794	72,876	74,958	77,040	79,122	81,204
12	74,872	77,368	79,864	82,359	84,855	87,350	89,846	92,341	94,837	97,333
13	89,033	92,001	94,969	97,936	100,904	103,872	106,839	109,807	112,774	115,742
14	105,211	108,717	112,224	115,731	119,238	122,744	126,251	129,758	133,264	136,771
15	123,758	127,883	132,009	136,134	140,259	144,385	148,510	152,635	155,500	155,500

Source: U.S. Office of Personnel Management, http://www.opm.gov/oca/11tables/pdf/DCB.pdf

After each factor is defined, the organization then sets a number of "degrees" of each. Just as it is important to have a sufficient number of benchmark jobs (from lower to higher value), it is important to have a sufficient spectrum of "degrees" to be able to easily distinguish among jobs. Martocchio (2001) notes a set of "writing ability: factor definition and degree statements." This includes first-degree writing ability that may include "print simple phrases and sentences, using normal order and present and past tenses," second-degree writing ability (which will obviously count for more in assigning points to the job than first degree) that may include "write compound and complex sentences, using proper punctuation and adjectives and adverbs," all the way up to the highest category, fifth-degree writing ability that may include "Write manuals and speeches" (Martocchio, 2001).

The next step is to define the weight of each factor, relative to the other factors. Say, for example, that the organization believes that among the categories responsibility, leadership, technical ability, communication, and working conditions, technical ability is by far the most important and working conditions is the least important. The organization can assign (say) technical ability 50 percent of the points and working conditions only 5 percent. Further, suppose the organization decided to assign 20 percent to leadership, 15 percent to responsibility, and 10 percent to communications. That makes 100 percent total.

Now suppose that the organization decides to assign at most a total of 1,000 points to any job and there is no way any job could have more than that many points. The number 1,000 is completely arbitrary. We could just as easily use 1,969, 7,254, or 345,839,201. But 1,000 is a nice round number. Given the percentages noted earlier, this would mean that at most 500 points are available to be assigned for technical ability, 200 points for leadership, 150 points for responsibility, 100 for communications, and 50 for working conditions.

The next step is to define the number of points within each compensable factor. For example, there are 500 points for technical ability. A degree 1 technical ability (say basic understanding of basic technical aspects of a machine at the workplace) could be worth 100 points. A degree 2 technical ability (say an understanding of the basics of the machine as defined in technical ability 1 but also the ability to repair the machine) is worth 200 points. This could go all the way up to degree 5 technical ability (which includes an understanding of all technical aspects of all machines and a visionary ability to develop new products and understand all appropriate engineering systems), which is worth 500 points. Note – although this is not

	Degree 1	Degree 2	Degree 3	Degree 4	Degree 5	Total
Technical Ability	100	200	300	400	500	
Leadership	40	80	120	160	200	
Responsibility	30	60	90	120	150	
Communications	20	40	60	80	100	
Working Conditions	10	20	30	40	50	

Figure 6.2. Example of a Job Evaluation Worksheet for an Organization

often discussed in many accounts in textbooks – that there is absolutely no reason there needs to be a linear progression in these degrees. For example, we could have assigned 50 points to degree 1, 300 points to degree 2, 310 points to degree 3, 350 points to degree 4, and 500 points to degree 5. This may make sense if there are obvious nonlinearities in how degrees are easily defined. However, for the purposes of this chapter, we will keep them nice and linear: degree 1 for technical ability is worth 100 points, degree 2 is worth 200 points, all the way up to degree 5, which is worth 500 points.

We then need to do the same with each of the other compensable factors. Take, for example, leadership, which has at most 200 points. Suppose the organization associates leadership degree 1 with 40 points, leadership degree 2 with 80 points, all the way to leadership degree 5, which gets 200 points. A sample complete description for this job family in this organization is in Figure 6.2. It is easy to see that in this example all five compensable factors are listed and, although the five factors are each given different weights (e.g., technical ability 50 percent), they each have five degrees within each factor and the degrees progress linearly.

The next step is to complete this "worksheet" (Figure 6.2) for each of the benchmark jobs. Suppose this is done for Engineer II. Suppose that Engineer II is expected to have technical ability of degree 4, leadership of degree 2, responsibility of degree 3, communications of degree 3, and working conditions of degree 1 (this means really good working conditions – those that don't require additional compensation[3]). This suggests that this job is assigned 400 points for technical ability, 80 points for leadership, 90 points for responsibility, 60 points for communications, and 10 points for working conditions, for a total of 640 points (see Figure 6.3). This forms the basis of a new horizontal scale for Figure 6.1, which we will no longer call "stuff that people do at work" but can relabel "Job Evaluation Points." Notice, however, that we still haven't discussed pay, so this isn't really on an X-Y grid yet. It is just a straight line as in Figure 6.4. Once we go through

	Degree 1	Degree 2	Degree 3	Degree 4	Degree 5	Total
Technical Ability	100	200	300	<u>400</u>	500	400
Leadership	40	<u>80</u>	120	160	200	80
Responsibility	30	60	<u>90</u>	120	150	90
Communications	20	40	<u>60</u>	80	100	60
Working	<u>10</u>	20	30	40	50	10
Conditions						640

Job Evaluation Points

Figure 6.3. Example of a Job Evaluation Worksheet for a Job

the job analysis and job evaluation process for each of our jobs, we can line them up on this horizontal line and visually observe their relative "value" to the organization. Dealing with the internal rankings is difficult (it is the subject of the next subsection). Chapter 7 then describes from where to get the right data and shows how to put the market data together with the internal system developed here to set up a pay system. The next step, then, is to generate pay on the vertical (Y) axis and job evaluation points – "stuff that people do at work" – on the horizontal (X) axis.

Developing a Structure for a Particular Organization: Internal Comparisons are Tricky

Have you ever felt satisfied with a particular deal, only to find out later that someone else got a better deal? And, as a result, did you feel particularly unsatisfied? Consider driving down the road and stopping to purchase gasoline at a "good price." But then, right after you fill up, you pass another gas station with a lower price. As I mention elsewhere in this book, when I taught at the University of Illinois, I was part of a salary-setting committee for eight of the ten years I was there. Often, individuals seemed relatively happy when they heard what their annual "adjustment" was. But, then (since Illinois is a public institution), when the salaries were released and individuals made *relative* comparisons, they were, in many instances, not

Engineer I	Engineer II	Senior Engineer
(530 points)	(640 points)	(935 points)

Job Evaluation Points

Note: This is just a line but will form the horizontal axis of an X-Y graph.

Figure 6.4. Job Evaluation Points

happy. It is not entirely clear why, but part of this could have been because of a lack of understanding of what their colleagues were doing and a lack of understanding (or communication) about how the compensation system worked.

The Parable of the Vineyard[4] appears in Chapter 20 of Matthew in the Bible[5]:

For the kingdom of heaven is like a landowner who went out early in the morning to hire men to work in his vineyard. He agreed to pay them a denarius for the day and sent them into his vineyard. About the third hour he went out and saw others standing in the marketplace doing nothing. He told them, "You also go and work in my vineyard, and I will pay you whatever is right." So they went. He went out again about the sixth hour and the ninth hour and did the same thing. About the eleventh hour he went out and found still others standing around. He asked them, "Why have you been standing here all day long doing nothing?" "Because no one has hired us," they answered. He said to them, "You also go and work in my vineyard." When evening came, the owner of the vineyard said to his foreman, "Call the workers and pay them their wages, beginning with the last ones hired and going on to the first." The workers who were hired about the eleventh hour came and each received a denarius. So when those came who were hired first, they expected to receive more. But each one of them also received a denarius. When they received it, they began to grumble against the landowner. "These men who were hired last worked only one hour," they said, "and you have made them equal to us who have borne the burden of the work and the heat of the day." But he answered one of them, "Friend, I am not being unfair to you. Didn't you agree to work for a denarius? Take your pay and go. I want to give the man who was hired last the same as I gave you. Don't I have the right to do what I want with my own money? Or are you envious because I am generous?" So the last will be first, and the first will be last.

The idea that people will be paid differently for the same work obviously made some in this bible passage and in many other work situations very upset. At the same time, it should be recognized that paying people the same for working for a period of time (for example) may make others upset, because some are more productive per period than others.

Internal Comparisons Really Matter

The bible passage is particularly interesting as it and the story from my days in Illinois both show that *relative* comparisons can matter as much or even more than absolute comparisons. For example, imagine the following situation where a worker is offered two choices. Assume for a moment that everyone in the organization is paid the same: $45,000 per year. In the first choice, a particular employee is offered a circumstance where he obtains a $4,000 raise and everyone else obtains a $5,000 raise. In the second circumstance, the worker obtains a $3,000 raise and everyone else obtains a $2,000 raise. (Don't worry about the fact that option A is much more expensive than option B or what that means for the organization).

Which of these options would you choose? If one is only looking out for his or her own interests (and those of his or her family), it obviously makes sense to go for the first option. And if one is the type that likes to see good things happen to other people, then that person would also prefer option A. But how many people do you think would *really* prefer option B? Can you think of at least *some* people who might prefer option B? I can. This type of person would rather earn *relatively* more than someone else than *absolutely* more himself.

Relative pay matters. In fact, there are instances where coaches or other employees have negotiated situations where they are guaranteed to earn more than some group, or more than the median or average of some group. So the issue is not really the *level* of pay; rather it is the *relative rank* that matters in these situations. This is certainly evidence that pay is not exactly equal to what the person is producing, and something else (e.g., psychology) is obviously involved.

One of the points I have been trying to make is that one can work very hard on a compensation structure before doing anything with actual compensation. It takes considerable time to develop the compensation strategy and organize the structure so that it makes sense *internally* before going to the outside market to think about actual compensation levels.

Imagine that an organization carefully goes through the development of its compensation strategy, then goes through job analysis and job evaluation and comes up with a set of three or four benchmark jobs in each of three different job families. Suppose the job families are administration, engineering, and legal.

We could have created the structure such that each of these job families has the same compensable factors as we used earlier: technical ability, leadership, responsibility, communications, and working conditions. But there is no real reason these five compensable factors should be used in each job family. Similarly, we could have used the same weighting scheme (technical ability – 50 percent, leadership – 20 percent, responsibility – 15 percent, communications – 10 percent, and working conditions – 5 percent) and "factor degrees" we used earlier, but again, that is not necessarily required for each job family.

In Figure 6.5, I have outlined a set of hypothetical job evaluation points for engineers, administrative staff, and legal staff of an organization. Notice that they each have different sets of job evaluation points. The idea is that

	Engineer I (530 points)	Engineer II (640 points)	Senior Engineer (935 points)

Job Evaluation Points

Admin I (211 points)	Admin II (411 points)	Admin Lead (657 points)	

Job Evaluation Points

Legal Assistant (385 points)	Junior Attorney (590 points)		Senior Attorney (895 points)

Job Evaluation Points

Figure 6.5. Job Evaluation Points in Different Job Families

this signifies the relative *within organization* value of these positions. As was noted, this is not to say that this means that these positions are worth the same relative amounts to other organizations. Further – and this is important – it does not necessarily mean that there is a linear relationship between the job evaluation points in Figure 6.5 and ultimate wages, salaries, and total rewards for the positions (or individuals in those positions). That discussion is to come in the next chapter.

It is important to understand that the jobs and these points will be combined using external market data in the coming chapter to map a unique compensation system for this organization. It is to that topic that we now turn.

SEVEN

Matching the Internal Organizational Structure to the Right Market Data

How and How Much to Pay

This chapter follows the lead of Chapters 5 and 6 and takes the internal structure developed for an organization and matches it to external data. It is important to have external data from places from where organizations will be drawing workers and to where workers might go if they leave. This leads to a discussion of how a large number of organizations develop their compensation systems. The chapter ends with a case study of how problems can arise with this sort of system. It is important to learn how organizations set pay systems, especially if you want to learn how to earn more.

Data and Surveys: How Do We Tell What Other Organizations Pay? Filling Out a Survey

Now that we have spent time in Chapters 5 and 6 describing how an organization can make its internal systems logically consistent, it is time to consider collecting some external market data. Collecting the data is a relatively straightforward process, but there are many, many ways that problems can arise. Therefore, it is worthwhile to be very careful about it. I often feel that when users of externally generated data obtain it, they think that the data are all nice and clean and clear. This is certainly *not* the case. This first came to me when I was helping some of my PhD advisors collect data for a statistical study of the relationship between earnings and education using data on twins at the Annual Twinsburg Twins Festival in Twinsburg, Ohio. As a graduate student at the time, I had frequently used data from the U.S. Census or the Current Population Survey in the past, and the initial tendency was to blindly march forward and use the data. Actually watching people answer questions led me to think carefully about the source of the data (even though we were collecting the data exactly the same way the Census Bureau was doing it).

The same can be true for market survey compensation data. Because I span the academic, business, and consulting worlds, I occasionally find myself in a business or practitioner conference or venue. As a result, survey companies have my name and contact information. No problem so far. But they then send me surveys and ask me to complete the surveys for my organization. The problem is that my organization is Cornell University and I am not the person in charge of the compensation systems at Cornell, nor do I know what most people at the university are paid. So who is filling these out? I suspect in some cases if the surveys get in the wrong hands (like mine), the potential respondents don't fill them out (that's just what I do – I don't fill them out). But some may

But this isn't the biggest problem with survey data. A bigger problem is that not all jobs that sound the same *are* the same. You will recall from Chapter 6 that one important aspect of doing the early part of job evaluation and job analysis is to consider "benchmark jobs." These are jobs that exist frequently (i.e., in many different kinds of organizations) and that have attributes that are widely known. But not all jobs fit this bill, and sometimes organizations provide information to compensation consulting firms that doesn't exactly match the job. Imagine that someone in HR for a company is filling out the compensation survey and has a job (e.g., carpenter) that is "close" to but not exactly like the job in the survey. Further, suppose that the job in the survey is slightly "less skilled" than the one the company has. Then, when the HR person fills out the survey, if she fills in information for her carpenter position, she will be inappropriately estimating the market value of the "carpenter" position in the survey. Please note that I certainly do not mean to be critical of all surveys – some are extraordinary. Rather, I am pointing out that one should be careful when using surveys to make sure they are appropriate for your situation.

Using a Compensation Survey

Imagine that you now have access to data from a compensation survey. How did this happen? Your organization, no doubt, purchased the data from a compensation consulting company that is in the business of collecting "market data." How will you use the data? Suppose you are in a company in the Seattle area and your company designs software to help people learn how to read. Would you want to use data from the survey only from the

Seattle area? Would you only want data from other software companies? These are difficult questions and they matter for your own pay.

If you are an employee and working in a company in Seattle, or San Diego, or Boston, you might not want your employer to be making comparisons using data from somewhere like Des Moines, Iowa. For most organizations, the data that are used depend on the kinds of positions being considered. For clerical positions, the local market may matter. For example, the Seattle software company will probably want to know what administrative assistants in Seattle earn and not what administrative assistants nationally earn. At the same time, the Seattle software company might be interested in having national data or even international data when hiring programmers for its software, because those kinds of positions may be associated with people who are more willing to move to a new position or can work via telecommuting.

The same kind of analysis goes for the kinds of organizations that are being compared. For example, if the Seattle software company is a small start-up, it may want to consider using data from only small or growing companies rather than compare itself with larger, more mature organizations.

This kind of question comes up often in organizations that span sectors or regions. Imagine a nonprofit hospital that is competing, in part, with for-profit hospitals and wants to consider hiring and compensating a new leader that will be more "business-like" (Bertrand, Hallock and Arnould, 2005). Should this organization use comparison data from for-profit hospitals, nonprofit hospitals, both, or neither? It depends. These questions are worth asking and considering, whether you are designing a compensation system for an organization for which you work, designing a compensation system for your own business, or an employee trying to negotiate for more, to better understand your compensation.

The Market Pay Line: Combining the Internal Structure With the External Data

Let's now suppose the organization has the "right data."[1] The simple idea now is to "merge" the analysis from Chapter 6 with the new external market data. Figure 7.1 is an example that does just this. In Figure 7.1, the horizontal axis represents job evaluation points for five jobs in the small Seattle software company – all are types of programmers. Reading along the horizontal axis, the first job has 185 job evaluation points, the second job has 200 points, the third job has 335 points, the fourth 400 points, and the fifth 460 job

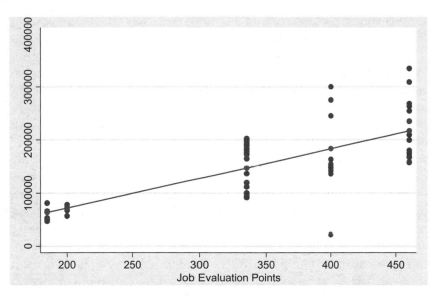

Figure 7.1. Market Pay Line. *Notes:* The horizontal axis represents job evaluation points for five jobs in the small software company. The dots each represent a point of data from the external market that match each of the five jobs (vertically).

evaluation points. Recall that the firm may have many people in each of these jobs.

Each of the 58 dots that go up vertically from each of the five job evaluation points (185, 200, 335, 400, and 460) represents a point of data from the external market that match each of the five jobs. Note that there are only six matches for the first engineering position (with 185 job evaluation points) but fifteen for the fifth engineer position (with 460 job evaluation points).[2] It is clear that the external company data associated with the second position (200 job evaluation points) are all very closely clustered vertically. That is to say that this job is paid very similarly across firms (in the survey). On the other hand, external company data associated with the fourth position (400 job evaluation points) and fifth position (460 job evaluation points) are much more dispersed. This could be for a variety of reasons. These could include that the jobs aren't defined perfectly (e.g., a company providing data to the compensation consulting company may have miscategorized jobs), the data are internationally dispersed and wages differ dramatically by country (see more in Chapter 12), or because there are more senior programmers, their pay is potentially associated with performance (see Chapter 9) and firms want to allow a lot of leeway in pay to coincide with potentially extraordinary performance.

You may also notice that one of the points seems way off. The low point in the vertical job evaluation point section of 400 seems to be at about \$35,000 on the vertical axis, when all of the other points are more than \$135,000. No doubt this is just an "outlier" and is probably a mistake. If you ever see something like this in the data, give it special attention to make sure it is not a mistake. *Always stare at your data for a long time.*

So again, each point represents data from some external company. All of the dots represent actual dollars (on the vertical axis) that companies somewhere are paying their employees. The idea now is to decide, using the external company data and internal structure developed in Chapter 6, how much to pay people in this company (*How* to pay them, or the compensation mix, is a bit more complicated and is discussed in Chapters 4 and 11, among other places).

Notice that the line in Figure 7.1 is straight. It doesn't have to be, but in this example, I have forced it to be straight. It could, for example, curve up (become steeper) as we go from left to right, but instead, in this example, I have kept the slope constant throughout.[3] The simplest way to think about this line is that it is the best line that "fits" through the data scattered in Figure 7.1.[4]

It turns out that the equation for this line is equal to $-39,651.77 + 556.931(JE)$, where JE stands for "Job Evaluation" points. Another way to say this is that if we "plug in" a number of job evaluation points into this formula, we will get the point wage that the internal and external structures suggest we should pay. Let's take the five examples we have considered in this example. If we plug 185 into the equation, we get $\$63,380.47 = -39,651.77 + 556.931 \times (185)$. So the "system" suggests that if we hold to our internally consistent structure (that developed the five jobs and levels of job evaluation points 185, 200, 335, 400, and 460) and used the right external market data, it would be reasonable to pay someone in the 185 job evaluation point job \$63,381 per year. The formula can be used similarly for the other positions. For example, for the second position, the point compensation level would be $\$71,734.43 = -39,651.77 + 556.931 \times (200)$. The other three jobs would yield \$146,920.12, \$183,120.63, and \$216,536.49, respectively.

Note that the "equation" $-39,651.77 + 556.931 \times (JE)$ should not be taken too seriously, especially "out of sample." What this equation literally means is that we would pay negative \$39,651.77, then add an extra \$556.93 for each job evaluation point. Since there is no data to the "left" of 200 job evaluation points, making such an interpolation would not be a good idea.

On the other hand, if the organization comes up with a new position, or has a position that is not part of the set of benchmark jobs, this equation can be used to price the job. Imagine, for, example a new position that is difficult to replicate externally (so it would not be a good benchmark job), but that easily fits the internal structure, and the organization decides it is "worth" 300 job evaluation points. This can easily be plugged into the equation, and we see that the point number for the job is $127,427.53 = -39,651.77 + 556.931 \times (300)$.

After the Line: Developing a System

After an organization has set up a market pay line, the job is not done. Obviously there is more to go. All the pay line tells is a *single* level of pay that corresponds to a given number of job evaluation points. If organizations ended there, then every single person in a particular job at a particular time would be paid at precisely the same level. And we know this not to be the case.

One step that an organization may want to consider is whether it wants to pay at, above, or below the market (Milkovich and Newman, 2008). That is to say, the organization may want to raise or lower the market pay line outlined in Figure 7.1. In a perfectly competitive labor market (as defined in introductory economics books), there is no reason to pay anything except exactly what everyone else is paying. But, as should be clear from this and the previous two chapters, things are more complicated than that.

Another issue to consider is the mix of pay that will go into the total levels that have previously been discussed. This is the idea of the difference between "how much" to pay and "how" to pay (see, for example, Jensen and Murphy, 1990). That is the subject of Chapters 4 and 11.

The next step is to put some sort of "leeway" into the system. This leeway is sometimes called grades and ranges, or bands and zones (or some other similar sets of terms which are basically describing the same thing). The idea is to provide a distribution of possible sets of compensation levels for each set of job evaluation points. The most obvious way to see how this would work is to consider two employees in exactly the same job – suppose they are both Administrative Assistants IV. Given what we have learned in Chapter 6, this particular job (Administrative Assistant IV) or any other specific job has a series of expectations and responsibilities associated with it.

Recall also the discussion earlier that we were focusing on the *job* and not the *person* (although other methods can do this differently). Well, now it is time to focus more on the person. Perhaps one Administrative Assistant IV is considerably more productive and has much more experience, leadership skills, and organizational ability than others. In this case, that person would naturally earn more than the others because he or she is performing in the same job but is more productive. However, once a *system* that allows leeway has been put into place, the next step is to decide how formalized the system should be. After an organization goes through all the trouble of developing a strategy (Chapter 5), considering job analysis and internal comparisons (Chapter 6), and matching with external data to develop a structure and then providing for minimum and maximum levels for each job, the organization may want to "stick to its plans" and not go outside of the structure (e.g., deciding that the span from the bottom to top for the lowest-level programmers should be 20 percent of pay and that for the top-level folks it should be 80 percent of pay). The case study that ends this chapter shows how difficult that can be.

A Case Study: Megalith

The Case of Megalith (Seeger, Harlan and Kotter, 1976) tells the story of a set of managers at the fictional company Megalith and problems with their compensation system. The four main characters are James Boyd (SVP Finance), Frank Nicodemus (VP HR), Edmund Rogers (Compensation Consultant), and Allen Whitfield (President). Yes, they are all men. It was written in 1976!

In the case, Boyd wanted to raise the salaries of his central finance staff a year earlier by 25 percent. The head of HR (Nicodemus) said no, that the people in question were too inexperienced for such compensation. And then two of the four people perceived to be central to the finance function left the company.

Boyd said he wanted more leeway to pay his finance people more, but Nicodemus countered that the structure was something that he and his staff (along with their external consultant) had worked hard to design.

In the case, Boyd asks the consultant (Ed) if the system can tell the "difference between talent and mediocrity." Ed's response is as follows:

That's a judgment no formal system can make. Only a responsible executive – the man in your own shoes – can tell how well his people are performing, or how high they can go. But a formal system can say something about the jobs themselves. We can compare the jobs in the Finance Group to each other, based on their contents, to give you a measure of internal equity – of how fairly you're paying your people relative to each other. Then we can compare your salaries to those paid for similar-content jobs by a broad spectrum of industry. We can help define what end results each position is accountable for, and the definitions can sharpen your management performance. That can help you decide what 'outstanding' means and how much you are willing to pay for it. (Seeger, Harlan and Kotter, 1976)

It turns out, in a follow-up to this case, that the people are leaving not because of money, but because Boyd hasn't given them enough responsibility. It does, however, indicate that the system can create some problems while masking others.

At the end of the day, I hope that the discussion in the past three chapters has given you a glimpse into one way that many, many organizations throughout the world pay their employees. When I first saw this, I was surprised and thought the system was too complicated, arbitrary, and formulaic. However, I think there are at least two important things to remember with respect to this. First, decisions have to be made about pay at some point. A formalized system is much less likely to lead to bias, inappropriate pay levels, and even discrimination. Why not write down the rules of the game in advance, as described here? Second, even if you don't like this system, it (and variants of it) is largely how a great number of people are paid. And even if your organization doesn't do this, so many do that they influence the rest of organizations in a meaningful way. Therefore, it is certainly worthwhile understanding it, especially if you are one who may be designing pay systems yourself, or even if you are a person who wants to make more in your own job.

EIGHT

Paying Executives, Athletes, Entertainers, and Other "Superstars"

The issue of executive compensation has become increasingly controversial in the past years, not just in the Unites States but throughout the world. This chapter is an attempt to introduce the reader to the "basics" of executive compensation, including main elements of executive compensation used by many companies and an overview of some current pay levels and the "mix" of pay for executives in the United States. The chapter then goes on to provide an example of why you shouldn't believe everything you read in the newspaper – which is a simple account of how and why it is often the case that seemingly simple issues are actually relatively complicated once they are examined more closely. The chapter then goes on to, in simple terms, discuss whether there is a link between pay and performance for executives and the topic of risk and executive compensation. Whether CEOs and other executives are overpaid is then discussed, in the context of other kinds of "superstar" compensation, for example athletes and entertainers. The chapter concludes with a section on what is on the horizon for executive pay.

Ways Executives are Paid

To begin, it is useful to consider the ways that executives are paid in the United States today. A large majority of executives are paid through one of seven different elements: salary, bonus, non-equity incentive, stock, stock options, change in pension and nonqualified deferred earnings, and other compensation.[1]

The Securities and Exchange Commission (SEC) recently began to require publicly traded firms to more carefully disclose compensation for the CEO, Chief Financial Officer, and three other most highly paid Named Executive Officers (NEOs). Prior to 2006, publicly traded firms were reporting this, but not in such a standardized and formalized way as they do today. The seven main elements that are required to be reported in detail are discussed further here. Salary, bonus, and non-equity incentive are often thought to be part of "cash" compensation, although some of it is guaranteed and some of it is not. Salary, of course, is the annual, fixed, and guaranteed compensation for the executive. Bonus and non-equity incentive compensation are sometimes confused and, intuitively, both can be considered a type of "bonus." Strictly speaking, the bonus as listed in the "summary compensation" table of proxy statements for publicly traded companies is formula-based pay beyond cash salary. Non-equity incentive is similar to a standard bonus but is somewhat different. In particular, non-equity incentive compensation can be both short-term or long-term pay that is based on some preset criteria (based on performance) the outcome of which is uncertain. Next comes equity compensation, which is most simply broken out into two categories: stock and stock options. Stock compensation is the value of the stock granted over the prior year, as of the time it is granted. Stock options represent the value of the options to buy stock over the prior year. Stock options pose a unique problem in valuing executive compensation contracts. The numbers included in firms' proxy statement "summary compensation tables" are accounting-based numbers and do not necessarily reflect the value of the options at the time of the grant.[2] Therefore, I recommend – and most researchers use – the value of stock options from the stock option grant summary tables, which are also included in firm proxy statements. Finally, "other" compensation refers to amounts of perquisites of $10,000 or more or to tax gross-ups, company contributions for security, private use of aircraft, financial planning, and so forth. At the end of the day, these are ways that pay reporting is required in proxy statements. In reality, most people probably think of the elements in the following categories: base, bonus, equity, benefits, retirement, and perquisites.

Table 8.1 is an example of a Summary Compensation Table for eBay for 2011. Several features of the table are noteworthy. The table lists compensation for the CEO, CFO, and four other executives. As noted earlier, firms are required to list the CEO, CFO, and at least three others. One reason for listing more than five executives is the fact that some may have retired or otherwise left the firm during the year. Another reason for the listing of more than five executives is the occasional listing of "co-CEOs." It is also clear from the table that information is included for each of the last three years. Table 8.1 also shows the seven different pay components that are required to be reported for each executive.[3] For example, eBay reported in its 2011 proxy statement that it paid its CEO $12,382,486. Of that, $920,673 was in the form

Table 8.1. eBay "summary compensation table" from 2011 proxy statement (from page 49 of eBay 2011 proxy statement)

Name of principal position	Year	Salary ($)(1)	Bonus ($)	Stock awards ($)(2)	Option awards ($)(3)	Nonequity incentive plan compensation ($)(4)	Change in pension value and nonqualified deferred compensation earnings ($)	All other compensation ($)(5)	Total ($)
John J. Donahoe President and Chief Executive Officer (7)	2010	$920,673	$736,538(6)	$5,586,045	$3,735,000	$1,158,575	$0	$245,655	$12,382,486
	2009	934,615	438,101(6)	4,450,388	2,483,682	1,653,568	0	172,394	10,132,748
	2008	879,808	500,000(6)	13,344,580	9,026,068	0	0	279,108	24,029,564
Robert H. Swan Senior Vice President, Finance and Chief Financial Officer	2010	768,606	584,303(8)	2,447,700	1,867,500	604,508	0	82,080	6,354,697
	2009	778,846	443,389(8)	1,362,375	2,323,600	918,649	0	73,530	5,900,389
	2008	697,442	200,000(8)	8,925,450	3,595,988	0	0	93,749	13,512,629
Scott Thompson President, PayPal (10)	2010	641,538	320,769(9)	7,652,625	1,307,250	504,570	0	9,841	10,436,593
	2009	635,288	174,704(9)	1,097,250	551,200	749,323	0	9,841	3,217,606
	2008	556,885	0	988,985	1,066,130	0	0	9,520	2,621,520

	Year								
Lorrie M. Norrington	2010	696,892	172,885(9)	1,522,350	1,120,500	543,895	0	705,951	4,762,473
Former President, eBay Marketplaces (11)	2009	700,962	192,764(9)	876,750	551,200	826,784	0	35,675	3,184,135
	2008	618,173	0	4,993,250	1,635,200	0	0	10,207	7,257,830
Elizabeth L. Axelrod	2010	497,404	139,895(9)	1,477,575	1,120,500	293,406	0	10,628	3,539,408
Senior Vice President Human Resources (12)	2009	503,654	102,305(9)	1,119,563	386,900	386,139	0	10,592	2,509,153
	2008	480,135	0	3,581,075	629,888	0	0	10,158	4,771,256
Mark T. Carges	2010	562,404	210,901(9)	1,059,675	747,00	331,748	0	10,736	2,922,464
Chief Technology Officer and Senior Vice President, Global Products, Marketplaces (13)	2009	571,154	117,801(9)	1,290,188	968,715	505,257	0	10,638	3,463,753

of guaranteed cash salary. They also paid him a \$736,538 bonus, \$1,158,575 in non-equity incentive, \$3,735,000 in stock options,[4] and \$5,586,045 in stock. The final category under which the CEO of eBay was paid that year was "other" and included a number of components, among them private use of aircraft. He was paid \$245,655 in other compensation.

It is interesting to see that at some companies, the CEO is not the highest-paid executive (at least as reported in the most recent proxy statement). Hallock and Torok (2011) report that of 2444 firms they studied, the CEO was the highest-paid executive in only 81 percent of them. There are many reasons why the CEO may not be the highest-paid person in the company, including one-time signing bonus for other executives, larger-than-normal option grants (commonplace when hiring new executives), or severance, among others. It is interesting to see, in Table 8.1, the diversity of compensation across pay elements and to see the diversity of pay within the top management team.

Main Data Sources

As I have noted, all publicly traded companies must report the compensation of the top five highest-paid employees with managerial control in the firm. This includes the CEO, the CFO, and three next most highly paid executives. In fact, if a company is publicly traded (more than 10,000 are in the United States), it is very easy to "look up" the pay of the senior managers. All one needs to do is go to the SEC Web site, www.sec.gov. Then under the "filings" tab, click on "search for company filings." This will give you a prompt to identify a "company name." Type in the company name and you will be provided with a list of all public filings to the SEC from the firm. Look for the one that says "DEF 14A" – this is the "definitive" proxy statement. The proxy includes the "summary compensation table" (like Table 8.1 for eBay), many other required tables, and a long discussion and analysis of the company compensation philosophy and justification for the executive compensation program.

There are three major commercial data sources on executive pay that are now relatively widely used. The first, ExecuComp (Executive Compensation database), is produced by Standard and Poor's Corporation and is surely the most widely used source of data for research on executive pay by academics. This source has data available from 1992 to the present on the compensation of the top five highest-paid employees of U.S. publicly traded firms (who have managerial control) in roughly 1,500 firms per year. These firms include those listed in the Standard and Poor's 500, the Standard and

Poor's SmallCap 600, and the Standard and Poor's MidCap 400. The data source starts in 1992, which was (until 2006) the last time there was a major change in executive pay disclosure rules.

Two other commercial executive pay sources are Equilar and Kenexa (formerly Salary.com). Each also provides comprehensive data sets of executive compensation but have a larger focus on marketing to the for-profit firm and compensation consulting market. These sources are frequently used by compensation design practitioners and consultants to help design executive pay plans (and to set comparison groups). Some academics are using data from these sources but they are much more widely used by practitioners.[5]

Executive Pay in 2010. A Summary and Overview of Facts

This subsection is designed to provide a descriptive overview of the basic kinds of pay levels, mix (types of pay across different components of compensation), and pay distributions for publicly traded firms in the United States today.[6] The data for this section are from Salary.com and comprise 2,444 publicly traded firms who reported executive compensation information in their proxy statements as of June 2010. The firms in this study range in size from less than $98 million in annual revenue (10 percent of the group) to more than $9 billion in annual revenue (10 percent of the group).

Figure 8.1 displays two measures of compensation. The first is defined as "cash" and is the sum of salary, bonus, and non-equity incentive. The second measure is "total compensation." This is defined as the sum of salary, bonus, non-equity incentive, stock, stock options, change in pension and non-qualified deferred earnings, and other. Figure 8.1 displays the median cash compensation and total compensation for CEOs by industry for each of twenty-two different industries. Notice the dramatic heterogeneity in compensation levels for the median-paid CEO across industries. For example, the median CEO in the Construction industry earned about $1,839,447 in cash pay and $3,371,968 in total compensation. At the extreme high end is the Food & Tobacco industry where the median CEO earned $2.6 million in cash compensation and $6.05 million in total compensation. These statistics alone mask another level of heterogeneity. Consider, for example, the Food and Tobacco industry (see Table 8.2). There, the CEO at the 10th percentile earned $635,192 in cash pay and $1,040,245 in total compensation, but the CEO at the 90th percentile of that industry earned $5.6 million in cash and $16.2 million in total compensation.

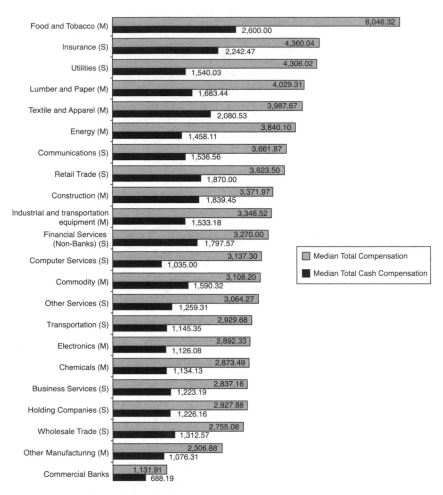

Figure 8.1. CEO Compensation by Industry (in thousands of dollars). *Note:* This is based on Hallock and Torok (2011). Data from Salary.com/Kanexa. A figure like this from the previous year is used in Florin, Hallock, and Webber (2010). (M = Manufacturing, S = Sales)

It turns out that the lowest average cash compensation and lowest average total compensation by industry is in Commercial Banking, where the average cash pay is $688,190 and the average total pay is $1,131,910. It may seem strange that Commercial Banks represent the industry with the lowest-paid median CEO. However, these numbers do not control for the size of the organization. In fact, there are a large number of Commercial Banks in the sample and many of them are quite small. Organization size (e.g., revenue, employees) is highly positively correlated with the compensation of the

Table 8.2. CEO compensation by industry in dollars

		Cash compensation						Total compensation					
	N	10th	25th	Mean	Median	75th	90th	10th	25th	Mean	Median	75th	90th
Business Services	98	543,672	900,000	1,608,476	1,223,191	1,800,300	3,257,820	991,134	1,534,953	3,668,602	2,837,162	4,657,403	8,407,644
Chemicals	205	540,346	717,848	1,731,938	1,134,128	2,506,000	4,004,521	882,100	1,356,301	4,845,255	2,873,491	6,736,012	12,400,000
Commercial Banks	188	360,000	469,082	1,080,409	688,188	1,198,315	2,266,667	476,758	716,903	2,352,754	1,131,910	2,477,335	5,241,902
Commodities	104	600,876	908,428	2,032,076	1,594,322	2,827,500	4,783,750	866,783	1,657,944	5,271,384	3,108,198	8,674,053	12,600,000
Communications	94	585,000	938,700	2,135,159	1,536,557	2,966,000	6,600,000	1,021,830	1,917,544	5,084,885	3,661,868	8,584,002	18,200,000
Computer Services	165	456,019	714,179	1,325,537	1,035,000	1,813,000	2,841,625	712,068	1,434,911	4,021,627	3,137,304	5,457,246	9,022,349
Cons- truction	33	690,000	785,000	1,916,965	1,839,447	2,831,015	3,500,000	1,148,108	1,932,012	4,325,751	3,371,968	6,730,381	8,933,005
Electronics	169	436,488	683,170	1,598,888	1,126,083	1,883,962	3,387,500	895,798	1,378,104	4,184,687	2,892,326	5,053,479	10,400,000
Energy	119	500,000	862,970	1,779,151	1,458,105	2,297,074	3,500,000	805,875	1,694,474	4,966,942	3,840,102	6,633,977	13,200,000
Financial Services (Non-Banks)	78	545,000	855,000	2,416,626	1,797,570	3,410,629	5,350,000	972,235	1,392,737	4,845,980	3,269,998	6,906,028	11,500,000
Food and Tobacco	52	635,192	1,163,383	2,752,409	2,600,000	3,622,905	5,569,521	1,040,245	2,534,854	7,041,743	6,046,318	10,100,000	16,200,000
Holding Companies	121	516,334	832,000	1,545,850	1,226,158	1,975,000	2,881,727	876,332	1,554,000	3,901,053	2,827,879	4,777,541	8,651,734
Industrial and transportation equipment	176	419,563	700,302	2,121,774	1,533,179	2,765,833	4,419,000	827,641	1,415,266	5,211,428	3,346,516	7,751,624	11,000,000
Insurance	108	825,002	1,276,837	2,647,694	2,242,471	3,412,500	5,200,000	1,288,945	2,457,896	6,350,036	4,360,036	9,085,577	14,300,000
Lumber and Paper	46	600,000	1,124,799	1,782,706	1,683,443	2,430,000	3,115,000	1,227,845	2,029,713	4,787,603	4,029,314	5,907,455	10,100,000
Other Manufacturing	161	500,000	695,000	1,437,589	1,076,312	1,873,129	2,668,554	749,152	1,173,880	3,616,480	2,306,880	4,637,120	7,948,211
Other Services	112	570,000	865,938	1,860,230	1,259,313	2,255,793	4,125,000	995,112	1,554,528	4,381,771	3,064,267	6,393,191	9,850,965
Retail Trade	157	532,308	888,104	2,172,466	1,870,000	3,220,453	4,154,689	1,009,148	1,735,619	5,220,517	3,623,499	6,747,800	13,100,000
Textile and Apparel	23	1,207,000	1,315,750	2,821,651	2,080,526	4,316,586	6,802,444	1,319,009	2,221,292	5,884,183	3,987,669	9,326,936	12,900,000
Transportation	66	450,000	747,500	1,602,538	1,145,350	1,827,800	3,341,168	707,100	1,316,504	3,558,744	2,929,685	4,926,236	8,041,271
Utilities (S)	99	644,615	985,975	1,930,303	1,540,031	2,825,000	3,774,400	1,231,916	2,288,372	5,179,510	4,306,017	7,868,720	9,956,433
Wholesale Trade (S)	70	640,000	789,167	1,593,504	1,312,572	2,270,093	2,904,250	967,697	1,451,405	3,809,358	2,755,084	5,548,738	7,538,616

Note: Adapted from Hallock and Torok (2011). Data from Salary.com. A table like this is also used in Florin Hallock, and Webber (2010).

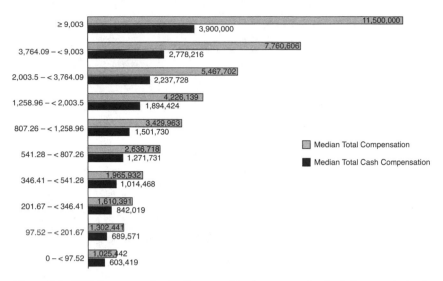

Figure 8.2. CEO Compensation by Company Size (compensation in dollars, vertical axis is revenue in millions of dollars). *Note:* This is based on Hallock and Torok (2011). Data from Salary.com. A figure like this from a previous year is also used in Florin, Hallock, and Webber (2010). Vertical axis in millions of dollars of sales.

senior leaders – this is one of the most widely known statistical facts in the executive compensation literature (Rosen, 1992). Figure 8.2 is a case in point. In this figure, the 2,444 companies are sorted by their level of annual revenue. The smallest 10 percent are in decile 1, the next 10 percent in decile 2, and so forth, up to the largest 10 percent in decile 10. It is clear that the median level of compensation rises monotonically with organization's size. In particular, for the smallest 10 percent of companies (those with annual revenues below $98 million), the median CEO earned $603,419 in cash pay and $1.03 million in total compensation. This rises monotonically up to the largest 10 percent of firms (those with annual revenues above $9 billion) where the median CEO earned $3.9 million in cash compensation and $11.5 million in total compensation. Again, the median masks the larger distribution. For example, for the largest 10 percent of companies, the CEO in the 10th percentile earned $4.1 million in total compensation, but the CEO in the 90th percentile earned $22.7 million in total compensation (see Table 8.3).

Understanding the levels of pay for CEOs is interesting and important but misses a more interesting and important part of executive compensation: *how* executives are paid. As noted earlier, this is an extremely important point

Table 8.3. *CEO compensation by revenue*

Revenue deciles in millions	Number of companies	Cash compensation						Total compensation					
		10th	25th	Mean	Median	75th	90th	10th	25th	Mean	Median	75th	90th
0 – < 98	244	337,457	458,322	694,945	603,419	792,588	1,039,520	468,589	712,252	1,445,600	1,025,442	1,549,625	2,955,261
98 – < 202	244	374,000	474,059	760,407	689,571	938,700	1,202,251	542,282	813,463	1,702,817	1,302,441	2,099,994	3,301,316
202 – < 346	246	420,000	589,439	933,887	842,019	1,074,304	1,500,438	618,415	1,000,803	2,036,095	1,610,391	2,619,066	3,904,151
346 – < 541	244	508,200	728,879	1,166,673	1,014,468	1,358,385	1,818,303	818,584	1,284,104	2,453,494	1,965,932	2,937,273	4,915,807
541 – < 807	244	649,384	889,802	1,469,078	1,271,731	1,777,383	2,250,000	1,022,102	1,607,856	3,112,977	2,636,718	3,794,117	5,967,995
807 – < 1,259	245	769,994	1,050,000	1,740,782	1,501,730	2,098,300	3,000,000	1,281,779	2,164,517	4,208,962	3,429,963	5,050,268	7,457,406
1,259 – < 2,004	243	873,148	1,269,507	2,037,602	1,894,424	2,510,557	3,196,502	1,562,381	2,582,046	4,836,696	4,226,139	6,180,996	8,401,040
2,004 – < 3,764	246	1,011,154	1,504,958	2,480,721	2,237,728	3,143,599	4,500,000	1,896,956	3,529,900	5,900,785	5,467,702	7,695,600	10,400,000
3,764 – < 9,003	243	1,248,490	1,877,352	2,936,170	2,778,216	3,467,905	5,066,000	3,260,980	4,916,534	7,899,076	7,760,606	10,300,000	13,400,000
≥ 9,003	245	1,595,000	2,710,000	3,986,757	3,900,000	5,426,761	7,700,000	4,119,384	8,096,968	11,900,000	11,500,000	17,300,000	22,700,000

Note: Adapted from Hallock and Torok (2011). Data from Salary.com

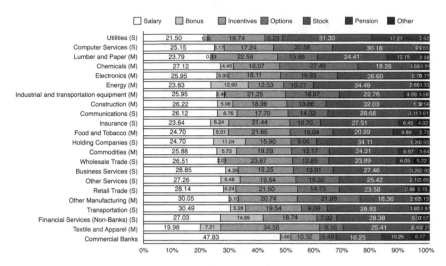

Figure 8.3. CEO Compensation Mix by Industry. *Note:* This is based on Hallock and Torok (2011). Data from Salary.com. A figure like this is also used in Florin, Hallock, and Webber (2010). (M = Manufacturing, S = Sales)

throughout this book, but especially with executive pay. In particular, we now explore how executives in general are paid across the seven components of compensation discussed previously. Figure 8.3 shows a great deal of heterogeneity across compensation components by industry. In fact, it is quite reasonable to expect diversity in compensation mix within industry. Note, for example, that in the commercial banking industry, on average, salary accounts for 48 percent of total compensation (this fraction is only 21.5 percent in the utilities industry). Figure 8.3 illustrates many other diverse numbers.

Figure 8.4 reports the pay mix distribution by firm size deciles (the same deciles reported in Figure 8.2). Notice that, as the average firm gets larger, a smaller fraction of the total compensation is paid in salary and a larger fraction is paid in stock and stock options. For example, for the smallest 10 percent of companies, the fraction of total compensation paid in salary is 42.64 percent, but for the largest 10 percent of companies, the fraction of total compensation paid in salary is only 13 percent. Conversely, the average CEO in the smallest 10 percent of companies earned 32.58 (18.09 + 14.49) percent of his or her total compensation in stock and options, but the average CEO in the largest 10 percent of companies earned 48.66 (16.93 + 31.73) percent of his or her total compensation in stock and stock options.

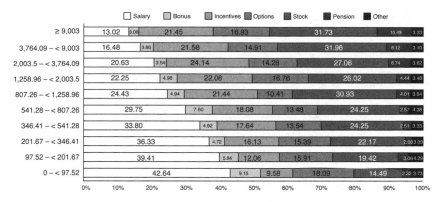

Figure 8.4. CEO Compensation Mix by Size Group (vertical axis is revenue in millions of dollars) *Note:* This is based on Hallock and Torok (2011). Data from Salary.com. A figure like this is also used in Florin, Hallock, and Webber (2010). Vertical axis in millions of dollars of sales.

Why You Shouldn't Believe Everything You Read in the Newspaper: A CEO Pay Example

In the mid-1990s, I found a press release that read "Workers Lose, CEOs Win" (Anderson and Cavanagh, 1994). The short report listed the thirty companies who laid off the most workers in the previous year as well as the level of pay and the level of total compensation and the most recent year-to-year raise for the CEOs of those firms. The study concluded that workers "lose" and CEOs "win" based primarily on one empirical fact: the *average* raise for the CEOs of the thirty firms who made these layoffs was 30 percent. Did the layoffs *cause* the large raises for the CEOs or were they just related for other reasons? I was curious about this fact and widely cited related news, and so decided to investigate it further.

The first part of my investigation led me to consider the *median* change in CEO pay for the thirty companies who had announced the largest number of job reductions in the previous year. It turns out that the median raise for CEOs from this group of thirty companies was 11 percent, much smaller than the 30 percent average raise. The median was so much smaller than the mean primarily owing to the fact that there were a few substantial outliers at the top end that obviously influence the mean in a substantial way, relative to the median.

The next step was to consider a much larger set of companies. Rather than start with thirty companies who made a large number of layoffs in a single year, I decided to follow the largest 800 companies for a period of seven years (this lead to 3,242 "CEO-years" of data). I collected information

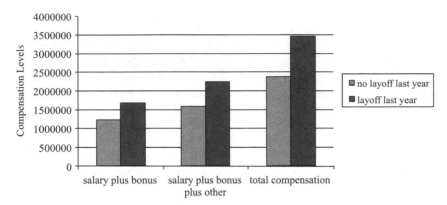

Figure 8.5. Pay Differences by Layoff Status (no control variables). *Source:* Hallock (1998, 2010).

on the CEO compensation for each of these firms as well as on each job loss announcement that each of the firms made in each year for this seven-year period.[7] It turns out that the median (and average) raise for this group of CEOs was 11 percent – exactly the median reported for the top thirty job-cutting firms.

Figure 8.5 separates the data into two groups: (1) the group of companies that did not make a layoff announcement in the previous year and (2) the group of companies that made at least one layoff announcement in the previous year. The figure also investigates three measures of CEO compensation: salary plus bonus, salary plus bonus plus "other," and total compensation.[8] The figure plainly shows that by each measure of compensation, those CEOs who led firms that made at least one layoff in the previous year are paid more than those who have not made a layoff in the previous year. This is perfectly consistent with Anderson and Cavanagh (1994).

Rather than just examine pay levels, I also considered raises. Figure 8.6 also clearly shows that CEO raises were higher in firms that made at least one layoff in the previous year relative to those firms that did not make a layoff at all. Again, this is true for all three measures of compensation. Again, this is perfectly consistent with Anderson and Cavanagh (1994).

Recall from the previous discussion that the single strongest correlate of CEO pay is company size (Rosen, 1992). Given this well-known fact, I decided to sort companies into "size" groups. I did this by taking the smallest 10 percent of companies (in terms of revenue) and putting them into group (decile) 1, the next 10 percent of companies into size group (decile) 2, and so on up to the largest 10 percent of companies into group (decile) 10. In Figure 8.7, I then plotted the level of total CEO compensation

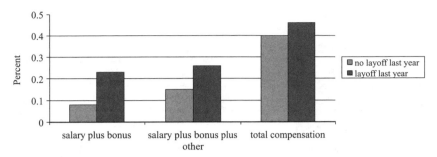

Figure 8.6. Pay Changes by Layoff Status (no control variables). *Source:* Hallock (1998, 2010).

(on the right-hand axis) versus the "size" (revenue) deciles. As is clear from the figure, on average, the larger the firm, the higher the level of total CEO compensation. I then plotted the fraction of companies in each decile who made at least one layoff announcement (on the left-hand axis) against the deciles (on the horizontal axis). Figure 8.7 also makes it clear that both pay for CEOs and the fraction of firms with at least one layoff rise dramatically as company size (revenue) rises. Only 4 percent of the smallest group (the 10 percent of companies with the smallest level of revenue) made a layoff. At the same time, fully 34 percent of the largest group (top 10 percent in terms of revenue) made a layoff. So perhaps it isn't layoffs that *cause* higher CEO pay or CEO raises but something is correlated with both CEO pay and the probability of making a layoff announcement. Figure 8.7 plainly shows that company's size is related to both the probability of a layoff (big companies are more likely to let workers go) and CEO pay (big

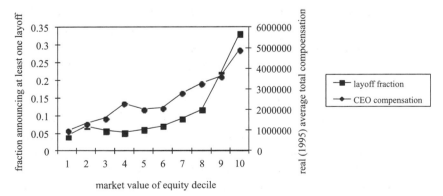

Figure 8.7. Fraction of Firms Announcing at Least One Layoff and Mean Total CEO Compensation by Company Size. *Source:* Hallock (1998, 2010).

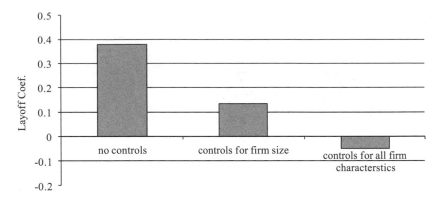

Figure 8.8. The Economic Relationship between Layoffs and CEO Pay. *Source:* Hallock (1998, 2010).

companies pay more to the CEO – and everyone else by the way). But perhaps there are other characteristics of companies that are related to CEO pay and to the probability of making a layoff announcement.

To investigate this further, I collected additional information on each company. This included details on a variety of firm performance (both financial and accounting) measures, characteristics of the CEO (such as age, seniority in the company, and seniority as CEO), time (years), and additional measures such as industry. I then performed simple statistical analyses of the relationship between CEO compensation and whether the firm made a layoff *controlling for* this wide variety of factors.[9] Figure 8.8 shows intuitively what was learned from this exercise. The first column shows the simple relationship between CEO compensation and whether the company announced a layoff in the previous year. This shows that CEOs who made a layoff in the previous year had 38 percent higher total compensation than those who did not make a layoff announcement in the previous year. However, once only firm size was controlled for, on average, CEOs who made a layoff announcement earned 13 percent more than those CEOs who did not make a layoff announcement the previous year; that is, in comparing firms of similar size, companies who made layoffs had CEOs with 13 percent higher total compensation than their counterparts who made no such layoffs. Finally, the last bar in Figure 8.8 shows that once we control for all of the characteristics of CEOs and firms, we find that, on average, those CEOs who did make layoffs actually earned about 5 percent *less* than those CEOs who did not make layoffs in the previous year.[10]

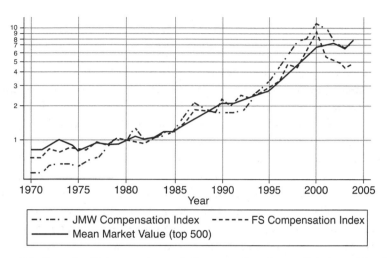

Figure 8.9. Executive Compensation and Company Size. *Source:* Gabaix and Landier (2008).

Executive Pay and Company Size

As noted previously, Rosen (1992) and many others have documented the extraordinary link between executive pay and company size. In fact, this is probably the single strongest finding in all of the literature on executive compensation (Murphy, 1999). Scores and scores of papers have written about it (Hallock, Madalozzo, and Reck, 2010). A question remains, however, as to why there is this strong link. Figure 8.9 from Gabaix and Landier (2008) shows the extraordinary growth in the average level of executive compensation over the past four decades.[11] What is also interesting about the figure is that average company size (measured as total market value of the firm) has grown similarly quickly. This is not to say, necessarily, that the growth in pay is causally related to the growth in company size – more complicated statistical analysis is required for such a claim (see later discussion) – but it is interesting to see this link.

Another interesting theory that is occasionally discussed with respect to executive compensation in known as "tournament theory" (Lazear and Rosen, 1981). The idea is that CEOs are paid actually more than they are producing.[12] However, all of the people working below them are working harder in order to compete for the ultimate prize – the job of CEO. This is a very clever and interesting idea and has been studied in many contexts. However, exploring the idea in the CEO labor market is difficult. The next section also considers the relationship between pay and the value of the CEO – is there a link between pay and performance for CEOs?

Is There a Link Between Pay and Performance? How Would We Know?

One might imagine that it is not particularly difficult to discover if there is a link between pay and performance for CEOs of publicly traded companies. It turns out, however, that this is actually considerably more difficult than it sounds. Of course, there are notable cases where a CEO is hired, stays only a very short time, and the company performs spectacularly poorly – or even goes bankrupt – and the CEO walks away with tens of millions of dollars in severance. But those kinds of cases are not as common as one might think. Further, the same constituents who are often outraged at the time of the collapse and payment of severance were quite happy to negotiate a contract that included a promise of severance if something went wrong. In this section, I offer a brief summary of some of the issues and findings on the relationship between pay and performance over the past few decades.[13]

I will only highlight a few famous examples of the pay and performance literature here, in order to give the reader a flavor for how the history of the CEO-pay-to-performance debate has changed over time. The academic study of executive compensation goes back at least to Roberts (1956) and even Bearle and Means (1932). There were also notable papers decades ago such as Masson (1971), Lewellen and Hunstman (1970), and Coughlin and Schmidt (1985), among others. The field really took off with the availability and use of better data (both in terms of quantity and quality) and Murphy's (1985) landmark study.

Murphy (1985) collected data on the compensation and performance of 461 executives at 71 firms over a number of years. But rather than estimating simple relationships (which showed no relationship between CEO pay and performance), Murphy (1985) introduced a slightly more complicated (but still widely known at the time) statistical method and found a strong relationship between pay and performance.[14] Murphy (1985), documenting a relationship between pay and performance, also wrote a paper in the *Harvard Business Review* at the time, stating that "Top Executives are worth every nickel they can get."

Five years later, Jensen and Murphy (1990) wrote an important paper using "first-difference" methods. In that paper, they found that for every $1,000 increase in shareholder value (measured as a change in the market value of equity), CEO pay went up by $3.25. Their interpretation of this was that, although there was a relationship between pay and performance, the relationship was rather weak and could be strengthened. In part stemming from Jensen and Murphy's work, and as a result of calls from practitioners, this led to the extraordinary rise in the use of stock and stock options in executive compensation contracts. Options and stock became much more important components of executive pay packages starting in the early 1990s.[15]

Later in the 1990s, Hall and Liebman (1998) asked whether CEOs were paid like "bureaucrats." They collected unique data on stock and stock options (that were at the time not as formally disclosed as they are now) and found stronger relationships between pay and performance than found by Jensen and Murphy (1990), on the order of $5.29 for every $1,000 increase in shareholder wealth. They concluded that while this may still seem like quite a weak relationship, their work suggests that even small changes in performance can have very large effects on the lifetime wealth of an executive.

More recently, Bebchuk and Fried (2004, 2006) wrote a provocative book called *Pay Without Performance*. This book carefully articulates the difference between the often discussed "arm's-length bargaining" framework and what they call the "managerial power" perspective, where, in essence, boards are "captured" by CEOs. They discuss many reasons why they think the system for setting CEO pay needs reform. Kay and Van Putten (2007) offer an interesting rejoinder. Both are executive compensation consultants. They make several arguments that the CEO pay-setting process is objective, independent, and fair.

Answering the pay-for-performance debate in executive compensation is obviously a difficult question. There are many complications. For example, researchers use different data sources, companies have different compensation and business strategies (even in the same industry), and there are many potential factors that are not easily measured by academic researchers. However, one of the main reasons one may think the debate has not yet been resolved is complications in methodological issues and data used by researchers in different fields.[16]

Risk and Executive Compensation

The recent financial crisis has led many to think about "risk" more carefully and for some to call for a closer look and potential regulation of risk when it comes to compensation, and executive compensation in particular. Given that some have argued that excessive risk has led to the recent financial crisis, others are calling for limits on risk taking by companies in the United States. My own opinion is that we should also be wary that this could go too far. To the extent that levels of risk are related to expected rates of return, limiting risk in a general way could lead to lower rates of return and potential different problems for the economy. In addition, because we are free to be diversified investors, individuals can choose a mix of investments that generates the right level of risk and expected rates of return to make themselves comfortable. Having a set of firms with heterogeneous levels of risk (some higher and some lower) allows investors to come up with their own optimal choices.

That said, in addition to the recession we have just experienced, there have been a wide variety of extraordinary executive compensation "disasters" in recent years. Considering some of them for a moment might be a useful way to avoid the same kinds of mistakes in the future.

In 2009, I presented as part of a "Webinar" sponsored by WorldatWork. In that webinar, three colleagues and I focused on three recent "disasters" in executive compensation and considered possible ways the problems may have been avoided. We focused on executive pay issues at the New York Stock Exchange (NYSE), United Health Group, and Walt Disney and Company.[17]

In the case of the CEO of the NYSE, many allegations were made regarding inappropriate pay and methods for determining pay. These included a law concerning alleged violation of the reasonable pay doctrine for nonprofits, lack of oversight by the compensation committee, questionable peer groups, and a lack of proper process. Richard Grasso of NYSE was awarded $139.5 million as a retirement benefit and $48 million in exit pay. Given that his "peer group" included some for-profit businesses that were not related to the mission of the NYSE, some called this compensation into question. In the end, Mr. Grasso was allowed to keep the pay, but not without an enormous public relations scandal for the NYSE.

The CEO of United Health Group received more than $2 billion in options during his tenure by allegedly choosing the lowest stock price of the year as the "strike price" of his stock options. This was part of the large stock options restatement scandal of the 2000s. It was also alleged that the compensation committee chair and the CEO were business partners and left the company on the same day in 2006. In March 2007, the company had to restate earnings by more than $1.5 billion over a twelve-year period. After the CEO left, the board instituted a variety of reforms including those related to eliminating severance payments to executives with respect to change in control and splitting the jobs of CEO and chair of the board.

An additional famous example of an executive compensation disaster is one that had to do with severance payments at Walt Disney and Company.[18] In this case, the CEO at the time, Michael Eisner, hired Michael Ovitz as a successor, allegedly in large part without the board's input. Ovitz left Creative Artists Agency and was earning between $25 million to $35 million per

defined as "independent." In any event, some firms have told me that they have turned away from some consultants – even though they trust them as being "independent" – because they may be perceived as not "independent" by the press, the public, and regulators. It will be interesting to see what happens to the executive compensation consulting practices in the coming years. In the middle of 2007, I spoke with a colleague who was then running a smaller executive compensation practice and I asked him what he thought about the fact that the head of the House Ways and Means Committee in Congress, Henry Waxman, was asking consulting firms about their billings for executive compensation services and for other services in the firms where they were doing executive compensation work. He was very excited and thought this was *great* news for firms like his, which specialized only in executive pay consulting, because they were a small independent organization. Related, just recently one well-known executive pay consultant left Mercer (a large, diversified HR consulting firm). Also, TowersPerrin and WatsonWyatt Worldwide merged to form TowersWatson, seemingly going in the opposite direction. However, leading consultants from WatsonWyatt and TowersWatson went out on their own to form a new independent group that focuses solely on executive compensation consulting.

Firms obviously face many kinds of risk. One is the how they set their compensation strategy and the compensation of their executives (and other employees). Even such seemingly noncontroversial issues such as who is selected as a compensation consultant can pose risks to firms.

Are Executives Really Worth that Much? What About Athletes and Other Superstars?

I am often asked if I think executives are overpaid. Given the wide disparity in income in the world and the United States in particular (see Chapter 2), it is not surprising that many people think executives are paid "too much" given that, in fact, they are paid much more than most people. Sometimes these questions come up at the time a firm is faltering and fired executives get severance, but for the purposes of this discussion, let's just consider normal times and normal levels of pay.

Whenever I am asked about whether executives are paid too much, we often talk about the difference between school teachers and executives. Both work very hard. Both play important roles in the lives of many. But executives are, generally, paid (up to) hundreds of times what school teachers are paid. Why?

When I travel around lecturing about compensation and this question comes up, I often put up pictures of people. I start with Bill Gates. Bill Gates has been paid a lot of money over his lifetime. However, he took the entrepreneurial risk and started his own company. Most people are okay with people like Bill Gates making a lot of money, and I think this is partly because of the fact that he was the entrepreneur and because of his generous philanthropic efforts. Many make the distinction between Bill Gates and "hired" CEOs who are really just employees of their companies. They argue that it can't be *that* difficult to run a company.

I then display a picture of Alex Rodriguez, the famous New York Yankee baseball player. Rodriguez earns on the order of $25 million per year playing baseball. Most people who have played baseball *know* that they can't play baseball anywhere as well as he can. But they assume that they could probably run a company well, relatively better than they could play baseball well.

Next, I propose Oprah Winfrey, Jerry Seinfeld, and Halle Berry as entertainers who have made many scores of millions of dollars. And I also propose famous contemporary authors such as John Grisham who are essentially paid by output – paid by the book!

Are Rodriguez, Winfrey, Seinfeld, and Berry paid too much? Or are they extraordinarily talented individuals who are paid in a competitive labor market? Most would suggest the latter. But then, what makes executives any different? Some (including Bebchuk and Fried, 2004) argue that the market for CEOs is not, in fact, a competitive labor market and that boards are "captured" by CEOs and that there is not, in fact, "arm's length bargaining" between boards of directors and CEOs. They argue that the system is unbalanced in favor of executives. On the other hand, others argue that because all firms are organized with the same structure, it is difficult to see that it is not a competitive market.

What's Next in Executive Pay?

Trying to predict what is next on the executive pay horizon is difficult, because the field is changing at a dizzying pace. However, there are some trends that are worth thinking about. These include calls for more common practices, pressure for continued governmental oversight or legislation, further discussion of risk, a stronger focus on "pay for performance," and new statistical methods.

In 2009, The Conference Board (a nonprofit group that studies issues of corporate leadership, human capital, economic markets, value creation, and high-performing organizations) organized a Task Force on Executive Compensation that issued a report with several recommendations.[19] Although many large firms in the United States already incorporate these practices, I suspect more will be in the near future.

Among the Task Force recommendations are that (1) "compensation programs should be designed to drive a company's business strategy and objectives and create shareholder value," and a "significant portion of pay should be incentive compensation" and "paid only when performance can be reasonably assessed;" (2) "payouts" should be "clearly aligned with actual performance;" (3) "companies should avoid controversial pay practices, unless special justification is present;" (4) "compensation committees should be independent, experienced, and knowledgeable about the company's business;" and (5) "compensation programs should be transparent, understandable, and effectively communicate to shareholders."

It will be very interesting to see the changes that are on the horizon for executive compensation in the United States and throughout the world. Issues of pay for performance, risk, and legislative oversight are very likely to be important topics for years to come.

PART III

HOW PEOPLE ARE PAID CAN MEAN AS MUCH AS HOW MUCH THEY ARE PAID

NINE

Evaluating Performance, Incentives, and Incentive Pay

When I teach managers or students about compensation, one of the first questions I ask is how many in the room have been professional cucumber pickers? And I slowly raise my own hand.[1] As of yet, I have not met anyone in *any* of these settings who, like me, has been a professional cucumber picker.[2] I grew up near farms in western Massachusetts and most of the other kids and I worked on the farms picking cucumbers that were processed and sold as pickles. Of course, this is a ridiculous, albeit true, example, but it highlights some important points in compensation design and strategy.

An Example: Picking Cucumbers

I then ask the group their opinion about the best way to pay a person who picks cucumbers. Many say "by the cucumber" or "by the pound" – the traditional piece rate idea. They say that this is the best method because "performance" matters and that those who pick more can be rewarded for their efforts and that it must be simple to just weigh the cucumbers. It turns out that paying cucumber pickers by the pound of cucumbers picked would be a disaster! Large cucumbers are nearly worthless (they can only be used for relish and the world only needs so much relish; in my own opinion, the world could do with a little less). Workers could just let the cucumbers grow and grow and pull out 2.5 pounders; big, heavy, and worthless.[3] So this then leads to all kinds of additional suggestions – by the week, by the hour, based on individual performance, based on group performance, and so forth. It turns out that most cucumber pickers in western Massachusetts are paid by the hour. Why?

Paying by piece or by the pound of cucumbers has some great virtues, including that it is tied to some measure of individual performance. The reason I bring this problem up is that it is a clear example that the *industry*

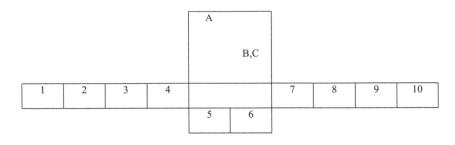

Figure 9.1. Aerial Schematic of a Cucumber-Picking Machine. *Notes:* This is a sketch of an aerial view of a cucumber-picking machine containing fourteen workers. Persons A, B, 5, and 6 are all on the frame of the "truck." Persons 1–4 and 7–10 lay on mattresses on top of plywood that are part of "wings" of the machine. It really looks like an airplane. Person A is the driver, persons B and C dump buckets full of "cukes" that persons 1–10 pick and throw in the buckets. Person D walks behind and constantly evaluates the performance of persons 1–10.

and *context* matter critically. Virtually no one knows how cucumbers are picked and the technology that is used. Employees who pick cucumbers lie down on a mattress and hang their arms in the vines searching for cucumbers to pick and then toss up into a bucket or (on more sophisticated machines) onto a tiny conveyor belt. Consider Figure 9.1, which is an aerial view of a cucumber-picking machine, which is an old truck that moves very slowly and has "wings." On this machine there are fourteen employees. One (A) drives the machine, two (B and C) empty buckets full of cucumbers into large (approximately 50 pounds each) bags, and ten (persons 1–10) pick the cucumbers. The best pickers are placed at positions #1 and #10 because they cover the edge and can help #2 and #9 (who are typically the weakest pickers). An additional employee (D) will occasionally walk behind the machine to monitor the quality of the picking. If he finds cucumbers behind any of employees 1–10, they obviously missed them and, he will take note of this poor performance.

Another way to monitor performance is to have some of the best employees rotate through different rows (cucumbers are picked about every 2.5 days). So, if a weaker picker worked in row 7 on Monday afternoon, by the time the machine got around to that spot again (probably on Thursday morning), a stronger picker would then be in row 7 to "make up for it." If one finds large (low-quality) cucumbers in a given spot, they must have been missed in the previous pass, because we know cucumbers can only grow so much in 2.5 days. It is really quite remarkable how many cucumbers one can pick in a day. At the peak of the season, it was not uncommon for a group of fourteen people as described in Figure 9.1 to pick 8 tons (!) of cucumbers.[4]

So why did we get paid by the hour? Paying by the "piece" was too cumbersome. It would have been too expensive to "monitor" us. The farm would have had to implement some sort of sophisticated system or pay someone who could easily determine who was doing what. In some sense, person D could have played that role and, perhaps, given bonuses. We were paid by the hour, and person D did have a say in telling those in charge who was "pulling their weight" and who was not. So, essentially, hourly wage adjustments were made based, in part, on performance. Another reason it might not be appropriate to pay workers of this type by their productivity was that productivity was not entirely based on effort. In fact, when I worked at the farm, enormous variation in the output per worker had absolutely nothing to do with employee effort. There were two reasons for this. The first was equipment malfunction. When the "picker" (the machine) was broken (e.g., flat tire, engine problem, broken conveyer chain), the workers couldn't work but continued to be paid. Many loved it when the machine broke down. The other was the weather. In hot, dry summers in the Connecticut River Valley of western Massachusetts, cucumbers didn't grow much so there just weren't that many to pick. Should that "weather" risk be placed on the workers or the firm owner (farmer)? In the case of the Kelly farm, the Kellys took the risk. Unless, of course, we didn't work. Often, in late August when the vines were drying up, we would skip a day and just not be paid. But this was expected once in a while.

Clearly this is a simple and modest example but it highlights the fact that industry matters a lot. Just as context and the way the company works in the cucumber industry matters, it also matters in many other industries and for many other occupations. Paying people in utilities or pharmaceuticals or energy or retail can all mean different things. In fact, as we learned earlier when we discussed strategy in Chapter 5, even in the *same* industry, from the perspective of paying people appropriately it is critically important to understand the organization's business philosophy and compensation philosophy. Again, even in a specific industry such as pharmaceuticals, it may make perfect sense for two companies to pay their workers quite differently.

Measurement Matters: The Classic Example of Installing Windshields

As I noted earlier, the context and the industry matter a great deal. In trying to discover whether pay for performance is a good idea, Lazear (2000) studied the interesting case of a windshield installation company. This is a great example for many reasons. High among the reasons is that even when one examines an extraordinarily specific task, and even when we know quite a lot about the business practices, really determining the best way to pay someone can be very difficult to determine.

There are many studies that claim to measure the effects of one particular Human Resource practice on some outcome – say firm profitability or organization productivity. The problem is that many (most) of them don't do anything to control for what else may be going on; so what about the "all else equal" part? For example, if one company pays piece rates (say each worker is paid a certain amount for a specific task performed) and the other firm pays time rates (here the workers are just paid by the hour), and say we know the first firm has higher profits, does that mean that piece rates *caused* the higher profits? Certainly it doesn't, for many reasons that we explore here and elsewhere in this book. I will mention a few right here, however. First, we don't know anything else about the companies. Maybe there is something about them that leads to these higher profits. Second, certainly it could be the case that certain workers may chose to work for the first firm because they offered a type of pay plan this type of worker may prefer. At the same time, perhaps some of those workers in firm B chose firm B precisely because they preferred that type of pay plan. These are a few among several issues considered in this chapter.

The Safelite Glass case study (Lazear, 2000; Hall, Madigan, and Lazear, 2000) describes a famous example where a company switched from paying people who install replacement windshields a time rate (paying the employees per hour) to a piece rate (paying by the windshield installed).[5] It provides very interesting results but also illustrates many of the issues one would need to consider to do a careful analysis of the effects of an HR practice on firm and worker outcomes. Safelite is an interesting case because it provided data access to a researcher and really tried to statistically test whether salaries or piece rates were better for them and their workers. They moved quite a step closer to a real experiment (say that a biology researcher would do in testing a drug) than is typically done in the area of Human Resource management.

In the early 1990s, Safelite was the largest autoglass installation company in the United States. The company included 500 stores, with more than 3,000 employees, more than 1,000 of whom were installers. The CEO of Safelite at that time, John Barlow, was very concerned that installers of windshields did not install very many windshields per day (they were installing about 2.5 per day). He believed that incenting them would help. He recalled working in the tire sales and installation business early in his career and how the people with whom he worked (those who put new tires on cars) put in extra effort when he gave them bonus payments for working more quickly.

Around the same time Safelite switched its pay system, it also moved from a system where they had stores (that competed with one another) to a central dispatch system that was more efficient. Safelite also organized systems with insurance companies where if a customer had a windshield in need of repair and called his insurance company to make the claim, the call would be routed directly to Safelite (Lazear, 2000; Hall, Madigan, and Lazear, 2000).

The firm believed that one of the reasons for the relatively low productivity of the windshield installers was the compensation system. This was based, in part, on the CEO's past experiences working in similar kinds of jobs, in part on the perceived relatively low level of productivity of the installers, and in part on comments made by some of the employees. As a result, Safelite instituted a new compensation system called the Performance Pay Plan (PPP).

Among the very important issues in the PPP plan are three that are really worth highlighting. First, although it is one thing to decide to design a new pay plan that is intended to motivate employees, it is entirely a different issue to actually *design* the plan. Second, *communicating* the new pay plan is a tricky undertaking and worth considering seriously. Third, after the plan has been designed and communicated, how can one tell if it actually worked?

The CEO wanted to provide a plan that would motivate installers to work harder and be more productive, so it was natural to consider a "piece rate" of some type. At the time of the change, Safelite installers were earning on the order of $10–$12 per hour (remember this was 1993). The new basic plan was to count up the number of windshields installed per week. If the installer completed more than a prespecified number of installations, he or she would earn a bonus. If he or she did not meet this quota for the first twelve weeks of the program, the installer would earn exactly what he or she earned earlier before the PPP was started. After the first twelve weeks, however, if the performance did not meet the minimum standard the "base" wage would be lowered by 30 percent.

The structure of the new plan was communicated in a memo to all installers. Many installers were upset because they perceived this as a potential way to cut their wages (and in fact, for those who did not install many windshields, their wages would be cut after the first twelve weeks). Others suggested that this was not a fair system, because the "risk" was now put on the workers. If, for whatever reason, customers did not come in to get windshields installed, the employees would potentially suffer lower earnings (this is equivalent to paying cucumber pickers by the cucumber – if a drought comes and the vegetables don't grow, a lot of the risk is on the workers).

Let's consider some of the costs and benefits of this type of plan. First – and assuming this is the type of incentive that motivates workers to work harder[6] – the plan is likely to motivate installers to work harder. Second, what about turnover? This plan is likely to lead to the voluntary turnover of less capable installers. If one is not very good at installing windshields, in the longer run he or she will earn less and be more likely to look for another job. On the other hand, the plan is likely to increase the probability that capable installers stay and likely to lead to the attraction of new efficient installers to the company. Third, what about quality? Clearly there is danger in workers working *too fast* and making mistakes, installing windshields improperly, or even breaking materials. This was counterbalanced with the idea that if something breaks or is not properly done, that the worker would have to fix it on his or her own time. Fourth, what about the fact that things aren't all in the worker's control? This is an important point. One could imagine the possibility that those who dispatch orders out to installers could be in a position to send them to their friends with higher frequency. This is something that this company and others with similar kinds of systems will have to try to guard against (Lazear, 2000; Hall, Madigan, and Lazear, 2000).

In the end, Safelite decided to implement the plan but without the lower wages if workers didn't perform above the minimum threshold. That is, the worker kept the wage floor at the level he or she would have earned before the PPP system and could enjoy bonuses for performance above a certain number of windshields per week. In the end, however, this did not really take all of the "teeth" away from the new plan, because this company and others can always let workers go if they do not perform up to a certain standard.

Trying to determine what happened to the company and whether it resulted from the implementation of the PPP plan is not as easy as it sounds. This is because other things were changing too – essentially it is quite difficult to "keep all else equal" (remember, for example, that the dispatch system and relationship with insurance companies also changed around this time). One problem is that different kinds of workers came to the firm and others left in part because of the PPP plan. For example, workers who would thrive in a bonus plan were attracted to the firm after the switch to the PPP and workers who did not earn bonuses may have been more likely to leave. In the end, after a careful statistical analysis (Lazear, 2000), it appears that the firm's productivity went up and the worker wages went up. Further, the productivity went up by enough more than the wages went up so that the firm became more profitable. So, in the end, by those measures, the firm and the workers were both made better off as a result of the new system.

Performance Appraisal

It doesn't seem like it should be too difficult to evaluate performance, but it is. It isn't particularly difficult for some occupations, such as Major League Baseball players – but even that isn't so easy (e.g., Lewis, 2003). Some occupations (e.g., windshield installers) may not be too difficult either, but as just discussed, even occupations where it may be seemingly straightforward to appraise performance, it can be quite difficult. My favorite example was when the National Basketball Association (NBA) player Dennis Rodman asked to be evaluated on and paid according to rebounds[7] only. Rodman was known for his extraordinary ability to rebound and rebounds are clearly easily measured. However, in the end, he never did sign a contract based solely on rebounds – even a simple case like this is more difficult than it seems. One of the problems the team ownership saw with this sort of contract was that he might be *too* focused on rebounds and not on other important parts of his job. This is a common problem with organizing an incentive contract based on only one measure of performance.

There is a large and broad literature in Human Resources management on what is known as performance appraisal. This research involves environmental influences, organizational influences, how to obtain information about performance, standards and goals, and errors in assessing performance (e.g., Latham and Wexley, 1980; Henderson, 1984; Murphy and Cleveland, 1995; Smither, 1998). Perhaps among the most important part of the performance appraisal process is potential errors in the system. It is very easy to see that errors can be made, and if those completing performance reviews (and those whose performance is being reviewed) understand potential biases, reviews are likely to be better. Murphy and Cleveland (1995) suggest a host of potential errors including leniency, central tendency, and halo errors. Other errors include strict/lenient rating, initial/latest impression, and status effect errors (Henderson, 2006).

Leniency errors can come about when managers rate employee performance more "softly" than they probably should, based on objective criteria.

A corollary is severity error that is just the opposite. Central tendency errors are common and come about when managers avoid extreme (high or low) ratings. Halo errors are interesting and come about when the rater attributes one aspect of the employee's performance to all aspects of the employee's performance. As an example, consider a forklift operator who is extraordinarily good and careful about most every aspect of his job. But he is not kind to people who come into the lumberyard to ask him questions. If his supervisor attributes these personal interactions to all of the forklift operator's performance, the supervisor would be making a (negative) halo error. Strict/lenient rating is about certain managers being more (or less) strict most of the time. If some supervisors are strict and some are not, it would obviously not be fair if all employees were rated only by their immediate supervisor, especially if appraisals were not adjusted for these differences in severity and were used in compensation decisions. Another error is initial/latest impression error. Those rating must be cautioned against and trained not to be swayed by their first impression or their last interaction with an employee. Raters must also be careful not to overrate those in high status jobs or underrate those in low status jobs.

Types of Performance Appraisal

Martocchio (2001) outlines four different formal types of performance appraisals: trait systems, comparison systems, behavioral systems, and goal-oriented systems. Even if you aren't designing such systems, it is useful to understand them because you may be evaluated (and paid) based on a similar method. The first step to making more is understanding how you are paid. I will explain each system very briefly here. In trait systems, those who evaluate are asked to consider each employee's "traits" such as dependability, initiative, cooperation, leadership, creativity, and quality of work. These types of systems are very easy to use and can apply to many jobs. A problem, however, is that relative to other types of performance appraisal systems, these are subjective, and one evaluator's opinion of creativity may be much different from that of another rater.

Comparison appraisals are another type of system. In a comparison system, employees are ranked relative to their peers. This can be done as a complete ordinal ranking or there could be some sort of "forced distribution," as some instructors do with grades in a course (e.g., 10 percent A, 20 percent B, and so on). Although this method is clearly straightforward, there can be problems. Often managers will argue that their employees are all better than average. And they may, in fact, be better than average. If this is the case, it is difficult to justify a forced distribution.[8] On the other hand, a forced distribution does help avoid other problems.

Behavioral systems are another group discussed by Martocchio (2001) and others. Some argue that behavioral systems help avoid some of the errors that are inherent in other methods. At the same time, they are more expensive because they require the appraisers to directly observe employees. Among the types of behavioral systems are critical incident techniques (which require raters and those being rated to pinpoint specific behaviors that mark good and poor performance), behaviorally anchored scales (like critical incident but based on the expectation of a completed task, not on an actual task completion), and behavioral observation scale (like behaviorally anchored scales but only tracks positive behaviors). An example of a critical incident technique for a forklift operator would be "The employee carefully cleans his or her work area before turning on the forklift" and would have answers such as very often, fairly often, sometimes, almost never, and never. These types of systems are much more detailed and expensive than other methods, but also provide much richer detail on performance. Another system is management by objective, which is a form of a goal-oriented system. In this type of system, an employee writes a review of his or her success at making certain objectives over the time period and the supervisor does something similar. This can be costly because it requires so much contact between the supervisor and the employee, but that can have benefits as a result of communication between the two (Martocchio, 2001).

There is one other issue that should be mentioned before we leave the issue of performance appraisals. When I was at the University of Illinois, a committee in the Department of Economics made performance and salary recommendations to the Department Head for each of the forty or so faculty. Members of the committee were asked to rank faculty on teaching, research, and service. All three are important activities of any faculty at a research university. But what weights should each get? Some felt that teaching should count for 30 percent, research for 60 percent, and service for 10 percent. But not everyone agreed. After scores were calculated by each committee member for each faculty member, means, medians, minima, and maxima were calculated.

An important second question is what to do with these scores after they are calculated. Should raises be based on a linear function of these numbers (so that if one scored a 3, he or she should get a raise that is half as large as one who earned a 6)? Or should it be nonlinear? Should people who get a 0 get no raise (or have their pay reduced)? Another interesting question is, should we expect *more* productivity from people who are already earning

Pay

	Level of performance (1 worst, 5 best)				
	1	2	3	4	5
Position in Pay Range					
Top 1/4 of pay	0%	0%	4%	5%	6%
Third 1/4 of pay	0%	0%	5%	6%	7%
Second 1/4 of pay	0%	0%	6%	7%	8%
Bottom 1/4 of pay	0%	3%	7%	8%	9%

Figure 9.2. Different Raises for Same Performance. *Note:* Some organizations expect more from highly paid employees than from lower-paid employees in order to earn the same percentage raise. This is one example.

more? Put another way, to get the same percentage raise, should someone who earns more have to produce more? An example of this is Figure 9.2. In this extreme example, those who are relatively high earners are only eligible for a 6 percent raise, no matter what they do. On the other hand, those who are below the median in annual earnings are eligible for a raise of up to 9 percent. Any given organization needs to figure out whether this is fair or appropriate in a given circumstance. In any event, it is best to *understand* how your organization does this. I suspect many employees don't know how their organizations do this. I also fear that many organizations themselves don't know how they do this.

Some Psychological Theory Related to Incentives and Pay

There is a host of psychological theories independent of (but complementary to) many of the economic theories I have mentioned elsewhere in this book. I will mention some of them here, including Mazlow's need hierarchy, Herzberg's two-factor theory, expectancy theory, reinforcement theory, and goal setting theory. Milkovich, Newman, and Gerhart (2011) outline each of these theories very clearly and provide a set of predictions for each. Mazlow's (1943) need hierarchy suggests that there is a hierarchy (pyramid) of needs from the most basic (e.g., food, water, breathing), to safety, love, self-esteem, and higher-order needs. An issue with respect to compensation is that, according to this theory, one can only be incentivized for higher-order needs once the most basic needs have been met.

Herzberg's two-factor theory (Herzberg, Mausner, and Synderman, 1956) made the distinction between "motivators" and "hygiene factors." One idea is that if hygiene factors (such as job security and safety) are not present, an employee is not satisfied, and if this is the case, it can be difficult to motivate a worker to higher levels of effort. The absence of hygiene factors can't motivate performance. However, motivators (such as recognition, responsibility, and interesting work) can motivate performance.[9]

Expectancy theory suggests that the combination of three factors make up motivation: expectancy, instrumentality, and valence (Milkovich, Newman and Gerhart, 2011). An employee must believe she is able to perform a task (expectancy), must believe she will be rewarded for completing the job (instrumentality), and must value the reward given (valence). Only when all three are present will an employee be motivated.

The idea behind equity theory (Adams, 1965) is that workers will be motivated when their perceived inputs (e.g., effort) match their perceived outputs (e.g., pay). If someone thinks she is being unfairly paid (e.g., others are being paid more for the same perceived effort), she will be uncomfortable and unmotivated. Further, one may try to create the match between inputs and outputs by engaging in counterproductive behavior such as "shirking" on the job.

Finally, reinforcement theory (Skinner, 1953) suggests that rewards must follow immediately from effort or behavior. If incentive payments are not tied directly to certain behavior or output, they will not have a motivating effect.

Some Types of Incentive Pay Plans

There is a very large set of incentive plans that are possible. I will mention just some of them here. Others are written about at various other places in the book (e.g., stock and stock options in the next chapter). Piece rate plans are obviously the most straightforward type of pay-for-performance plan and these have already been mentioned in many places in the book, including windshield installation earlier in this chapter. Another obvious piece rate plan is related to how authors are paid by publishers (and some actors are paid by movie studios). Many authors are paid a fixed rate up front and then earn royalties on each additional sale above some point. This really is among the most vivid and stark forms of incentive pay. The better the book sells, the more the author earns. The interests of the author and the publisher are aligned. The trick is the negotiation over the up-front payment and the subsequent per-book payment after that. Sometimes there are multiple different "kinks" in such a plan. For example, an author could earn one fraction on gross sales of the first 30,000 books sold and another fraction on books sold after the first 30,000.

Some real estate agents are compensated with incentive pay, but not all, and this is typically negotiable. In the "standard" case, agents for the seller are paid 3 percent of the purchase price and agents for the buyer are paid 3 percent of the purchase price. However, because many agents are employed by agencies, those agents don't take home the entire 3 percent of the commission. Some agents take home a smaller part of the commission in exchange for a higher guaranteed salary (just as an author may take a smaller cut per book in exchange for a larger advance). It is interesting to think about what kinds of agents and what types of agency owners would prefer one form of compensation over another. For example, those agents who expect they will sell many homes would prefer the larger commission (piece rate) relative to a larger base. On the other hand, those agents who are uncertain of their ability to sell or who are relatively more risk averse would prefer a larger base as a trade-off to a higher commission rate.

The person who cuts my hair owns the company where she works. But what are her options for paying everyone else in the business? One option is to have all of the other people who work there "rent" chairs from her and then keep all of the revenue they earn. This would give her a set and relatively known income and allow the others to keep all of their marginal profits. It might also be the way to ensure that those others who work there work incredibly hard. Another option would be for her to rent chairs but for much less and then take some part of the revenue from each of her staff. The most extreme form of pay on the other end would be to pay her staff either by the hour or by the haircut or as some fraction of the revenue they generate for the business. A discussion of taxi drivers could be nearly identical to this discussion of people who cut hair.

There are many other ways that individuals can be paid incentive pay. These include stock and stock options, which are described elsewhere in this book in detail. Other forms of incentive pay could be merit pay, based on, for example, the performance someone has had in the previous year. This type of incentive is often added to the base pay from the previous year to form a new base pay the following year.

A form of pay similar to merit pay is a bonus. The major difference between a bonus and the typical merit pay is that the bonus is only one-time, in the sense that it is not added to the base. So a person earning $41,000 who is granted $1,000 in merit pay has a base pay of $42,000 the following year. Someone earning $41,000 and being granted a $1,000 bonus still has $41,000 base pay.

There are a series of "group" incentive plans such as stock and stock options (if employees are granted stock or stock options or hold stock or stock options, then when the firm's stock price goes up, they all benefit –

this is a real group incentive plan). Some firms also offer profit-sharing programs where all workers may share in some fraction of the profits. This fraction is usually predetermined and can be capped, depending on the arrangements.

Critics of Incentive Pay

Although many people are great fans of incentive pay, and I have described several success stories of paying with incentive pay in this chapter and elsewhere in this book, there are some strong critics of incentive pay. Chief among these critics are Kohn (1993), Pfeffer (1998), and Pink (2010). (Also see Hamner [1975] who suggests there is nothing wrong with the theory of incentives plans but argues that they are not executed correctly by managers). Kohn and Pfeffer wrote articles in the *Harvard Business Review* in the 1990s and were extremely critical of incentive pay.

Kohn (1993) outlines a series of points including that "rewards don't motivate, rewards punish, they rupture relationships, they ignore reasons, they discourage risk-taking, and they undermine interest." He goes on to suggest that rewards only secure "temporary compliance" and not long-term results. This is an extreme position and certainly interesting. In fact, in some circumstances I agree with him, but in others not. For example, the argument that rewards discourage risk-taking is too extreme a point. In fact, there are many cases where rewards or incentives may encourage too much risk-taking. Imagine, for example, an executive who gets a $1 million bonus for reaching some financial goal. Further imagine that he is very close to the goal but not quite there. This might lead him to take extraordinary and inappropriate risks for the firm and himself.

I did see a recent example of what I think Kohn (1993) was writing about. I was with one of my children in a retail clothing store and asked if I wanted to sign up for a store credit card to save 10 percent on my purchase (I know, this happens frequently). I asked the clerk if he was paid for each additional person he signed up. He said that he was not. However, he and his colleagues were previously paid $1 for each sign-up. He said he signs up a lot more now because the pressure is off and he isn't uptight about it anymore – an interesting point.

Pfeffer (1998) has also been a strong critic of incentive pay. Among the points he makes in a 1998 article is that the claim that "individual incentive pay improves performance" is a myth. There certainly may be evidence that is consistent with that view. There is also a great deal of evidence (including Lazear, 2000) that differs, however.

Pink (2010) is the most recent well-known critic of incentive pay. In a provocative new book, he offers a host of new examples that are critical of incentives. In particular, he makes the distinction between types of tasks that can be incentivized (basic, repeatable tasks) and those that are more difficult to incentivize (higher-order tasks where visionary thinking might be necessary). In the next chapter, we examine much more closely two forms of incentive pay: stock and stock options.

TEN

Stock and Stock Options

Executives in most American companies are paid some form of their compensation in stock and stock options. Stock is a fractional ownership in a company. If a company has 1,000,000 shares of stock and you own 100,000 shares than you own one-tenth of the company. You can vote for board directors and shareholder proposals and can sometimes earn dividends (like interest) on your share ownership.

Some executives are paid in part in company stock. Suppose the stock is trading at $30 per share. If an employee is given 100 shares of stock as part of her compensation, then this is equivalent to paying her $3,000. In many circumstances, stock offered to employees is restricted in some way or another. A common restriction is for the stock to require vesting. A common form of vesting is time vesting, in which the stock cannot be sold by the employee for some time, for example a year. Some companies require what is known as performance vesting. In this case, the stock cannot be sold until some measure of performance is met (for example, the stock price increases to a certain amount or some other performance e.g., a level of profitability metric). Some companies pay in stock so as to make the employees feel like owners. Some companies require executives to keep (hold) a certain multiple of their company stock. This is called a holding requirement.

Stock Options Defined

Stock options are similar to stock but distinct. A stock option is the right to buy a share of stock at a set price at some time in the future. Consider the example of a very close friend of mine. He started to work for a high-tech company in California in 1997 and, in addition to his salary, was offered 30,000 stock options at a "strike price" (sometimes called exercise price) of

$20. This means he had the guaranteed right (but certainly no obligation) to purchase 30,000 shares of stock at $20 per share at some point in the future. At the time he was granted the stock options, the company stock share price was also $20. So anyone could buy the stock for $20. It is common to offer employees stock options "at the money" – that is, with the strike price of the stock option exactly equal to the current price of the stock. Given that the strike price and the exercise price were identical, he would have no incentive to exercise his option to buy stock at $20 per share, because anyone could buy stock at $20 per share in the open market. However, when the stock price rose to $23, for example, then he could approach the company, exercise an option to buy stock at $20 (his promised strike price), and then turn around and sell the stock in the market for $23 and pocket $3 per option.

Vesting and Expiration of Options

There are two other interesting complications. First, stock options typically must "vest." This means that my friend could not exercise his options for some time. In his case, which is typical, he could only exercise one-third of the options after the first year, another third after the second year, and the final third after the third year. There are other possibilities such as one-quarter each year for four years. The second twist is that one cannot hold on to options forever. It is typically the case that options "expire" after ten years. This means that if they are not exercised after ten years, they become worthless.

I have heard of several cases of poor souls who have actually *forgotten* to exercise their options! I was sitting at lunch in Ithaca with the head of HR from a large global company based in the Midwest. During lunch he received an urgent call on his cell phone. One of his staff told him that a senior-level employee simply forgot to exercise options to buy shares and the options expired. This employee left nearly $300,000 on the table! The firm had no obligation to make up the difference to the employee, but they did. They gave him some of the difference in new options as a new incentive.

Stock Option Craziness

There is more to the story of my friend with the 30,000 stock options offered at a strike price of $20 per share.[1] He was first granted his 30,000 options in November 1997. The following October he was visiting me in Illinois where I was then living. He asked my advice about whether he should stay at his job or take a new job where he was offered 45,000 stock options in the new company and a salary and set of benefits roughly equivalent to those in his current job. He seemed to find the new job quite interesting but felt he was "stuck" at the old one because the stock price in the original company had moved up to $23 per share from the $20 per share price when he was given the 30,000 options.

He felt stuck because, although he had a profit of $90,000 = (30,000 × (23–20)) = (30,000 × 3) from his options "on paper," none of his options had yet vested. In fact, the first set of options would not vest for another month, and if he left for the new job and new options in the new company, he would have to forfeit all of the options in the original company. So he stayed. Guess what happened?

The stock price went up some more! By the end of the year, the stock price was up to $50 per share, and he asked me what he should do. Remember, he had options to buy 30,000 shares of stock at $20 per share and the current price was $50. So he was "in the money" for $900,000 = (($50–$20) × 30,000) = $30 × 30,000. This was assuming that the options had all vested (which they had not all done yet). Another way to think about the numbers is that he could essentially buy shares for $20 × 30,000 = $600,000 and then immediately sell them for $50 × 30,000 = $1,500,000 for a profit of $900,000. In reality, firms offer a "cashless" exercise, where an individual can come in with a vested option, hand it over and be given the difference between the current stock share price and the strike price of the option ($50–$20) = $30, minus a bit for the transaction.

A while later, in the spring of 2000, my friend asked me what I thought about buying a new house. I told him I was just coming up for tenure and what sort of nut would buy a new house right *before* coming up for tenure! He said, "Not you, me!" I told him to do whatever he wanted. He bought a new house – a big and really, really nice one, in northern California. At the time the stock price was about $150 per share. So, on paper, my friend had ($150–$20) × 30,000 = $3,900,000 in wealth in the company. He asked my advice on what to do. I said "sell."

He didn't sell and called me back when the price was at $200 to tell me that if he cashed out at $150, the difference would have cost him $1.5 million. He was right, of course. But this scared me. He worked for the company, his wife worked for the company. His gorgeous house was near the company. What if something happened to the company?

In fact, every time I talked with him, the price had gone up higher and higher. Of course, the stock didn't always go up. Some days it went up, others it went down. But in general, it was on a steady upward pace, just like many high-tech stocks at the time. Ultimately the price went to about $600 per share![2] So my friend had ($600–$20) × 30,000 = $17.4 million in wealth in the company. In just a few years, he had gone from a guy with a good professional salary (a wicked smart guy and great person by the way, but his story is not unique to smart or good people nor to people loaded with [potential] money) to a guy with gobs of money.

The stock price on the day he left the company was $4 per share. That's right, not four hundred, or forty, but four *dollars!* What does one do with a stock option to buy a share of stock at $20 per share when the stock price is $4? The short answer is "not much." But it is wrong to say the options are "worthless." It is true that an employee would never exercise a stock option to buy a share of stock at $20, when he could buy the same share in the open market for $4. So an employee wouldn't exercise the options, but that doesn't mean the option has no value. This is the subject of the next section.

Stock Option Valuation

Valuing stock options is tricky business. However, there is, in fact, a straight-forward way to value market-traded options – those that can be bought and sold by investors. In 1973, two papers were written that outlined the basics of these ideas. One was written by Merton (1973) and the other by Black and Scholes (1973). Merton and Scholes won the Nobel Prize in Economics in 1997 (Black had passed away and was, therefore, not eligible). I will not go into the technical details of their work here but they essentially laid the groundwork for options prices that lead to an enormous industry in options trading.

Black, Merton, and Scholes showed that one need only know six factors to determine the value and price of a stock option: (1) the "strike" price (sometimes called the exercise price) of the option, (2) the current price of the stock, (3) the time left until the stock can be exercised (also known as the expiration date), (4) the risk-free rate of interest, (5) the variance of the stock price, and (6) the dividend rate.[3]

As an example of how these characteristics are related to option prices, consider Table 10.1. In column 1, consider a stock option with a strike price (exercise price) of $15, a current stock price of $25, 2 years (730 days) until it expires, a stock price volatility of 10 percent, and assume the risk-free rate of return (that which one could get by investing in safe government securities) is 5 percent. In such a case, although the "intrinsic value" – the value that one could get by immediately exercising the option and then selling the stock is $10 (the $25 stock price minus the $15 exercise price), the actual value of the option is higher – $11.43. Intuitively, it makes sense that the option value would be higher than the intrinsic value, because there are still 730 days over which the price of the stock could go up.

Table 10.1 *Stock option prices, based on various assumptions*

	(1)	(2)	(3)	(4)	(5)	(6)	(7)	(8)
Stock Price	25	25	30	30	30	30	4	4
Exercise Price	15	20	20	20	20	20	20	20
Days to Expiration	730	730	730	365	365	365	365	1825
Volatility (%)	10	10	10	10	35	35	35	35
Risk-Free Interest Rate (%)	5	5	5	5	5	3	3	3
Option Value	11.43	6.90	11.88	10.97	11.43	11.02	0.00	0.07

Note: These examples assume there is no dividend.
Source: Numbers calculated using options pricing formula based on Black and Scholes (1973) and Merton (1973).

If the exercise price of the stock goes up, then the value of the option should fall. In column 2 of Table 10.1, only one change is made to the assumptions relative to column 1. In this case, the exercise price is $20 (and not $15). All of the remaining characteristics of the stock option remain the same. Because the exercise price is now higher, it should be no surprise that the value of the option is lower. It is now $6.90. Another way to think about this is the following: the market would be willing to pay exactly $6.90 for an option to buy a share of stock at $20 per share, when the current stock price is $25, there are two years left over which to exercise the option, assuming the stock volatility is 10 percent, and the risk-free rate of interest is 5 percent. Notice again that one would be willing to pay more than the intrinsic value of $5 ($25 – $20) because, although one could immediately exercise the option for $5, there is the chance that over the next two years the price of the stock may rise.

We should also expect that as the price of the stock goes up, so should the value of the option to buy the stock. In column 3 of Table 10.1, the only assumption that changes, relative to column 2, is that the price of the stock goes up by $5, from $25 to $30 per share. This causes the value of the option to increase from $6.90 to $11.88.

The switch from column 3 to 4 of Table 10.1 illustrates that as the time left until the option expires decreases, so does the value of the option. This is intuitive because there is less time over which to experience a jump in the stock price. As we move from column 3 to column 4, the days to expiration falls from 730 (2 years) to 365. The value of the option accordingly falls from $11.88 to $10.97.

Another interesting feature of options that is sometimes not immediately obvious is that the higher the stock price volatility (how much the price historically moves from day to day), the *higher* the value of the option. This is not immediately obvious to most people because they expect that as something is more volatile, they think it is more risky and, therefore, should probably be worth less. However, with options, remember that you don't have to exercise them, so you are, essentially, "protected" on the bottom end. Large fluctuations in price (volatility) mean there are decreases and increases in stock prices. Because with options one is protected from large decreases, she is just left to enjoy the advantages of increases. As an example, as we move from column 4 to 5, the only assumption on our option that changes is that the volatility increases from 10 percent to 35 percent. The option value accordingly increases from $10.97 to $11.43.

The risk-free rate of interest is the rate of interest that can be earned from super-safe assets such as government-backed short-term treasury bills. The higher this safe interest rate, the higher return we should expect from other financial investments such as stock options. As we move from column 5 to column 6 in Table 10.1, the one assumption that changes is the risk-free rate of interest that falls from 5 percent to 3 percent. The value of the option falls from $11.43 to $11.02.

To summarize, the value of an option increases as the stock price increases, the strike price decreases, the time to expiration increases, the volatility increases, and the risk-free rate increases. Remember back to the earlier story of my friend who had 30,000 options to buy at $20 and the fact that his company stock price went up to $600 and then fell to $4 per share? It is natural to think that an option with a strike price of $20 and a stock price of $4 is "worthless," but that is actually not entirely true. Certainly the intrinsic value is zero because you would not exercise the option to buy at $20 when you could buy in the open market for $4. But the value of the option with these two characteristics obviously depends on the other assumptions we make. In fact, if the option has a strike price of $20, a share price of $4, expires in a year, the volatility is 35 percent, and the risk-free rate is 3 percent, the value of the option is less than 1 cent (it rounds down to $0 – see column 7). However, if we change one assumption and assume the time to expiration is 5 years (1,825 days), then there is more time for the stock price to potentially go up over $20 and the value of the option goes up to $0.07.

Why do Companies Give Options? Why do Some Companies Give Options to *All* Employees?

There are many kinds of reasons managers use to justify providing options to employees. Among these are that the firm may not have enough cash, as a retention device, for accounting reasons, as a way to "pay for performance," to align the interests of the workers with those of the owners and to sort workers. This section will briefly discuss each of these.

Up until 2006, many large firms and many small high-tech firms liberally granted stock options. This was, in part, a result of an unusual accounting rule that basically allowed companies to count options as an expense (in order to lower tax burden) but did not require companies to count them as an expense in terms of reporting profits to shareholders. So some firms thought options to be "free," when they obviously were not. This is the subject of the next subsection.

As Oyer and Schaefer (2008) note, options are tied to a single firm and thus give employees quite a bit of risk (e.g., my friend with the 30,000 options). They argue, therefore, that there should be some offsetting benefits. It is these benefits to which we now turn.

Many companies give lots of stock options and even stock as a form of compensation. This is, in part, because in the early days of the company it may have little or no revenue with which to pay workers. This obviously worked very well for early employees of companies such as Microsoft and eBay.

Another significant reason for giving options is that they align the interests of the employees with those of the shareholders. This is particularly true for executives, but some companies give options to all of their workers. Starbucks is an example of a company that traditionally gave options to nearly all employees. Does this make sense? From a purely economic point of view it may not seem to make a lot of sense. Some provide the reason that options align the interests of the worker with those of the firm. But it is hard to believe that the person who serves coffee in an airport Starbucks will work harder and more carefully if she is provided options rather than not. However, there may be psychological reasons that Starbucks does this. Workers may essentially feel a commitment to a larger team and, as a result, work harder.

The issue of sorting is interesting. It rests on the notion that employees may have different ideas about the value of a firm's option grant (Oyer and Schaefer, 2008). Those employees who are most enthusiastic about the future of the company (and therefore value options more) may be more likely to take options in exchange for cash.

Another clear reason firms may give options is that it is a way to retain workers. Imagine a worker who is "in the money" with options but the options have not yet vested. This worker may stay at a firm longer than she otherwise would, just to keep the opportunity of the option payoff. Recall my friend who agonized over the decision to leave his company, given that he would have to leave some money "on the table" if he did so.

The Change in Accounting for Stock Options

Up until 2006, there was an enormous disconnect between the tax and accounting treatment of employee stock options. If the number of options and the strike price of the options were fixed in advance, then options were not treated as an expense in the firm's balance sheet. This means that although they did have cost to the firm and value to the recipient employees, they did not count against the firm's profits. This seems like a strange situation. Some argued that it was extremely difficult to calculate the value of options to an employee because employee options are actually a bit more complicated than the market-traded options mentioned earlier. However, just because something is difficult to value does not seem to be a good reason to value it at zero.

Consider the following example that would have been how options were accounted for prior to 2006. Suppose there is one employee in the firm, that employee is paid $100,000 per year, and the firm has annual revenue of $100,000. Consider two possible scenarios. In scenario A, the employee is paid $100,000 in cash. In scenario B, the employee is paid $100,000 in stock options. Under "old" pre-2006 accounting rules, in scenario A, the company would report $0 in profit for tax purposes because they paid their employee $100,000 and they had $100,000 in revenue. So profit was exactly $0. They would also report to shareholders that their profit was $0 because they brought in $100,000 but paid their employee $100,000 in cash. In scenario B, however, the firm pays the employee entirely in stock options. So the company has $0 in profit for tax purposes (just as in scenario A) but had $100,000 in profits when it reports to shareholders! This is because options were counted as $0 as an expense in the balance sheet prior to 2006. This was changed so things are more uniform and clearer now. Now taxing and accounting treatments are identical whether employees are paid in cash or stock options.

How do Employees Value Options?

As was discussed in Chapter 4 and as you will see again in Chapter 11, pay mix and the value employees place on compensation is of particular importance in this book. This is easily highlighted with stock options, which can be much more complicated than they first appear.

At the end of the previous section, you may have noticed that I referred to *employee* stock options as opposed to *market-traded* options. This distinction is very interesting and important. A market-traded option is the option to buy a share of stock and that option can be bought and sold on options exchanges just like stock can be bought and sold on the open market. Employee options are different for a few reasons, which will be made clearer later. For now, understand that employee options are given to employees in the firm for which they work.

In the early 1990s, Lambert, Larcker and Verecchia (1991) pointed out that the original Black and Scholes's (1973) option pricing formula valued options for risk-neutral, diversified investors who could trade their options. But the formula was not designed for employee options, like those of my friend with the 30,000 options. Among the reasons the Black and Scholes's (1973) model doesn't work for employees is that employees are neither risk neutral nor diversified. Consider again my friend with the 30,000 options. His human capital and a great deal of physical capital were tied up in one organization and he was unable to diversify it away. As a result of this clear insight, Lambert, Larcker and Verecchia (1991) suggested that employees must value employee stock options at a level less than the Black and Scholes (1973) model values them.

Following this, Hall and Murphy (2002, 2003) in a series of clever papers set out to test these ideas. Their method, based on a mathematical formulation of "certainty equivalents," made assumptions about individual "utility functions" and the level of risk aversion of employees. They, too, concluded that employee must value options at a level considerably less than the Black and Scholes (1973) level.

More recently Craig Olson and I (Hallock and Olson, 2007, 2010) have worked on this problem. In our work we highlight a few issues. First, the Black and Scholes's (1973) model was developed for market-traded stock options and not for employee stock options. Second, market-traded options are *never* exercised prior to expiration, but they can be traded (sold). This was part of the point of Table 10.1. There is always a market for market-traded options and the intrinsic value (the difference between the current market price and the exercise price – or the value one could get if one exercised the option immediately) must be less than the value of the option. On the other hand, employee options are *often* exercised prior to expiration (e.g., to buy a car or house, to pay for a child's college education, etc.), but can *never* be traded because employees are restricted from trading them. So market-traded options are never exercised early but can be traded, and employee options can be exercised early and can never be traded. So they are different, like apples and oranges (although often worth more).

In recent work, Olson and I (Hallock and Olson, 2007, 2010) have used these ideas to estimate the value of options in a single firm.[4] Recall that employees cannot sell their options for any reason. Instead, they can exercise them if they want to meet some budget issue, prepare to leave the company, or want to purchase something. So they must exercise their options to purchase stock or complete a "cashless" exercise transaction (as discussed earlier).

Olson and I reason that important information is revealed every time (day, week, or hour) an option is kept or exercised. Recall that the intrinsic value is the current stock price minus the exercise price – that is, the cash one immediately gets when exercising an option. If an option is not exercised by an employee at a point in time, we reason that the value to the employee of holding the option and reserving the right to exercise it later is greater than the intrinsic value of exercising now. At the same time, if an employee does exercise right now, we reason that the value of holding the option another period is less than exercising now and receiving the intrinsic value.

We use this idea and some interesting statistical methods to follow employees in a multibillion-dollar nonmanufacturing firm in the Midwest to determine the value of options to the employees. We find in this firm for these workers at the time we studied them, that they value options at *more* than the Black-Scholes (Black and Scholes, 1973) value. At first, this is surprising, but not when we remember the earlier discussion about how market-traded options for which the Black and Scholes's (1973) model was developed are different from employee options. There are a number of reasons for these interesting results, including that this is one particular firm, optimism of the employees, the time in the business cycle, and many others.[5]

Stock and stock options are two innovative and important ways employees can be compensated. But they are somewhat complicated and difficult to administer. There are many reasons employees are granted options, including retention, sorting, pay and performance, and others. Options are an unusual and extreme form of compensation. The next chapter discusses some others and even asks whether we should pay employees anything other than cold hard cash.

ELEVEN

Pay Mix

Why Offer Benefits? Would Employees Prefer Cash?

An important puzzle with respect to how people are paid is the issue of why some organizations offer benefits and others do not. Or, more specifically, why some organizations offer certain benefits and others do not. One example, which we will get to later, is health insurance. Why are some employees "paid" with health insurance benefits whereas others are not? One of the ways I am paid as a professor at Cornell University is salary. I am also provided ("paid") health insurance. In addition, as stated earlier, Cornell has agreed to pay one-half of each of my children's college tuition for each child who attends Cornell. The university has also agreed to pay thirty percent of tuition if my children attend another college or university.

Why does Cornell offer a lower "rate" if my kids go elsewhere? Probably because it is relatively less expensive (for Cornell) if my kids go to Cornell rather than somewhere else, because the additional cost of my kids attending Cornell (or any additional student) are relatively low to Cornell. This isn't entirely correct because Cornell can always fill all seats with other paying students.

Why does Cornell offer this benefit at all? Consider the benefit they have offered me. My wife and I have two children. If they both go to college for four years each, that makes for eight years of college tuition. As of the writing of this book, Cornell's tuition is around $43,000 per year (room, board, and fees bring the total annual bill up to around $57,000, but the deal is that the university pays a portion of tuition only). If both of our kids go to Cornell, this means that Cornell will pay for 8 years $\times$ \$43,000 $\times$ (1/2) = \$172,000 of their tuition. If both of our children go to other expensive colleges, Cornell will pay for 8 years $\times$ \$43,000 $\times$ (0.30) = \$103,200. And if one child goes to Cornell and the other to another institution, Cornell will pay a total of 4 years $\times$ \$43,000 $\times$ (1/2) + 4 years $\times$ \$43,000 $\times$ (0.30) = \$137,600.

So in addition to my salary and all of the other benefits Cornell University pays me, I will be paid this "bonus" of between $103,200 and $172,000 if my kids go to expensive colleges. Notice that the size of this bonus does not depend on my performance *at all*. In fact, it depends on if and where my children go to college. Further, it depends on how many children I have. In effect, if we decided to have more children and they decided to go to college too, Cornell would pay me even more.

This is an extraordinary benefit and I am delighted that I have it. But why do I have it and why does the university provide it to all employees? Some might argue that this plays to Cornell's competitive advantage, in that the benefit is related to the university's "business" – education. Others might add that this benefit "costs" Cornell less than I (and other parents) value it, because an extra student on campus may not be that expensive for the university. On the other hand, Cornell can easily fill the available slot with a "full freight" student if my children decide not to go or don't get in.

This is an interesting example for a variety of reasons. Chief among them in my mind is the fact that two otherwise equivalent employees are paid differently, strictly because of the structure of their family. So, in effect, I am paid between $103,200 and $172,000 more than a colleague of mine who has an office a few doors away but has no children. As an alternative, Cornell could take all the money it spends on this benefit and distribute it evenly across all staff at the University. This would lower my "benefit" from between $103,200 to $172,000, to something much lower but would raise my childless colleague's benefit from zero to something substantially higher. But, would this be a better way to pay? For faculty with children, no. For faculty without children (or for faculty whose children have already been through college – prior to 1983, Cornell paid the entire tuition bill!), yes.

This chapter is essentially about why firms offer benefits versus wage and salary only. Oyer (2008) wrote an interesting paper about this issue and notes a number of reasons. He suggested at least three reasons for the value of benefits paid for by employers. The first is firms have an advantage in providing them relative to employees purchasing them. The second is that different kinds of employees value benefits differently and it is hard for workers to find employers that offer benefits that the employees prefer. Firms may be interested in hiring a particular type of worker (Lubotsky, 2011). The third reason is that some benefits reduce "costs" of workers of extra time at work. An additional reason is the tax advantage enjoyed through certain benefits (Lubotsky, 2011). I explore each of these and discuss some evidence for each later.

The idea that organizations have an advantage in providing certain benefits relative to workers purchasing them is probably the best-known and first reason most would think about when considering why firms offer benefits directly to workers. Rosen (1974) and others have suggested that firms can often purchase goods and services more cheaply than individuals can. As an example, firms can get much better rates (per worker) when negotiating with health insurance companies than the workers could get for themselves individually, for a number of reasons. First, when an individual walks through the door (or goes to the Web site) of an insurance company, the insurance company may appropriately fear that the worker needs insurance because she is sick, and therefore charge higher rates. On the other hand, when a firm negotiates rates on behalf of hundreds, or thousands, or hundreds of thousands of workers, the insurance company knows they are getting a set of healthy and unhealthy workers and therefore can spread the risk and costs around. Secondly, firms can take advantages of the fact that they are buying in "bulk." Just as it is cheaper (per ounce) to buy 2 gallons of peanut butter relative to the per-ounce cost of buying 8 ounces of peanut butter, buying health insurance on behalf of a few hundred thousand people is much less expensive (per person) than buying health insurance for only one person, or for one family.

The second reason for employers providing benefits has to do with employee valuations of benefits. If companies want to recruit workers who value certain benefits relatively highly, then those firms will provide more of that benefit. As a result, workers who value that benefit may be more likely to go to that firm. An example of this would be that faculty who particularly value the college costs contribution offered by Cornell are more likely to find Cornell a more attractive place to work. Oyer (2008) and others show that employees with families are much more likely to select jobs that have employer-provided health insurance than those without families. He also shows evidence for this for other benefits such as childcare.

An additional and very interesting reason firms may provide benefits is that they may reduce the "cost" of effort at work. Starting about a decade ago there was an explosion in providing all sorts of amenities to employees in the workplace. To name a few, these benefits included dry cleaning, dentists, doctors, banking, and cafeterias. The idea is that if it is relatively less costly for the worker to leave (e.g., he can eat at work, get his laundry done at work, he can do his banking at work), then the workers will be relatively more likely to stay at work. An often-discussed example of a company with these types of perks is Google. Obviously this is a two-edged sword. Many thought these to be generous perks, often associated with high-tech firms. On the other hand, some have been very critical of this sort of benefit. "Concierge services, petsitting, nap rooms and the option to telecommute are really just sneaky new ways to get already overworked employees to toll even harder, says Jill Anresky, author of *White-Collar Sweatshop*. 'These perks are often illusory. They exist just for their publicity value,' she says. 'In reality, staff face resentment if they try to work from home or take family days. And free food, nap rooms and home computers just keep people tied to their work" (*Economist*, 2001).[1]

An additional reason that firms may offer benefits is that they are tax advantaged (Lubotsky, 2011). In fact, many benefits are provided to workers "tax" free. Suppose that a tax-exempt benefit is offered to an employee. An example would be some type of health insurance. Assume the "cost" of the benefit is $3,000. Let's say for now that the cost is the same $3,000 if the worker buys the insurance or if the firm buys the insurance (so assume for now that the firm doesn't get a "deal" owing to the fact that the firm buys in "bulk" – that makes this example even more stark). Because the "income" from this employer-provided benefit is not taxed, it is as if the employee gets all $3,000. If, instead, the firm paid the worker in cash and then the worker had to buy insurance, the worker would have to pay 30 percent in tax or $900 (0.30 × $3,000) and only have $2,100 left over.

A few years ago, I worked with a company that had a very unusual compensation system (also mentioned in Chapter 4). Each year, the firm told all employees the value of their "total compensation." The firm then offered employees total choice over their method of pay. Employees could take their pay in one of three forms: cash, at-risk bonus, or stock options. Suppose the employee's pay was exactly $100,000. She could take all $100,000 in cash. She could also take $50,000 in cash, $30,000 in stock options (where the employees were told the exchange rate for options versus cash in advance), and put up $20,000 to be "at risk" in a bonus. The bonus could pay out anywhere between 0 percent and 250 percent of the amount at risk (depending on individual and group performance). Employees could also pick any other combination of compensation.

When a new head of HR came to the firm, he changed the plan, for several reasons. First, it was somewhat administratively difficult. More importantly, he thought it offered risk to the firm in the following sense. If workers chose the stock options alternative and that didn't pay off in the long run, then they may sue the firm claiming that they didn't understand the sophisticated financial issues behind stock options. In any event, the new head of HR suggested the firm go almost completely in the other direction – get rid of nearly all benefits. He did not do this as a way to cut costs; in fact, the firm compensated its employees very generously both before and after the change. After the change, they essentially increased all salaries by the cost of the benefits that were taken away. He simply believed that workers should have a choice over their pay and that the firm would just pay appropriately higher cash pay in exchange for the benefits and noncash financial pay taken away.[2] He believed workers should just get to choose exactly what they want. There were two types of pay that were kept from the old system. One was health insurance, given the extraordinary tax advantage described earlier. The other was the cafeteria. Employees loved the cafeteria and it wasn't very expensive for the firm to keep it.[3]

The cafeteria example is an interesting one. I have done work for several companies that have "free" (to the employees) food. In one, a small high-tech firm, it was all you could eat for free. In another, a large beverage firm, you could have any soft drink for free; there were dispensers in lounges all around the building and you could have as much of it as you wished. In another, drinks were free in the cafeteria but other food was not. I *always* have some sort of soft drink with me when I teach (ask my students – they tease me about it). Once in class I was asked if I would like to consult for the company that produced the soft drink in exchange for all the soft drink I could drink. I told the students that I don't drink *that much* of the stuff for this to be worth it in any way. At the same time, when I was in the place where the soft drinks were free, I consumed way too much.

There is an interesting, related literature in economics about "compensating differentials" (Rosen, 1974). The idea is that workers expect to be paid more when they face unpleasant or risky conditions at work. For example, although a worker may normally be willing to mow a lawn for $40, she may demand "extra" payment if the weather is particularly hot and humid. She may also demand more pay if there are beehives near where she mows. Another example is that workers may expect higher wages when they work at night, relative to working during the day (Hallock, Lubotsky, and Webber, in preparation). The compensating wage differential literature is very interesting, but it is extraordinarily difficult to actually detect such differentials in large data sets (see Viscusi and Moore, 1991). For example, many low-wage jobs are also associated with quite unpleasant working conditions such as heat or cold and unpleasant odors (e.g., sanitation workers) and many high-wage jobs are associated with pleasant working conditions such as air conditioning (e.g., attorneys). Of course there are other trade-offs that people make in terms of accepting lower wages and salaries in exchange for something else. Many people are willing to accept more stable jobs that pay less than less stable jobs that pay more.

Although this book does not delve deeply into the subject of "benefits," this chapter is about the trade-off between wage and salary income and benefits. There are a variety of reasons why firms offer benefits. These include the large tax advantages, the large potential "economies of scale" where firms, by buying in "bulk," can purchase benefits more cheaply than workers can, that firms may be trying to recruit and attract certain types of workers that may prefer certain benefits, and that firms may try to reduce the costs to workers for being at work, for example by providing childcare and banking services in the workplace. In the next chapter, we explore the complicated world of international compensation.

TWELVE

International Compensation

International compensation is an interesting and complicated subject.[1] This includes the pay of people from one country who take a one-time assignment overseas, those who work for a company that is based in another country, those who work for an international company but as workers move from country to country, and a host of other examples. This chapter discusses a number of issues important to paying employees internationally, including culture, institutional issues, and specific types of workers. We should keep in mind that these differences by country could also be true within organizations. When considering international pay, people sometimes lose sight of a company business strategy and compensation strategy. Focusing on international issues could inappropriately overshadow other important internal issues (Milkovich and Newman, 2008).

Culture

Culture is fundamental to the issue of international compensation. Many discussions of culture with respect to international compensation start with Hofstede's (1980) big four issues: (1) power distance, (2) uncertainty avoidance, (3) individualism versus collectivism, and (4) masculinity versus femininity. Each of the four is considered more carefully here. Marin (2008) offers a clear outline on which some of the following country examples are based.

The power distance issue is particularly interesting. The question is how accepting people are of a given hierarchical structure. I first saw this in striking fashion when I was teaching at the University of Illinois at Urbana-Champaign. One semester I was teaching two graduate courses. The first was a lecture to about 70 international students (only one student in the entire class was an American) and the subject matter was econometrics and

141

statistics. When I approached the classroom, I would hear the typical noises of people talking, shuffling papers, and moving around. But as soon as I appeared in the room, the entire place fell silent, immediately. Everyone faced forward, waiting for class to begin. In a second lecture, I taught a group of (largely) American graduate students a course in Finance for HR Managers. As I approached that classroom, I also heard the typical noises of people talking, shuffling papers, and moving around. But the noise did not stop until after I organized myself at the front of the room, wrote the outline for the day on the board, and even began my lecture! The American students had a drastically different view of the "hierarchical" structure of the professor-student relationship. This relationship persisted in different semesters with different students. I do not think it was the subject matter, or the time of day of the lecture, or anything but the average difference in cultural norms. It is interesting to note that as the semesters wore on, the group of international students became more like the American students. This could have been from a combination of cultural assimilation into the country (most of the international students came to Illinois directly from their home countries) or from my own way of running class in an informal way (e.g., everyone using first names – including me).

In any event, there is evidence of substantial differences in culture views of power distance. Marin (2008) discussed that countries such as Mexico and Malaysia rank very high on power distance rankings and countries such as the Netherlands, Sweden, and Australia rank very low. Of course, this is not to say that everyone from those countries should be associated with these norms; rather, on average, these countries are known to be extreme on these scales. Broad-based options and ownership are more likely to be used is low-power-distance countries (Schuler and Rogovsky, 1998; Gerhart, 2008).

Another important cultural issue is uncertainty avoidance. Some people have very low tolerance for risk. I count myself among these. For example, I would *never* consider a variable rate mortgage.[2] I have enough things to worry about and adding uncertainty about the size of my mortgage payments would not be a good thing. Countries that are thought to have, on average, high levels of risk tolerance include Greece, Portugal, and Italy. Countries known to have low tolerance for risk include Sweden, Denmark, and Singapore (Marin, 2008). Examples of forms of compensation that could be used in low uncertainty avoidance situations include variable compensation and incentive pay.[3] Seniority-based pay is something that could be used in a high uncertainty avoidance situation (Schuler and Rogovsky, 1998; Gerhart, 2008).[4]

Another of Hofstede's (1980) issues with respect to culture is individualism versus collectivism. The idea is the difference between having a lot of independence versus the importance of being part of a group. Highly individualistic societies are the United States, the United Kingdom, and Canada. On the other hand, countries with a great deal of social cohesion include Japan, South Korea, and Indonesia (Marin 2008). Individual performance-based compensation and extrinsic rewards are relatively more likely in individualistic societies, whereas in less individualistic societies, seniority, intrinsic rewards, and internal equity are more likely (Gerhart, 2008; Gomez-Mejia and Welbourne, 1991). Lowe, Milliman, De Cicri, and Dowling (2000) note that "because of their strong respect for elders and the need to maintain harmony and cohesion among all employees, collectivistic cultures are generally thought to emphasize seniority in human resource decisions to a much larger degree than individualistic cultures" (p. 60).[5]

The last major cultural issue is masculinity versus femininity. These can appear, for example, as a care for material possessions or, conversely, for an emphasis on care and health. Germany, Austria, and the United States are known as more masculine societies, whereas Norway, Finland, and the Netherlands are thought to be more feminine (Marin, 2008).

Be careful, however, when thinking about cultural issues. Culture means a lot more than differences in norms and standards across countries. Cultures can differ by neighbors, family, colleagues, and organizations.[6] When I was teaching at the University of Illinois, I drove a seminar speaker to dinner. She was a professor at another major university. I was driving a pickup truck. Quite aloof, she said "I have never been in a truck before." I told her she should get out more. In another example, it is interesting that Cornell University has traditionally been extraordinarily decentralized by "College." This means, for example, that undergraduate admissions decisions for, say, the College of Arts and Sciences students are done completely independently of those for students in the College of Engineering. Compensation decisions for faculty are similarly independent. If, for example, one College and Dean had a more "egalitarian" culture and one a more performance-based culture, one could imagine that one had a more compressed distribution of salaries than the other.

It can be very easy to fall into the trap of worrying about individualism versus collectivism, or uncertainty avoidance by country. Milkovich and Bloom (1998), Bloom, Milkovich, and Mitra (2000), Herod (2008), Milkovich and Newman (2008), and others discuss that it is important to not lose sight of non-national culture (i.e., the organizational culture) when thinking about compensation.

Institutional Issues

Culture isn't the only major issue to consider when thinking about international compensation. Obviously, there are dramatic institutional differences across countries. These include differences in levels of unionization, differences in the minimum wage, differences in worker protections, and dramatic differences in marginal tax rates. An example of how differences in worker protection can have substantial effects is a discussion I had with a CEO of a high-tech company based in the United States. We were talking about international differences in hiring and firing workers. He told me that it was so difficult to fire workers in France that he would never hire any additional workers there in the future (Hallock, 2009).

Table 12.1 shows differences in marginal tax rates for twenty-two countries (the data are from Towers Perrin, 2005). It is quite remarkable that there are such large differences in marginal personal income tax rates across countries. In Hong Kong, the highest marginal personal income tax rate is only 20 percent, in Singapore it is 22.0 percent, in Brazil it is 27.5 percent. At the other end of the spectrum, France's highest marginal personal income tax rate is 48.1 percent. It is 50 percent in Japan, 52 percent in the Netherlands, 53.5 percent in Belgium, and 56.4 percent in Sweden. Remember, however, that these numbers are not all directly comparable. For example, sales and property taxes, which are prevalent in the United States, also differ dramatically by country (and state and locality in the United States).[7]

There are other institutional differences that are masked by these differences in highest marginal tax rates. For example, in some countries, such as Germany, Austria, and Switzerland, stock options and restricted stock may be taxable at the time they are granted (Cui, 2006). So, even if one gets no immediate cash from the grant, he or she may owe tax at the time of the grant.

A host of other institutional differences and differences in norms also exist across countries. For example, in some European countries, wages for large sets of workers are collectively bargained. This is obviously not true in the United States, and the numbers of union members have been declining in the United States for some time. There are also dramatic differences in how even specific forms of compensation are paid to workers. Although the data are based on a survey from one consulting company (Towers Perrin, 2005)[8], it is interesting to see the dramatic differences in the fractions of companies offering long-term incentives, the typical stock option vesting times, vesting schedule, and terms of the options across countries in Table 12.1.

Table 12.1. *International differences in marginal tax rates and typical long-term incentives*

| | Max marginal tax rate | Estimated percentage of companies offering long-term incentive plans | | | Typical years to vesting | Typical vesting schedule | Typical term of stock option |
		2001	2004	2005			
Argentina	35.0	40	60	60	8	33,33,33	8
Australia	48.5	85	90	90	5	0,0,100	5
Belgium	53.5	75	95	95	10	0,0,100	10
Brazil	27.5	40	60	65	10	33,33,33	10
Canada	46.4	100	100	100	10	25,25,25,25	10
China (Hong Kong)	20.0	50	65	80	9	33,33,33	9
China (Shanghai)	45.0	20	25	35	10	33,33,33	10
France	48.1	90	95	95	9	0,0,0,100	9
Germany	47.5	60	80	85	5	0,0,0,100	5
India	33.6	10	20	20	10	25,25,25,25	10
Italy	43.0	50	80	85	8	0,0,100	8
Japan	50.0	15	35	35	7	0,100	7
Mexico	30.0	15	50	55	10	33,33,33	10
Netherlands	52.0	90	100	100	8	0,0,100	8
Singapore	22.0	70	80	90	10	0,100	10
South Africa	40.0	55	70	70	5	20,20,20,20,20	5
South Korea	39.6	15	20	25	8	0,0,100	8
Spain	45.0	50	70	70	5	0,0,100	5
Sweden	56.4	70	65	60	5	33,33,33	5
Switzerland	33.7	60	90	95	10	0,0,100	10
United Kingdom	40.0	100	95	95	10	0,0,100	10
United States	35.0	100	95	95	10	33,33,33	10

Note: All numbers are for 2005, except where noted.
Source: Various tables from Towers Perrin (2005).

Who Are We Talking About?

Before we get too far into the issue of international compensation, it is worth considering who, specifically, we are talking about. Martocchio (2001) and others mention three types of workers who are worthy of special attention: (1) expatriates, (2) host-country nationals, and (3) third-country nationals. I discuss each from the U.S. perspective, although, obviously, this could be done from any country's perspective.

Expatriates are U.S. citizens working in foreign lands for companies that have their headquarters in the United States. An example would be a U.S. citizen working in the London office of American Express. To make up for the cost of living away from "home," expatriates are often compensated in additional and sometimes interesting ways. For example, it is not uncommon in some countries for expatriates and their families to have drivers, laundry services, cleaning services, relocation assistance, rest and relaxation compensation, and special funds for children's education. Suutari and Tornikoski (2001) suggest that among the more difficult issues for expatriates are how to deal with taxation, the availability (or lack thereof) of information about the local standard of living, fears about currency rate risks, pension issues, and spousal-related issues. It may be for exactly these kinds of reasons that expatriates are paid relatively well. Nevertheless, more recently there is some evidence that there is a movement toward less lucrative expatriate compensation packages (e.g., Paul, 2007).

A second type of worker in the international compensation area is a host-country national. A host-country national is a foreign national citizen who works for a U.S.-headquartered company in his or her own country. An example of this would be a Japanese citizen working for General Mills in Japan. Of course, this type of arrangement does not have the critical issue of expatriates, namely compensating someone to live and work outside of their own home country. But it does have a set of associated costs. For example, as discussed elsewhere in this chapter, culture matters. A U.S.-based firm may have a certain compensation philosophy and that may not perfectly mesh culturally in all other countries. It is also worth noting that there is evidence that host-country nationals may resent the perceived-to-be lucrative packages that some expatriates are paid (Toh and DeNisi, 2003). This is particularly difficult when host-country nationals and expatriates are working side by side.

The final type of worker covered here is a third-country national. A third-country national is a foreign national citizen who works for a U.S.-based company in neither the United States nor his or her home country. An example would be a Swiss citizen working for General Electric in Germany.

Major Methods of Paying Workers Across Countries

How do companies keep track of paying workers around the world and what is the best way to do this? Three of the main methods for paying international workers are the (1) home-country-based method, (2) the host-country-based method, and (3) the headquarters-based method (Martocchio, 2001).

In the home-country-based method, a company would pay an employee as if he or she were doing that kind of work in the United States. This would perhaps make most sense for someone on a particularly short assignment.

The host-county-based method pays expatriates based on the pay scales for the country in which they work. If a U.S. citizen is working for Ford Motors in France, then that person would be paid in a similar way to the others working for that company in France. This would obviously make most sense for someone who is on a long-term assignment in France. If a U.S. citizen were working for ten years in France, it wouldn't make much sense to pay on the U.S.-based scale given that, by being there that long, the employee would be essentially assimilated in France.

The final main method for compensating workers internationally is called the headquarters-based method. By this method, employees are compensated at the level and mix that is used at the headquarters of the company. This means that neither the citizenship of the employee nor the location of job influences compensation. This obviously would be relatively most appropriate for those employees who move around a lot and who only infrequently (at most) work in their own home countries (Milkovich and Newman, 2008).

The State Department and Compensation Allowances

The U.S. Department of State is an excellent source for considering what employees from the United States might be paid during overseas assignments. The State Department considers five different types of allowances: (1) post (cost of living) allowance, (2) post (hardship) allowance, (3) living quarters allowance, (4) education allowance, and (5) danger pay allowance.[9] It is important to understand that these are independent allowances. Therefore, some cities may prompt additional compensation, for example, for cost of living, hardship, and danger pay. Next, I define each of these categories in more detail.

Foreign-cost-of-living allowances are designed to be given to those in a foreign country that has a cost of living (independent of housing) that is "substantially higher" than in Washington, D.C. The allowance is "designed to permit employees to spend the same portion of their basic compensation for current living as they would in Washington D.C., without incurring a reduction in their standard of living because of higher costs of goods and services at the post."[10] In Table 12.2, using data from the U.S. Department of State, I display the cost-of-living adjustments for selected cities. It is interesting to see the diversity in the data. For example, the cost-of-living

Table 12.2. *U.S. Department of State allowances for working abroad*
(selected locations)

Country	City	Cost of living	Hardship	Living quarters	Education	Danger pay
Belgium	Brussels	42%	0%	$41,800	$42,500	–
Bosnia-Herzegovnia	Sarajevo	5%	20%	$26,800	$19,400/ 57,200	10%
Canada	Vancouver	42%	0%	$41,200	$19,900	–
Canada	Winnipeg	30%	0%	$27,800	$15,750	–
China	Beijing	35%	15%	$58,200	$30,800	–
Egypt	Cairo	0%	15%	$18,800	$20,950	–
France	Lyon	70%	0%	$41,900	$15,200/ 55,100	–
France	Paris	70%	0%	$55,500	$43,550	–
Haiti	Port-au-Prince	25%	30%	$9,200	$10,450/ 55,500	5%
Iraq	Baghdad	0%	35%	$14,600	$5,050/ 58,450	35%
Israel	Tel Aviv	35%	0%	$41,200	$29,000	15%
Italy	Milan	70%	0%	$62,100	$39,850	–
Italy	Rome	60%	0%	$38,600	$28,750	–
Japan	Kyoto	90%	0%	$15,300	$8,900	–
Japan	Tokyo	90%	0%	$104,400	$35,000	–
Kenya	Nairobi	35%	30%	$16,200	$21,150	–
Lebanon	Beirut	10%	20%	$14,600	$11,200/ 57,000	25%
Libya	Tripoli	5%	35%	$14,600	$19,000/ 56,850	25%
Mexico	Mexico City	0%	15%	$39,200	$19,000	10%
Netherlands	Amsterdam	42%	0%	$43,200	$38,100	–
New Zealand	Auckland	50%	0%	$29,300	$11,150/ 58,900	–
Poland	Warsaw	15%	0%	$13,200	$26,550	–
Russia	Moscow	50%	15%	$45,900	$26,950	–
Senegal	Dakar	25%	15%	$14,600	$20,050	–
South Africa	Johan-nesburg	20%	10%	$14,600	$31,300	–
Turkey	Istanbul	10%	10%	$8,900	$29,900	–
United Kingdom	London	50%	0%	$68,800	$41,200	–

Notes: Living quarters is the amount listed for the middle category ("Group 3") for one living "without a family." For "Education," when two numbers are listed, these are for instances where the amount for "post" (the first number) and "away" are different. In the "Danger Pay" section, a city is listed as "–" if the State Department didn't list a number for that city, presumably because the number is zero.

Source: From the U.S. Department of State Web site on allowances: http://aoprals.state.gov/Web920/ allowance.asp?menu_id=95. This is a small subset of cities listed in the Department of State database. These data were collected on October 26, 2011, and specific numbers may have changed since that date. The State Department updates allowance numbers frequently.

allowance is 35 percent for Tel Aviv, 50 percent for London, and 90 percent for Kyoto. At the same time it is 5 percent in Tripoli and zero in Cairo, Baghdad, and Mexico City.

An additional allowance is suggested by the State Department for "hardship." The State Department suggests allowances from 5 percent to 35 percent, in 5 percent increments, for "service at places in foreign areas where conditions of environment differ substantially from conditions of environment in the continental United States and warrant additional compensation as a recruitment and retention incentive."[11] As I have noted elsewhere in this book, some people earn a lucky bonus for certain types of pay. For example, imagine being employed in Washington, D.C., but wanting to live in Istanbul for family or any other reasons. According to column 2 of Table 12.2, the State Department suggestion is to pay a 10 percent allowance for this assignment. Some may not want to go there and would need a bonus so as to be "recruited or retained" by the organization. Others may not; they may actually have a preference to go to that city. They can enjoy the bonus and the assignment in the new city. Other examples include Sarajevo and Beruit, with hardship pay of 20 percent and Baghdad with 35 percent (the highest possible for any country). Note, also, that many countries have no danger pay at all.

The State Department also calculates specific numbers for living quarters while spending time on assignment in other countries. Numbers in this category are counted for individuals or families into three groups each. I have recorded the middle of the three numbers for each city for a single person ("Group 3"). The allowance is intended to cover the annual cost the average "employee's costs for rent, heat, light, fuel, gas, electricity, water, taxes levied by local government and required by law or custom to be paid by lessee, insurance required by local law to be paid by the lessee, and agent's fees required by law or custom to be paid by lessee."[12] These numbers, too, vary dramatically by location through the world. Two cities in Table 12.2 have living allowances under $10,000 for the year: Port-au-Prince and Istanbul. Others are extremely high, including Paris ($55,500), Milan ($62,100), London ($68,800), and Tokyo ($104,400). The education (for children) allowance similarly varies dramatically across countries.

The final category in Table 12.2 is danger pay. Danger pay is independent from hardship pay. The State Department defines danger pay as an "allowance to provide additional compensation above basic compensation... for service at places in foreign areas where their exist conditions of civil insurrection, civil war, terrorism or wartime conditions which threaten physical harm or imminent danger to the health or well-being of an employee. These conditions do not include acts characterized chiefly as economic crime."[13] Danger ranges from 0 up to 35 percent of basic compensation. Among the cities listed in Table 12.2, the allowance ranges from 5 percent in Port-au-Prince to 35 percent in Baghdad.

It is interesting to note that many companies pay "extra" if someone goes off to an area where the cost of living and related costs are higher. In fact, this even happens as one moves within the United States. Consider, for example, an employee working in Ithaca, New York, at a high-tech start-up. Consider that person moving to San Diego, California, where costs of living are much higher. It would be quite expected that the person would get a raise at the time of the move. But it is a lot more difficult to go the other way. Firms are much less likely to lower pay as one moves from San Diego to Ithaca. It is sensible to raise pay when costs are higher. It could be equally sensible to go the other way. However, this is likely another example of "sticky wages." Wages rarely fall. It is difficult to accept lower wages, even if the *purchasing power* of those lower wages may lead to a higher standard of living in a new low-cost area.

A related example is from a company for which I did some consulting work. The company moved a set of workers from Texas to New York. Because the cost of living was substantially higher in New York, it was easy to argue for higher wages for the employees as they moved to New York. Shortly thereafter, the firm decided to send everyone back to Texas – including some who were always in New York. It was nearly impossible to get anyone to go back to Texas at wages lower than they were earning in New York.

Just Because You Are Focused on International Issues, Don't Lose Sight of Everything Else

Milkovich and Newman (2008) cleverly point out that many companies are so focused on the kinds of "international" issues, I have described in this chapter, that they may lose sight of all of the other things that make up a good pay system. Consider again the issues discussed in Part II of this book, including strategy, job analysis and job evaluation, internal comparisons, market data, and the market pay line. If people are so concentrated on international differences in culture, hardship, cost-of-living differences, and the like, it is certainly possible to lose sight of other important, and perhaps fundamental, parts of paying employees. In some cases, international differences in culture (for example) may be much smaller than cultural differences across firms in the same industry in the same country.

I end this chapter with an interesting example from professional baseball. Picker (2007) describes "fight money" that is paid to professional baseball players in Japan. This is given by some Japanese professional baseball teams after a game for extraordinary play. An amount, on the order of $1,000 (in cash), is handed to a player by the manager in an envelope. One of the players, Kei Igawa (formerly of the New York Yankees), when he pitched for the Hansin Tigers in Japan, described it as follows: "It's like you're the horse and they put a carrot in front of you and you try to go for it. . . . It's like bait" (Picker, 2007).

It is very interesting that "fight money" is paid to players in countries where it was illegal, until the mid-1990s, to pay stock options to any employees. Why is this done in Japan and not the United States – especially given that the United States is known as much more of an individualistic culture and Japan a much more collectivist one? One might argue that $1,000 is too little to motivate highly paid players in the United States. But, the numbers could be adjusted – how about $200,000 for a job well done? In Japan, the player is often given the envelope in a kind of ceremony in front of his teammates, accompanied by applause. Hideki Okajima (formerly of the Boston Red Sox and the New York Yankees) was paid fight money when he was with the Yomiuri Giants. He said the financial reward was no match for the feeling of being recognized. Would that be true in the United States?

THIRTEEN

Compensation in Nonprofit Organizations

Even though an extremely large number of people work in the nonprofit sector, surprisingly little is known about how people there are compensated,[1] relative to what we know about the for-profit sector. This chapter aims to fill this gap by presenting a simple description of the employees in the nonprofit sector and describing some differences in the pay of those in the nonprofit, for-profit, government, and self-employed sectors. The chapter also discusses different kinds of nonprofits, the size of the sector, and possible reasons why people in the nonprofit sector are paid differently than those in the for-profit sector. These reasons include: labor donations (some argue that workers in nonprofits are effectively making donations to their organizations in the form of lower wages), compensating differentials (some have argued that workers in nonprofits accept lower wages in exchange for better working conditions, more job flexibility, etc.), and differences in returns to characteristics or selection (some have suggested that perhaps different kinds of workers choose to work in the nonprofit sector). The chapter also discusses gender in the context of nonprofits and includes a discussion of managerial compensation in nonprofit organizations.

Before considering differences in the way those in the nonprofit and for-profit sectors are paid, this section provides a brief outline of the nonprofit sector in general.[2] In this section, I define the nonprofit sector, explain simple details of the structure of the nonprofit sector, and describe Hansmann's (1980) "nondistribution constraint." This constraint is central to organizations' choice of the nonprofit form, as well as the pay gaps and issues of incentive compensation discussed later. The nonprofit "industry" classification system, the National Taxonomy of Exempt Entities (NTEE), is also explained later in the chapter.

Institutional Details

Defining the nonprofit sector is not as easy as it might seem. In fact, even settling on a simple set of terms for the sector can be difficult. Salamon and Anheier (1992a) describe six different terms or phrases that all seem to have some important aspects related to the issues discussed later in the chapter. First is the "charitable sector," which survives on support from donations. Second is the "independent sector," which is independent from the government or the private sectors. Third, the "voluntary sector," is so termed because of its extensive use of volunteer labor. Fourth is the "tax-exempt sector," receiving its name from the fact that, following certain conditions, organizations in this sector do not have to pay income taxes as for-profit organizations do. Fifth includes nongovernmental organizations (NGOs), which are often social and developmental organizations but outside of the government. Finally there is the "nonprofit sector." Organizations in the nonprofit sector can earn profits but can't distribute those profits to those in charge of the organization.

For the purposes of this book, I consider an organization to be nonprofit if it adheres to the definition as outlined by the Internal Revenue Service (IRS). However, in most of the main discussion of the possible theoretical reasons for differences in compensation between for-profit and nonprofit organizations, this definition need not be so strict. For an organization to become officially designated as a nonprofit in the United States, it must file forms with the IRS for nonprofit status.[3] Officially designated nonprofit organizations do not have to pay tax. However, if they have more than $25,000 in annual net revenue, they must file IRS Form 990. Among the twenty-eight possible groupings for nonprofits, by far the most frequently designated are 501c(3), "charitable and religious." Organizations in group 501c(3) are considered charitable because, according to the IRS, they serve "broad public purposes [including] educational, religious, scientific, and literary activities, among others, as well as the relief of poverty and other public benefit actions." In Table 13.1, it is clear that of the roughly 2 million nonprofit organizations in the United States in 2009, more than 75 percent have the 501c(3) designation. Other major groups include social welfare organizations (501c[4]), of which there were about 110,924 in 2009, and fraternal and beneficiary societies (501c[8]), of which there were about 58,065 in 2009). Those designated 501c(3) have the added benefit that contributions made to the organization are tax deductible to the contributor. I make this distinction because the majority of all nonprofits are 501c(3)

Table 13.1. *Tax-exempt organizations registered with the IRS in 2009*

Section		Number in 2009
501(c)(1)	Corporations Organized Under Acts of Congress	98
501(c)(2)	Titleholding Corporations	5,639
501(c)(3)	*CHARITABLE AND RELIGIOUS*	*1,535,151*
501(c)(4)	Social Welfare	110,924
501(c)(5)	Labor, agricultural organizations	55,629
501(c)(6)	Business leagues	71,887
501(c)(7)	Social and recreational clubs	55,838
501(c)(8)	Fraternal and beneficiary societies	58,065
501(c)(9)	Voluntary employees' beneficiary associations	9,428
501(c)(10)	Domestic fraternal beneficiary societies	20,044
501(c)(11)	Teachers' retirement funds	10
501(c)(12)	Benevolent life insurance associations	5,857
501(c)(13)	Cemetery companies	10,031
501(c)(14)	State chartered credit unions	3,245
501(c)(15)	Mutual insurance companies	1,127
501(c)(16)	Corporations to finance crop operations	14
501(c)(17)	Supplemental unemployment benefit trusts	271
501(c)(18)	Employee funded pension trusts	1
501(c)(19)	War veterans' organizations	32,592
501(c)(20)	Legal service organizations	9
501(c)(21)	Black lung trusts	28
501(c)(23)	Veterans' associations founded prior to 1880	3
501(c)(24)	Trusts described in section 4049 of ERISA	1
501(c)(25)	Holding companies for pensions, etc.	1,059
501(c)(26)	State-sponsored high risk health insurance organizations	10
501(c)(27)	State-sponsored workers compensation reinsurance	11
501(d)	Religious and apostolic organizations	161
501(e)	Cooperative hospital service organizations	17
501(f)	Cooperative service organizations of operating educational orgs.	1
501(c)(71)	Charitable risk pool	1
501(c)(81)	Qualified state-sponsored tuition program	1
501(c)(82)	527 political organizations	8
501(c)(90)	Split interest trust	463
501(c)(92)	Private foundations	3,984
TOTAL		1,981,608

Source: National Center for Charitable Statistics at the Urban Institute.

but, again, the discussion throughout this chapter easily applies to a wider variety of organizations.

Hansmann (1980) categorized nonprofits into four groups. Doing so helps understand the missions and institutional detail of the sector in general. A much more detailed classification system, much like industry codes for firms, is described later. Hansmann (1980) suggested that nonprofits can be either "mutual" – that is, controlled by patrons – or "entrepreneurial," which are free from tight control by patrons. Nonprofits can also be categorized as "donative" if the majority of income comes from donations or "commercial" if the majority of income comes from charging for services. Hansmann (1980) also provided some well-known examples of nonprofits and placed them into each of four categories: (1) mutual and donative, such as Common Cause, the National Audubon Society, and political groups; (2) mutual and commercial, such as the American Automobile Association, Consumers Union, and country clubs; (3) entrepreneurial and donative, such as CARE, March of Dimes, and art museums; and (4) entrepreneurial and commercial, such as the National Geographic Society, The Educational Testing Service, and nursing homes.

After framing the nonprofit sector, I now focus on a central issue in nonprofits, which appears frequently throughout the remainder of this chapter – the "nondistribution constraint" (Hansmann, 1980). Hansmann (1980, 1996) pointed out that nonprofit organizations are free to make profits but what distinguishes them from for-profit organizations is that the profits may not be distributed to those with formal control over the organization (see also the Taxpayer Bill of Rights II, 1996). It turns out that the "nondistribution constraint" is critically important to several issues mentioned later in the chapter, including the choice of for-profit versus nonprofit form and incentive compensation. Enforcement of the nondistribution constraint is difficult and is usually left in the jurisdiction of the Attorney General's office of each state in the United States.

Just as for-profit firms have an industry classification system, there is a system for categorizing nonprofits – the previously mentioned NTEE. Hodgkinson (1990) outlined an interesting history of the NTEE. In 1984, the Independent Sector and the National Center for Charitable Statistics began to develop a unique classification system for nonprofits. At that time, there were at least nine different classifications and none seemed satisfactory (Hodgkinson, 1990). Developing such a system will ultimately prove quite useful in trying to decide whether there is a nonprofit versus for-profit wage gap, and in trying to determine exactly what workers in the different sectors are doing with their time.

NTEE can be categorized in several ways. There are twenty-six "major groups," such as Animal Related and Medical Research, which comprise the first part of the code (see the left-hand column of Table 13.2). The twenty-six major groups can be further generalized into 10 major categories. These categories are: (1) Arts, Culture and Humanities, (2) Education, (3) Environment and Animals, (4) Health, (5) Human Services, (6) International and Foreign Affairs, (7) Public and Societal Benefit, (8) Religion Related, (9) Mutual/Membership Benefits, and (10) Unknown. Further groupings include two digits of subcodes beneath each of the twenty-six major groups. The last part of the NTEE code is what is known as the Common Code and includes such classifications as Alliance Organizations, Management and Technical Assistance Services, and Public Education. There are a total of 645 unique subgroupings in the NTEE. Hodgkinson and Toppe (1991), Turner, Nygren, and Bowen (1992), Gronbjerg (1994), and Stevensen, Pollack, and Lampkin (1997) have provided many more details on the NTEE.

Why Organize as a Nonprofit Versus For-Profit?

Although there are nearly 2 million nonprofit organizations in the United States today, most organizations are not nonprofits. This section discusses potential reasons why organizations choose to form in a particular way and hints at how these forms may influence the pay of the workers in the different kinds of organizations. Obviously, the emphasis is on why groups choose to form nonprofits, and the costs and benefits of doing so. This entire literature is based on the pioneering work of Hansmann (1980) and many others.[4] Hansmann (1996) provided a thorough up-to-date synopsis of the field. This part of the chapter aims to discuss the costs and benefits of the nonprofit form of organization.

Hansmann (1980) outlined several reasons why nonprofits arise. The first is that the buyer of an item and the recipient of the item are not the same person. He considers the case of food donations. If one donates food to a relief organization, he or she cannot tell whether the food actually makes it to its intended destination, say to the survivors of an earthquake. The problem is that it is nearly impossible for the one who donates the goods to monitor those working for the relief organization. If that relief organization is organized as a nonprofit, then, because of the "nondistribution constraint," those in charge of the organization will be much less likely to abscond with the money. Recall that the nondistribution constraint does not ban the nonprofit organization from making profits per se. However,

Table 13.2. *Nonprofit "industry" classifications, National Taxonomy of Exempt Entities (NTEE)*

Major groups (26 of these)	Major categories (10 of these)
A. Arts, Culture, and Humanities	I. Arts, Culture, and Humanities
B. Educational Institutions and Related Activities	II. Education
C. Environmental Quality, Protection, and Beautification	III. Environment and Animals
D. Animal Related	III. Environment and Animals
E. Health – General and Rehabilitative	IV. Health
F. Mental Health, Crisis Intervention	IV. Health
G. Disease, Disorders, Medical Disciplines	IV. Health
H. Medical Research	IV. Health
I. Crime, Legal Related	V. Human Services
J. Employment, Job Related	V. Human Services
K. Food, Agriculture, and Nutrition	V. Human Services
L. Housing, Shelter	V. Human Services
M. Public Safety, Disaster Preparedness, and Relief	V. Human Services
N. Recreation, Sports. Leisure, Athletics	V. Human Services
O. Youth Development	V. Human Services
P. Human Services – Multipurpose and Other	V. Human Services
Q. International, Foreign Affairs, and National Security	VI. International, Foreign Affairs
R. Civil Rights, Social Action, Advocacy	VII. Public, Societal Benefit
S. Community Improvement, Capacity Building	VII. Public, Societal Benefit
T. Philanthropy, Voluntarism, and Grantmaking Foundations	VII. Public, Societal Benefit
U. Science and Technology Research Institutes, Services	VII. Public, Societal Benefit
V. Social Science Research Institutes, Services	VII. Public, Societal Benefit
W. Public, Society Benefit: Multipurpose and Other	VII. Public, Societal Benefit
X. Religion Related, Spiritual Development	VIII. Religion Related
Y. Mutual/Membership Benefit Organizations, Other	IX. Mutual/ Membership Benefit
Z. Other	X. Unknown

Notes: The NTEE codes are similar to industry codes for firms. The NTEE codes are four characters. There are 26 "Major Groups," which comprise the first digit of the codes. Below each of these 26 groups are two digits of subcodes with finer organization-type classifications. The final digit is called the "Common Code." There are a total of 645 unique subgroups. There are 10 "Major Categories" (see column 2 above), which comprise the broadest organization classifications. See Stevenson, Pollak, and Lampkin (1997) Appendix B for more detail on the NTEE.

Source: Stevenson, Pollak, and Lampkin, *State Nonprofit Almanac 1997: Profiles of Charitable Organizations,* 373–400.

the managers of the nonprofits are not allowed to benefit from those profits directly.

Nonprofits are also likely to arise in the case of public goods. The fact that one person enjoys the services of a public good does not preclude others from doing so at the same time (Rosen, 1988). Examples of public goods include radio broadcasts and lighthouses. Consider more carefully the case of public radio. Public radio is free to all and one person listening to his or her radio does not stop others from doing the same. Hansmann (1980) argued that public radio is likely organized as a nonprofit so that it can more effectively raise funds for programming. Because a given donor cannot monitor the use of funds donated to public radio, he or she is probably more willing to donate to an organization where it is clear that the incentives for absconding with the profits are lower.

Nonprofits are also more likely to appear in the case of museums and operas where there is considerable heterogeneity in the value individuals place on the performance or exhibit, and where the ratio of fixed to variable costs is extremely high (i.e., the cost of adding an additional audience member is extremely low relative to the cost of setting up an exhibit or performance). In this case, Hansmann (1980) suggested that nonprofits are more likely to form because of a type of what he calls "voluntary price discrimination." In this case, ticket prices are actually set quite low, but those who value performances more will be willing to donate additional money to the museum or opera company just as in the case of public radio. If the organization is organized as a for-profit firm, then the high-valuation donors will be less likely to want to donate funds because of the worry that the managers will be residual claimants on any profits. Hansmann (1980) argued that we are much less likely to see television stations and sports teams organized as nonprofits, because, although the marginal costs of adding an additional "seat" are small relative to the fixed costs of starting the production or organization, the costs can be spread over a much larger audience.

Another example of this type of situation is "implicit loans" in the higher education arena. This works precisely the same way as implicit price discrimination. In this case, colleges set tuition costs low relative to the true costs of schooling. However, those students with particularly high valuation of their college's services are free to voluntarily donate back some of the tuition money that they "borrowed" earlier. If universities were not organized as nonprofits with the nondistribution constraint, donors would be much less likely to give.

A final, and perhaps most striking, example of choice of organizational form comes from organizations such as hospitals, nursing homes, and daycare centers. All three are similar, but only daycare centers are discussed here. Given that it is particularly difficult for a parent to monitor what goes on inside a daycare center, a parent might be more willing to place his or her child in a nonprofit daycare center than a for-profit one. This is also because of the nondistribution constraint. Because, in the case of the nonprofit daycare center, the managers are not the residual claimants (they cannot keep any excess profits), managers in nonprofit daycare centers may be less willing to cut corners on the quality of the food, for example. Arrow (1963) also pointed out that consumers may prefer hospitals to be organized as nonprofits because of some preferences against the motive for profits in such organizations.

There have been some criticisms of Hansmann's (1980) ideas about the nondistribution constraint and the reasons for certain types of organizational forms. For example, for it to be credible that families choose nonprofit nursing homes over otherwise identical for-profit nursing homes, it must be the case that people can tell which organizations are for-profit and which are not. Permut (1981) attempted to do this through a telephone survey of 225 households. The survey also "asked if they felt that nonprofits were likely to be more trustworthy, fair, or personally concerned than a for-profit organization" (p. 1626). The survey additionally inquired about whether respondents would prefer to have an elderly relative in a nursing home or a child in a summer camp that was a nonprofit relative to a for-profit. The survey found that more than half of the respondents could not tell whether five local nonprofits were nonprofit or not. Also, 68 percent of respondents said that they did not care about the nonprofit status of the nursing home, and 58 percent did not care about the nonprofit status of the summer camp for children. While just suggestive, these results are interesting in light of Hansmann's (1980) well-known work.

Several papers subsequent to Hansmann (1980) have built on his ideas from a theoretical economics point of view, including Easley and O'Hara (1983, 1986) and Glaeser and Shleifer (1998). Easley and O'Hara (1983) examined the solution to an optimal contracting problem. They demonstrated that the nonprofit form of organization may be preferred when there is a cost to observing output. It may in fact be optimal, not just another form of organization. Glaeser and Shleifer (1998) described a case where perfectly self-interested entrepreneurs might choose nonprofit status for their business even though they are aware of the nondistribution constraint that may limit the profits they get from the organization. The main point is that the nonprofit signals to customers that there may be weakened incentives to maximize profits.

It is in the context of the nondistribution constraint and the choice of organizational form that pay differences between nonprofits and for-profits in general are discussed in this chapter. In particular, from the point of view of a consumer, even though the nonprofit form may seem most appropriate for certain services, "nonprofits may succeed in distributing some of their net earnings through inflated salaries, various perquisites granted to employees and other forms of excess payment" (Hansmann, 1980, p. 844). In addition, to the extent that managers and employees of nonprofits are motivated by personal financial concerns, employees of nonprofits may be less willing to work efficiently and quickly than those in for-profits.

Possible Reasons For Differences in Pay Between For-Profit and Nonprofit Sectors

Much of the literature on pay in nonprofits concerns the perceived gap in pay between employees in nonprofits relative to those in for-profit organizations. The following section on empirical findings on the pay gap more carefully examines the facts on differences in pay between those employed in the two sectors. It seems instructive, however, to first explore possible theoretical reasons for differences in compensation between the two sectors.

Of the many reasons discussed for differences in pay between the for-profit and nonprofit sectors, four seem to be most relevant. First, many have argued that those in nonprofits earn less because they are "donating wages" to the organizations for which they work (e.g., Preston, 1989). That is, employees are basically donating back to the nonprofit the difference between what they would have earned in the for-profit sector and their actual wages in the nonprofit sector. The second main reason for differences in pay surrounds the well-known discussion of compensating wage differentials in economics. In this case, workers accept lower wages in nonprofits in exchange for a host of pleasant amenities on their job, such as flexible hours, more stable job prospects, and a slower pace of work. The third reason is the well-known efficiency wage hypothesis where workers who are difficult to monitor are paid more and work harder so as to avoid losing their jobs and having to take new ones at the lower competitive wage. The fourth reason that some have argued for is that differences in pay for employees in nonprofits may be because their skills are more useful elsewhere, or that they are in general less appropriately matched to the for-profit sector. These differences are extremely difficult to separate with most existing data sources. The remainder of this section discusses each of these topics and several related ones such as the extreme case of a wage gap – the case of volunteering. Note that, although this section seems to be centered on the decision to work in the for-profit versus nonprofit sector, Burbridge (1994) pointed out that workers probably select an occupation first and then chose a sector in which to work.

The idea of labor donations is easily seen in a paper by Preston (1989). In her example, workers are willing to trade lower wages for higher social benefits.[5] As part of her model, workers' utility is a function of their wage and of "social benefits" provided by the organization for which they work. For a given level of utility, organizations that provide society with greater benefits can pay given workers lower wages.[6] Preston (1989) argued that the limiting case of this is complete labor donations whereby workers donate all of their time to an organization; that is, they volunteer.

There are several interesting implications of Preston's (1989) ideas. As jobs are more likely to generate social benefits, there is a greater chance of a for-profit/nonprofit wage gap. Consider some ranking of jobs by the social benefit that they provide. An employee managing a nonprofit may actually help provide a great deal of social benefit relative to a for-profit employee. However, as one moves further away from the top of the hierarchy of the organization (e.g., mail room workers), occupations are less likely to have a nonprofit versus for-profit wage gap (Young, 1987). Preston (1989) provided some empirical support for this. A second interesting implication is that because managers are not constrained to keep wages low (i.e., as they would be by competition from a for-profit firm), they may push wages up because it is simply pleasant and easy to do so.[7] On the other hand, the idea of social benefit provision and donation of wages suggests that wages are expected to be lower in nonprofits. Mirvis and Hackett (1983) reported that those in nonprofits "are more likely to report that their work is more important to them than the money they earn" (p. 7).[8] However, this could be rationalizing the employment situation.

A related example to labor donations is a study reported by Frank (1996). Reporting on a sample of 680 Cornell University graduates 9 months after graduation, Frank (1996) demonstrated that even controlling for gender, course mix while at Cornell, and GPA, there was still a very large wage gap between those who entered the nonprofit sector relative to those who went into for-profit organizations. Frank (1996) decided to add a measure of "social responsibility" to each of the occupations to which the respondents belonged. The responsibility scale was created by asking others how they would rate certain occupations on a social responsibility scale from 1–7 (after standardizing, stockbrokers received a –1.44 and teachers a 1.98). Frank (1996) found that salaries fell with increases in the social responsibility scale, even controlling for gender, courses, GPA, and sector (i.e., nonprofit, government, for-profit).

Obviously, the extreme case of labor donations is volunteering, and Menchik and Weisbrod (1987) developed two economic models of volunteering. The first model is based on consumption (i.e., people enjoy volunteering), and the other is based on experience (i.e., people view volunteering as a means to gain valuable experience that they may use later in the paid labor market). They demonstrated that both models imply that as wages increase, volunteering declines. Weisbrod (1988) estimated that the number of volunteers in the United States is very large. He reported previously unpublished results from the group called Independent Sector that the number of full-time-equivalent volunteers over age 14 increased from 4.2 million in 1974 to 6.7 million in 1995. Hodgkinson, Weitzman, Noga, Gorski, and Kirsch (1994) and Hodgkinson, Gorski, Noga, and Knauft (1995) reported on trends in household giving and volunteering, including trends in given sectors such as environmental, health, human services, religious organizations, and youth development. Vladeck (1988) and James and Rose-Ackerman (1986) described the case where individuals may be willing to donate time to religious organizations. Steinberg (1990a) and Bilodeau and Slivinski (1996) also considered the case of volunteering.

A related explanation for differences in wages for those in the nonprofit sector versus the for-profit sector is related to screening and is carefully explained in the appendix to Hansmann (1980). This theory is also related to the choice of organizational form as discussed earlier. Hansmann (1980) considered a model where there are only two types of individuals: those who are only greedy and those who seek money and quality of service. He further assumed that both types have similar opportunities for work – that is, they are of the same level of ability. Greedy workers will only work for the market wage because they gain no utility from the quality of service provided by their organization. The other workers, on the other hand, have a preference for providing good service and are willing to earn less while working for an organization that provides good service. Therefore, service-oriented workers (not greedy) will work for less than the wage of the greedy-minded workers so long as the level of service is sufficiently high. Steinberg (1990a) also discusses that the downside of paying high wages to managers of nonprofits is that you may attract a particular type of worker that may not have interests in line with the organization.

For an organization to maintain a given level of service, it must pay service-minded workers the lower wage and, as always, pay greedy-minded workers the "market" wage. One way for consumers to be assured that they are receiving service of a certain level of quality is for the organization to organize as a nonprofit. If an organization (e.g., a food relief organization, as described earlier) organizes as a nonprofit, then in this model only service-minded workers will volunteer to work because the organizations can only pay the lower wage. By virtue of being set up the way they are, nonprofits may be able to attract precisely the kinds of employees they seek.

A host of authors including Young (1984), James and Rose-Ackerman (1986), Burbridge (1994), Glaeser and Shleifer (1998), and Handy and Katz (1998) have suggested that one reason we may expect lower wages in nonprofits is because of the amenities associated with nonprofit jobs (Borjas, 1996).[9] The typical case of compensating differentials is the one where workers are paid more when they must face higher risks of death. The higher pay is simply to compensate for the increased risk. Classic examples of equalizing difference are those of Rosen (1974, 1986). There are many suggestions that nonprofits provide amenities for their workers such as more pleasant work environments, greater job flexibility, more stable positions, and more control over the job.

Steinberg and Jacobs (1994) suggested that there is a much higher rate of turnover in nonprofit organizations than in for-profit organizations. They say that this represents a "problem" (p. 86) for the compensating differential explanation for lower wages in nonprofits. If it were the case that turnover were the only job characteristic to differ between the for-profit and nonprofit sectors, this problem would exist. However, given the other evidence on differences in jobs across the sectors, this is probably not the case.

Another theoretical reason why one might expect to see different wages in nonprofits has to do with efficiency wages. In this case, workers who are difficult to monitor are paid more and work harder so as to avoid losing their job and having to take a new one at the lower competitive wage. Ito and Domian (1987) described the case of symphony orchestras that are nonprofit organizations where monitoring of workers is difficult and workers are paid high wages. Ito and Domian (1987) attributed the high wages to efficiency wages but didn't consider the potential (in this case) positive ability bias.

Clearly, labor donations and compensating wage differentials are interesting theoretical reasons for differences in pay between the for-profit and nonprofit sectors. However, these are sometimes "residual arguments" that serve as reasonable explanations for a gap that exists after certain careful attempts have been made to remove it. The idea here is to consider the simple case of selection bias. If an omitted variable (e.g., motivation, organization, or ability) is correlated with nonprofit status and with compensation, and if this measure of motivation, organization, or ability is not taken into account when estimating the relationship between wages and nonprofit status, the estimated effect of nonprofit status on wages will be biased. Using cross-sectional data (at a single point in time), Heckman (1978) and Lee (1978) offered possible ways to consider these issues. Weisbrod (1983) discussed selection, in a paper described in detail later, but argued that the assumptions required to deal with the selection are strong. Goddeeris (1988), in a follow-up to Weisbrod, considered selection and found it to be quite important.

Because one way to interpret the issue of this bias in measuring the for-profit versus nonprofit wage gap is that the true difference simply lies in the fact that workers with different unmeasured characteristics are more likely to choose to work in nonprofits, one way to deal with this issue is to collect data on individuals who switch from the nonprofit to the for-profit sector or vice versa. Preston (1989) also argued that one possibility for the gap is that women are more likely to work in nonprofits and that the gap may simply be a gender effect. This is discussed in more detail later in this chapter. We now turn to considering pay for performance in nonprofit organizations.

Pay and Performance in Nonprofits

The concept of using measures of performance to compensate employees is not new. However, given the nondistribution constraint in nonprofits, performance pay in nonprofits has historically not been very significant. In fact, many have thought that it is not legally possible to pay employees in nonprofits based on performance. This is not the case.[10] Steinberg (1990b) noted that profits can be made and distributed to outside contractors or employees, but not to those in charge.

This section explains some basics of incentive pay generally and the increased use of incentive pay in nonprofits specifically. It also covers benefits and costs of such a system for the organization and other workers and constituents. In addition, the concept of the difficulty of measuring performance in a nonprofit is discussed along with the associated problems it might create for performance pay. Pynes (1997) discussed several forms of compensation in nonprofits, including broadbanding, skill-based pay and pay for knowledge, merit pay, and gainsharing. Her book is a summary of HR practices in nonprofits. This section deals exclusively with pay for performance.

Hansmann (1980) wrote that money given to a manager that varies with "annual surplus achieved by the firm is likely to be viewed as a distribution of profits either by the state authorities charged with policing nonprofit corporations or by the Internal Revenue Service" (p. 900). However, there is now increased attention in the nonprofit sector on using monetary incentives to motivate nonprofit employees (Bailey and Risher, 1996). Abelson (1998) cited Stacey Palmer, the managing editor of *The Chronicle of Philanthropy*, discussing the fact that nonprofits are becoming increasingly innovative in how they pay managers in order to attract and retain them. Casteuble (1997) reported on a survey on Association Executive Compensation and Benefits conducted by the American Society of Association Executives (association executives manage trade associations, individual membership societies, voluntary organizations, and other nonprofits). The survey suggested that many participating associations currently provide and will continue to provide incentive pay for top managers. In addition, Ernst and Young's Not-for-Profit Business Services group conducted a survey of 250 nonprofits in the New York area and found that 16 percent had some sort of incentive pay in 1990.[11] However, Elaine Allen, the National Director for Ernst and Young's Not-for-Profit Business Services group, stated, "I think these trends toward innovative total compensation plans serve as a testament to the resourcefulness, commitment, and determination of the nonprofit community" (Incentives, 1992, p. 10). Ms. Palmer also stated that "[i]n the face of a crunch that has sent some highly successful businesses into an economic tailspin, the not-for-profit community has demonstrated its administrative acumen by making every effort to reward and retain its most vital resource: the people who make the organization work" (p. 11).

Oster (1996) noted that franchises (where a local affiliate pays a fee to use the national name but keeps all extra revenue it generates) may be important in nonprofits. Just as the franchise is important for helping guard against managerial shirking (see Martin, 1988; Krueger, 1991), franchises may be particularly important in nonprofits where performance is particularly difficult to measure. Oster (1996) noted that franchises are widely used in nonprofits, including Planned Parenthood with 171 affiliates, the Boy Scouts of America with 400, Goodwill Industries with 179, and the United Way with 2,300.

Now that it has been demonstrated that incentive pay exists in at least some nonprofits, this section turns to a discussion of incentive pay generally and benefits of paying for performance in particular. Some useful and important questions to ask when considering how to pay workers include whether to pay by time (salaries) or by output (piece rates) (Lazear, 1986, 1996a, 1998, 2000). There are obvious advantages to paying "by the piece," such as the fact that workers work more quickly, produce a higher level of output, and have less incentive to shirk (Steinberg, 1990b; Rose-Ackerman, 1996).

In addition to piece-rate workers, one place where the relationship between pay and performance has received a great deal of attention is in the compensation of top managers of firms. Rosen (1992) and Kostiuk (1990) examined the relationship between organization size and CEO pay and found that the size of a for-profit firm is one of the greatest correlates of pay of the top manager. As noted in Chapter 8, Murphy (1985) and Jensen and Murphy (1990) are two classic cases where the relationship between stock price and CEO pay have been studied. The idea is that the perfor-mance of the CEO can be measured based on the firm's stock price, and as the stock price rises, so should the pay of the manager. Murphy (1985) found convincing evidence that the pay-to-performance link was strong, but Jensen and Murphy (1990) argued that it was once much stronger and could be made stronger still. Hall and Liebman (1998) carefully examined the pay-to-performance link between firm performance and executive pay while considering the importance of stock options.

Two other issues in considering pay and performance for managers in for-profit firms have been the issues of relative performance (Antle and Smith, 1986; Gibbons and Murphy, 1990) and tournaments (Lazear and Rosen, 1981; Main, O'Reilly, and Wade, 1993). Because a great deal of risk is involved if an employee's pay is based entirely on output, Antle and Smith (1986) and Gibbons and Murphy (1990) examined relative performance. The idea is that if a firm were to simply tie a manager's pay to firm performance, the manager may take on too much risk, especially in times of a volatile economy. The firm stock price may drop in a recession through no fault of the manager. The solution to the problem is to pay managers relative to how they do in comparison to other similar organizations (e.g., in the case of for-profit firms, those in the same industry). There is no reason that such methods could not be applied to nonprofits as well, although the makeup of the comparison group may be more difficult to determine.

Although there are many positive features of compensating employees based on performance, there are many difficulties imposed by the use of incentive pay, especially in the case of nonprofit organizations, as described in the following section. These problems include the fact that it is difficult to measure output, that managers may focus on the wrong objectives, that implicit contracts may exist along other dimensions, that risk is too high for the employees, and that donations may fall if donors feel that there is an incentive contract in place for employees of the nonprofit.[12]

Weisbrod and Schlesinger (1986) discussed the case of performance measurement and performance pay in nonprofits. Clearly, for managers of nursing homes, it would be easy to focus on a measure such as mortality. Say, for example, that the top manager of a nursing home is paid more when people in the institution live longer. This is clearly an important and easily measured outcome. However, it may be the case that managers focus on such a measure and then only admit healthy people so as to increase their compensation rather than admitting people who really need help. Weisbrod and Schlesinger (1986) suggested using "trustworthiness" as a measure of performance, but pointed out how difficult this is to measure. Herzlinger (1994) reported a related situation where a particular museum had revenues from its gift shop that were seventeen times revenues from admission. This alone does not suggest that there is a problem (e.g., admission to the museum is just a nominal fee, and the bulk of institution's revenue is from the gift shop), but if too much focus is placed on the revenue and not enough on the original mission of the museum, this could prove problematic.

Another issue that arises from performance pay or even high pay of employees in nonprofits may come from the trustees. Young (1984, 1987) suggested that because trustees are working without pay for nonprofits, they might expect something similar from managers of their organization and, therefore, may not want to pay for performance. In addition, Young (1987) described that there may be implicit contracts between nonprofits and their workers that although the pay is relatively low, the work environment is "intentionally secure and relaxed" (p. 175). He suggested that switching to a system that pays for performance and might even punish those who do not perform well would not be fair. Young (1987) additionally pointed out that it may be difficult to find managers of nonprofits who know that much about pay for performance. The kinds of payment techniques used in for-profit firms (e.g., bonuses) have not historically been used in nonprofits. However, new strides have been made to educate managers specifically for the nonprofit sector (e.g., Young and Steinberg, 1995).

The final issue is concerned with the exempt status of the institution itself, and whether incentive pay may cause an organization to lose its exempt status. If an organization fails in upholding the nondistribution constraint, it could lose its exempt status and then formally no longer be a nonprofit. Emory, Swenson, Lerner, and Fuller (1992) and *World Family Corp v. Commissioner of the Internal Revenue Service* (1983) provided two interesting examples. Emory et al. (1992) described a situation of a nonprofit daycare center that is facing some financial difficulties. This organization then hired a for-profit firm to help it with certain tasks including management, staffing, and the development of a curriculum. The major decisions, however, were left to the original staff of the nonprofit. Obviously, the for-profit firm was paid for the services it provided. The IRS found in this case that the daycare center could keep its exempt status because the main control of the organization was kept in the hands of those in charge of the nonprofit and the for-profit firm did not have substantial authority.

The second example is older (from 1983) and concerns an organization that granted money to missionaries of the Church of Jesus Christ of Latter Day Saints (LDS) while they were on mission. The organization, World Family Corp. (WFC), is a nonprofit organization that hires people to do fundraising and pays them as much as 20 percent commissions on funds they collect. Additionally, one of the managers of WFC collected a 10 percent commission. "The issues presented here are whether petitioner (WFC) is operated exclusively for religious, charitable, scientific, or other exempt purposes, and whether part of petitioners net earnings inures to the benefit of private individuals" (*World Family Corp. v. Commissioner of the Internal Revenue Service*, 1983, p. 959). In this case also, the organization was allowed to keep its nonprofit exemption. "Accordingly, we find that petitioner's (WFC) commission system does not constitute private inurement in violation of the proscription contained in Section 501(c)(3) [of the IRS code]" (*World Family Corp. v. Commissioner of the Internal Revenue Service*, 1983, p. 970). Further, "a contingent-fee arrangement made by a tax-exempt entity is not per se unreasonable" (*World Family Corp.v. Commissioner of the Internal Revenue Service*, 1983, p. 968).

Paying employees, managers in particular, based on performance is interesting in theory. However, paying based on performance when performance is difficult to measure (as is clearly the case in nonprofits) can be very problematic (Cleaverly and Mullen, 1982; Weisbrod, 1988). Oster (1996) argued in the case of nonprofits that if performance measures are not clear, then pay-for-performance contracts are not efficient. In fact, as Weisbrod (1988) argued, it may be better not to base pay on performance at all than to base it on a poor measure. Kanter and Summers (1987) concluded that nonprofits have multiple constituencies and must, therefore, focus on performance along many dimensions.

Actual measures of performance in nonprofits are numerous. For example, the Council of Better Business Bureau (undated) publishes a pamphlet called *The Council of Better Business Bureau's Standards for Charitable Solicitations.* Among the many useful pieces of information is the suggestion to consider the ratio of program service expense to total expenses. For example, if program service expenses are very low relative to, say, fundraising or administrative expenses, one might want to be more careful about charitable donations. Other measures include income growth, increased funding, cost savings, increased public awareness, quality of service, and fundraising volume (Rocco, 1991), customer satisfaction (Bailey and Risher, 1996), or trustworthiness (Weisbrod and Schlesinger, 1986). Note that obviously some of these performance indicators are extremely difficult to measure. Bowen (1994) cautioned against using certain variables such as total revenue minus total cost as a measure of performance for nonprofits. This is because total revenues may include "very large amounts of noncurrent income" such as a large gift to build a new building.

Empirical Findings on the Nonprofit Versus For-Profit Pay Gap

Although there is a substantial amount of literature on nonprofits and compensation in nonprofits, there is surprisingly little convincing empirical work on the subject. This section surveys a few of the better-known examples. I separate the discussion in this section into those cases that document a pay gap, including papers by Mirvis and Hackett (1983), Johnston and Rudney (1987), and Shackett and Trapani (1987), and those that attempt to consider issues of causality slightly more deeply such as Weisbrod (1983), Goddeeris (1988), and Preston (1988). Although these papers are interesting and enlightening, it is clear that a great deal more effort needs to be put into the empirical study of pay gaps in nonprofits.

To begin, it is useful to examine some simple descriptive statistics from the 2000 census of population. In Table 13.3, I have presented simple mean characteristics for a set of workers from the 2000 PUMS Census 5 percent person's sample. Note that this discussion only includes workers with annual income in 1999 of at least $1,000, who worked at least 40 weeks in 1999, who "usually" worked at least 35 hours per week, and who were between the ages of 16 and 65, inclusive. Given these selection criteria, there are 2,712,456 observations in the 2000 census. These individuals have the following characteristics. The average age is 40.06. Forty-two percent are female. Eight-four percent are white. The average annual income is $41,878 and average hourly

Table 13.3. *Sample means and standard errors from 2000 census data*

	All	Nonprofit	For-profit	Government	Self employ
Demographics					
Age	40.06(0.01)	42.19(0.03)	39.05(0.01)	42.25(0.02)	44.51(0.03)
Female	0.42(0.0002)	0.65(0.001)	0.40(0.0004)	0.48(0.001)	0.20(0.001)
White	0.84(0.0002)	0.86(0.001)	0.84(0.0003)	0.82(0.001)	0.91(0.001)
Compensation					
Annual Income	41,877.57	39,700.24	41,209.76	39,546.04	70,948.61
	(24.50)	(77.62)	(29.24)	(32.78)	(263.16)
Hourly Wage	18.23(0.01)	17.71(0.03)	17.79(0.011)	18.25(0.01)	27.71(0.10)
Education					
Less High School	0.09(0.0002)	0.03(0.000)	0.11(0.0002)	0.03(0.0002)	0.07(0.001)
High School	0.26(0.0003)	0.14(0.001)	0.30(0.0003)	0.18(0.001)	0.22(0.001)
Some College	0.33(0.0003)	0.30(0.001)	0.34(0.0003)	0.34(0.001)	0.30(0.001)
College	0.20(0.0002)	0.28(0.001)	0.18(0.0003)	0.24(0.001)	0.22(0.001)
College Plus	0.12(0.0002)	0.26(0.001)	0.08(0.0002)	0.22(0.001)	0.19(0.001)
Sector					
Nonprofit	0.07(0.0002)	1.00(0.00)	0.00(0.00)	0.00(0.00)	0.00(0.00)
For-Profit	0.71(0.0002)	0.00(0.00)	1.00(0.00)	0.00(0.00)	0.00(0.00)
Government	0.18(0.0002)	0.00(0.00)	0.00(0.00)	1.00(0.00)	0.00(0.00)
Self-Employed	0.04(0.0001)	0.00(0.00)	0.00(0.00)	0.00(0.00)	1.00(0.00)
N	2,712,456	200,180	1,933,556	479,417	99,303

Note: Standard errors are in parentheses. Included only those between ages 16 and 65 inclusive, those with at least $1,000 in annual wage and salary income, those working at least 35 usual weekly hours, and those with at least 40 weeks worked last year.
Source: 2000 PUMS Census 5% sample person's file.

wage is $18.23.[13] Twenty-six percent graduated with exactly a high school degree and 20 percent had a college degree. Only 7 percent worked in the nonprofit sector, 71 percent worked in the for-profit sector, 18 percent in the government sector, and 4 percent were self-employed.

It is clear from Table 13.3 that nonprofit workers (column 2) are different from other workers in several ways. For example, they are slightly older than the average worker, and much more likely to be female. Note that while only 42 percent of these "full-time" workers are female, 65 percent of the nonprofit workers are female. Also, in these raw data, it is clear that workers in the nonprofit sector earn a slightly lower hourly wage than workers in any other of the sectors (including for-profit, government, and self-employment). The final thing to note is that nonprofit workers are much more highly educated than workers in any of the other sectors. Workers in the nonprofit sector are much less likely to be in the bottom two education categories (i.e., less than a high school education or exactly a high school education), and much more likely to be in the top two categories of college education or more than college. These differences between nonprofit and other workers are also documented by others as described later in the chapter.

Mirvis and Hackett (1983) provides a well-known example of relatively early empirical work on nonprofits. They use the 1977 Quality of Employment Survey created by the Institute of Social Research at the University of Michigan to document a large unadjusted gap in pay between workers in the for-profit and nonprofit sectors. They found, for example, that the unadjusted wage gap between the nonprofit and for-profit sectors was very large as the average nonprofit income for full-time workers was $10,200 and that for for-profit workers was $14,981. Note, however, that the 1977 Quality of Employment Survey does not specifically identify workers by "sector" (e.g., nonprofit, government, for-profit, etc.), but that Mirvis and Hackett (1983) categorized workers into sectors based on the industries for which they worked. Among the other findings of Mirvis and Hackett (1983) are that the very young (less than thirty years of age) and the relatively old (greater than fifty-five years of age) are more likely to work for nonprofits than for-profits. They also stress that the better educated are more likely to be found in nonprofits, wages are lower in nonprofits, and that there is "more variety and challenge" in nonprofit jobs.

Johnston and Rudney (1987) published a similarly descriptive paper on the characteristics of nonprofit workers in the *Monthly Labor Review* only a few years after Mirvis and Hackett (1983). Johnston and Rudney (1987) used the 1980 census to study worker characteristics by sector. In the 1980 census, there is also no question that asks workers about the sector in which they directly work. Johnston and Rudney (1987) used the same kind of method as Mirvis and Hackett (1983) and assigned workers employed in industries with a large fraction of nonprofits to nonprofit status. They also found substantial evidence that workers in nonprofits are better educated than workers in other sectors. In addition, they found that the fraction of workers in professional and executive occupations was much higher in nonprofits. For example, 47.9 percent of workers in nonprofits are in executive, administrative, professional, and technical occupations compared with only 26.5 percent in for-profits. Also, 31.9 percent of those in nonprofits are considered professionals as compared with only 11.8 percent of those in for-profit firms.

Johnston and Rudney (1987) also considered the 1982 Census of Services. Using these data they documented that in many service-sector jobs, those in nonprofits actually earned more than those in for-profit firms. They also

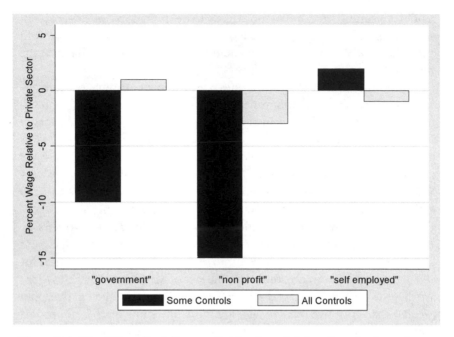

Figure 13.1. The "Wage Gap" Between For-Profit and Other Organizations. *Source:* 2000 PUMS Census 5% sample person's file. *Note:* Included only those between ages 16 and 65 inclusive, those with at least $1,000 in annual wage and salary income, those working at least 35 usual weekly hours, and those with at least 40 weeks worked last year. Control variables include age, age-squared, gender, white, nonwhite, five educational categories (less than high school, high school, some college, college and college plus). Two-digit industries and occupations and controlled for in "all controls bars." Dependent variable is log annual earnings.

found that nonprofits had, on average, more employees per organization than for-profits, which is contrary to findings in Mirvis and Hackett (1983).

In Figure 13.1, I display the results of some statistical analysis of "organization form sector differences in wages." After controlling for a set of characteristics (see note to Figure 13.1) including age, gender, race, and five educational categories, those in the government sector earn about 10 percent less than those in the for-profit sector. Also, those who work for nonprofits earn about 15 percent less than those who work in the for-profit sector. Self-employed workers actually earn slightly more than workers in the regular for-profit sector. However, although these differences do control for age, education, race, and some other characteristics, they still do not take into account specific occupations and industries. Once we control for these, Figure 13.1 makes very clear that the "penalty" for being employed in the nonprofit sector goes way down. That is to say, controlling for a host of

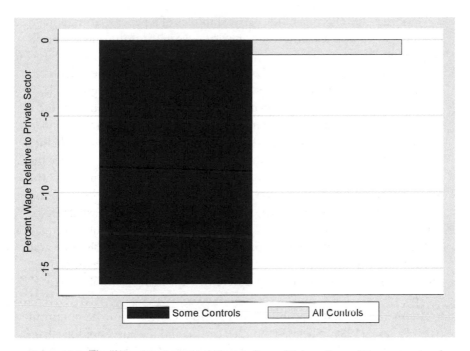

Figure 13.2. The "Wage Gap" Between Nonprofits and Private Sector (Government and Self-Employed Excluded). *Source:* 2000 PUMS Census 5% sample person's file. *Note:* Included only those between ages 16 and 65 inclusive, those with at least $1,000 in annual wage and salary income, those working at least 35 usual weekly hours, and those with at least 40 weeks worked last year. Control variables include age, age-squared, gender, white, nonwhite, five educational categories (less than high school, high school, some college, college and college plus). Two-digit industries and occupations are also controlled for in "all controls" bar. Dependent variable is log annual earnings.

characteristics, including occupation and industry, the penalty for working in the nonprofit sector is only about 3 percent. Note, however, that this has not *fully* controlled for differences in workers and job characteristics across sectors. As noted earlier in this chapter, it could be the case that part of the remaining wage penalty to those in the nonprofit sector could be because workers there enjoy better amenities, non-wage benefits, and satisfaction from their jobs, for example.

Figure 13.2 shows the results form a similar analysis where only those in the private for-profit and nonprofit sectors are considered; those in the government or who are self-employed are left out of this analysis. The figure is very similar to Figure 13.1 in that the wage penalty for working in the nonprofit sector is about 15 percent. Once industry and occupation are controlled for, however, this gap falls to about 1.5 percent.

Weisbrod (1983) is one of the early examples of a paper that tried to go beyond the simple mean differences in pay between for-profit and nonprofit employees. As mentioned earlier, he examined 737 private lawyers. Fifty-three of these were identified as "public interest lawyers" as they identified themselves as working for a "private nonprofit law firm engaged in class-oriented activities of a left, reformist sort" (p. 250). He controlled for a set of easily measurable characteristics such as experience, race, gender, whether the individual was on the editorial panel of the law review, whether the individual served as a clerk, the quality of the law school, whether the person was in the top or bottom quarter of his or her class, and the size of the organization for which the lawyer worked. He then used this information to predict pay for lawyers in the "public interest." He tested whether the "predicted" and actual wages for "public interest" lawyers would be equal. In fact, he found that predicted pay for lawyers in the public interest was $24,350 and that actual pay was only $20,300. He concluded that, therefore, there may be some compensating differential for being a "public interest" lawyer.

Another important contribution to the empirical literature on nonprofit pay is Preston (1989). She used the 1980 census and the Survey of Job Characteristics to consider the pay gap between for-profit and nonprofit workers. Recall that the 1980 census does not identify the nonprofit status of a worker directly, but that Preston (1989) used industry to identify nonprofit status. The Survey of Job Characteristics does identify nonprofit status. She found that even after adjusting for a set of covariates, there seems to be a penalty for being in the nonprofit sector of between 5 percent and 20 percent depending on the occupation of the worker. However, because the gap is not completely explained by measurable characteristics, it is consistent with the "labor donations" hypothesis developed in Preston (1989) and discussed earlier.

Preston (1989) also attempted to consider the compensating differential explanation for lower wages in the nonprofit sector by including a set of "work life controls" in her analysis. The idea is that part of the nonprofit pay gap may be owing to the better working conditions in nonprofit jobs. She did not find much evidence for this, but this could have been the result of the quality of her compensating differential measures.

Preston (1989) went on to consider whether the pay gap may be resulting from selection or quality of workers. To get some bearing on these issues, she explored various selection techniques and used longitudinal data (matching across years) from the Current Population Survey. She found that it is very difficult to tell whether the results are stemming from selection.

The fact that the gap may be resulting from motivation, organization, ability, or other "unmeasured" characteristics is compelling. Weisbrod (1983) thought that the fact that "public interest" lawyers may earn less than private lawyers could be explained by some of the theoretical issues described earlier in this book, including the quality of the office and surroundings, the intensity of work, the types of people one has to interact with, and the types of activities one has to engage in. Clearly, "public interest" lawyers may have more pleasant hours, nicer working conditions, and prefer to work for "public interest" causes, but one other issue prominent in the theoretical discussion was not directly addressed by Weisbrod (1983) – "ability" bias. Goddeeris (1988) addressed this directly using Weisbrod's (1983) data.

Goddeeris (1988) explored the possible "ability" issue more deeply and showed, using a simple statistical model, that Weisbrod's (1983) result that lawyers in the "public interest" make less "and know it" may be masked by selection. He also suggested that those who work in the public interest have different preferences. Goddeeris (1988) simultaneously estimated earnings and choice of job sector functions to more carefully consider the wage gap between public interest and private lawyers. The point is that it is possible that those in the nonprofit sector would have earned less even if they were in the private sector, and this may explain their choice of nonprofit sector in the first place. He noted that the previous work assumed that workers were identical in wage preferences, and that non-wage job characteristics and selection into a sector are not related to ability or productivity. He thought that neither of these assumptions was very strong, and went on to develop a model where he simultaneously estimated the choice of sector and wages for lawyers and found that the large wage gap was owing to selection. That is, once selection is considered, the nonprofit/for-profit wage gap disappears.

There is a large unadjusted nonprofit/for-profit wage gap that is now clearly documented. However, as a result of data constraints, it is very difficult to disentangle the various theoretical reasons for this gap. The empirical evidence is potentially consistent with the "labor donations" hypothesis, compensating differentials, efficiency wages, and ability bias. Hopefully, more large national survey data sources will be used that carefully consider nonprofit status of workers as the census has done. Perhaps panel data surveys will follow suit so that we may obtain a clearer picture of the reasons behind the true wage gap.

Executive Pay in Nonprofits

Although there has been increased discussion of pay for performance in nonprofits, there has been surprisingly little work on the pay of managers of nonprofits, primarily because of a lack of data. This section reviews the importance of and legality of performance pay for managers of nonprofits, and reports on some of the empirical findings of recent studies on pay of top managers of nonprofits. It reviews the motivation for paying managers of nonprofits in certain ways, and surveys the empirical evidence on managerial pay in nonprofits by describing a set of studies of small data sets collected by consulting firms and others, and one large set of data collected from IRS Form 990 tax returns (and that nonprofit organizations are required to file).

Just as there has been increased scrutiny over CEO pay in firms in the United States in the last few decades, there is increasing pressure on non-profits to disclose compensation and report financial statistics carefully. For example, Young (1987) stated that "charitable agencies are relatively open organizations, subject to scrutiny by government on behalf of the contributing public. In this fishbowl environment, it can be difficult to pay high managerial salaries, which might look out of line and embarrassing in the context of charity, despite whatever justification exists for the need to attract and retain superior administrative talent" (p. 173). Freeman (1975) and O'Connell (1992) also stressed the importance of retention. Freeman (1975) stated that "If we assume that the supply of 'able' managers depends on their records, and that nonprofit institutions do not substitute salary or prestige for ownership income by enough to counterbalance the absence of the latter, nonprofits will be unable to attract high quality management talent" (p. 99). O'Connell (1992), who was then president of the Independent Sector, wrote, "Overshadowed by the tiny proportion of the highly paid are the vast majority of nonprofits whose people are so inadequately compensated that all but the most dedicated leave through exhaustion or better offers" (p. 34).

Newer rules suggest that nonprofit organizations must disclose compensation of top managers and that charities must justify the pay. Parts of the new law require that organizations 1) document how much they pay their heads, 2) report financial information about the charity quickly, and 3) document how the salaries of the chiefs were determined (Taxpayer Bill of Rights II, 1996).[14] At the IRS, Marcus Owens, head of the Exempt Organizations Division, stated, "[W]hat the IRS will accept as reasonable compensation is probably a lot more than the general public will stand" (Casey, 1996, p. B1). There has also been increased emphasis on pay for performance in nonprofits.[15] In addition, there has been a great deal of discussion of the pay of managers of for-profit firms. It is interesting to consider whether the pay of managers of nonprofits differs, both in levels and in determinants of pay.

Although there has been a great deal of discussion of the pay of managers in for-profit firms (e.g., Murphy, 1985; Hall and Liebman, 1998), much less attention has been paid to managers in nonprofits. This is probably because, among other things, pay of managers in nonprofits is much lower, as discussed later, and that far less data have been available to study compensation in nonprofits. This section briefly describes earlier work using data from a variety of sources, and then focuses more detail on a study of mine (Hallock, 2002) that used data from IRS Form 990 tax returns.

In a careful and interesting study, Oster (1998) investigated the link between managerial pay and organization size in nonprofits using cross-sectional data from five different nonprofit industries; universities, social service organizations, hospitals, foundations, and a broad set of organizations, with sample sizes between thirty-one and ninety-five. She documented a strong positive link between organization size and managerial pay, which agrees with Rosen (1992) and others who found a strong link between firm size and CEO pay in for-profit firms. She also reported that "both ideology and the composition of revenues substantially affect executive compensation levels" (p. 207). The great virtue of Oster's (1998) results is the care she used to focus on specific industries and to select an appropriate organization size measure. However, the sample sizes are small and the data are cross-sectional and so do not solve some of the problems of ability bias discussed earlier.

Pink and Leatt (1991) studied 213 nonprofit Hospitals in Ontario and found only a weak relationship between management compensation and hospital surplus or deficit, but found a strong link between pay and hospital size as measured by the number of beds. Their paper only examined the sum of the compensation of the top five managers. Additionally, there seems to be wide variation in the mix of compensation and performance data. Clarkson (1972) represents an early study that discusses pay and performance in nonprofit hospitals. He reported that nonprofit hospital administrators are much more likely to give across-the-board raises than performance-based raises using data from 1956. Langer (1989) examined 1,142 nonprofit organizations that were surveyed by Abbott, Langer, and Associates. He only reported simple correlations, but many are instructive. He showed that experience, education, numbers of workers supervised, and budget all were positively correlated with managerial pay.

In my research using panel data from IRS Form 990 tax returns to study the pay of 32,144 nonprofit managers over five years (1992–1996), I found the average pay of top managers across many industries to be about $160,000, which is much less than the average pay of managers of for-profit firms. In Table 13.4 it is clear that by 2003, the average pay for the officer of a nonprofit had risen to $352,996. Table 13.5 shows that a large fraction of

Table 13.4. *Sample means and standard errors for pay of top managers of nonprofits from IRS data*

	2003
Compensation[a] (in 1996 dollars):	
Officer/Director #1	352,996(2,290,731)
Officer/Director #2	208,952(117,524)
Officer/Director #3	171,475(149,610)
Employee #1	220,529(556,333)
Employee #2	185,427(518,611)
Employee #3	166,399(311,554)

Note: Standard errors are in parentheses. (a) Compensation defined as the sum of base pay, benefit plan contributions plus expense accounts.
Source: IRS tax form 990 for individual organizations for 2003.

the compensation of managers of nonprofits came in the form of benefit plans and expense accounts. Also, there is a great deal of pay variability at the top of charities within charities (the top manager often makes much more than the second in command, and so on) and across charities as defined by their National Taxonomy of Exempt Entities (pay differs dramatically by industry) (see Table 13.5).

In my 2002 study, I examined the effects of organizational performance on managerial pay in nonprofits using several measures of performance. For example, I found that the median "profit" level (revenue – expenses) for the organizations in the sample was $1,117,222, the median "return on assets" ("profits"/assets), was 7.01 percent, and the median change in assets was $991,317. I also suggested the ratio of program service expense to total expense as described above. Results for tying pay of nonprofit heads to performance are not particularly clear. I did, however, find a strong relationship between organizational size and managerial pay as in Oster (1998).[16]

I also examined several other aspects of pay in nonprofits, including the effects of government grants, governance in nonprofits, and tournaments. It is possible that as managers increase the numbers and size of grants to their organizations, they are paid more, and that nonprofits with higher levels of government grants pay their managers more. However, because the data are arranged in a panel, organizational fixed effects can be taken into account. Once organizational fixed effects are controlled for, there is a weak negative relationship between grants and pay of managers in nonprofits. This may be because government agencies monitor managerial actions and, within organizations, managers can be paid less in the presence of this monitoring.

Table 13.5. *Pay for top managers of nonprofits by industry group*

	Number organi-zations	Top officer or director			Top employee		
		Base pay	Benefits package	Expense account	Base pay	Benefits package	Expense account
A. Arts, Culture, and Humanities	403	227,122	23,892	7,815	111,337	10,381	638
B. Educational Institutions and Related Activities	2,510	221,384	32,623	8,390	191,515	16,680	1,299
C. Environmental Quality, Protection, and Beautification	76	215,612	19,562	1,008	107,194	10,216	0
D. Animal Related	53	187,294	13,294	5,446	98,900	9,011	54
E. Health – General and Rehabilitative	3,588	455,837	57,016	6,128	294,405	20,968	698
F. Mental Health, Crisis Intervention	168	203,883	22,912	1,738	130,976	10,191	436
G. Disease, Disorders, Medical Disciplines	86	311,348	28,725	3,525	200,431	26,204	2,124
H. Medical Research	72	291,133	26,310	1,856	213,897	18,637	265
I. Crime, Legal Related	30	180,393	13,453	2,445	96,752	7,958	144
J. Employment, Job Related	95	167,417	20,843	392	54,971	5,163	18
K. Food, Agriculture, and Nutrition	19	122,392	15,065	0	51,416	26,083	0
L. Housing, Shelter	82	165,700	17,977	1,241	56,858	5,162	1,229
M. Public Safety, Disaster Preparedness, and Relief	8	391,851	11,103	993	49,110	7,982	0

(continued)

Table 13.5 *(continued)*

	Number organi- zations	Top officer or director			Top employee		
		Base pay	Benefits package	Expense account	Base pay	Benefits package	Expense account
N. Recreation, Sports. Leisure, Athletics	62	175,657	15,190	3,640	88,400	13,586	1,258
O. Youth Development	46	140,562	12,498	2,369	55,319	6,845	0
P. Human Services – Multipurpose and Other	779	148,875	14,790	2,257	77,077	7,303	663
Q. International, Foreign Affairs, and National Security	156	214,030	28,867	6,116	113,301	13,705	8,481
R. Civil Rights, Social Action, Advocacy	33	157,479	19,227	3,021	85,208	6,481	16
S. Community Improvement, Capacity Building	96	220,533	26,349	1,947	88,593	9,654	438
T. Philanthropy, Voluntarism, and Grantmaking Foundations	260	155,873	21,780	2,255	69,055	9,007	295
U. Science and Technology Research Institutes, Services	132	365,090	43,221	20,290	191,031	24,578	13,572
V. Social Science Research Institutes, Services	45	335,570	26,557	4,644	154,993	19,403	57
W. Public, Society Benefit: Multipurpose and Other	113	302,630	48,561	4,508	107,086	11,723	3,651

Table 13.5 *(continued)*

	Number organi- zations	Top officer or director			Top employee		
		Base pay	Benefits package	Expense account	Base pay	Benefits package	Expense account
X. Religion Related, Spiritual Development	113	131,794	12,541	9,103	67,439	6,640	2,248
Y. Mutual/Mem- bership Benefit Organizations, Other	19	397,965	39,674	1,010	209,587	18,160	286
Z. Other	0						

Notes: Total of 24,626 organization years represented. The rows represent the 26 major categories of the National Taxonomy of Exempt Entities (NTEE).
Source: IRS tax form 990 for individual organizations for years 2003.

There is a literature on the influence of boards of directors on the pay of managers of firms in the United States. Hallock (2002) also focused on the relationship between managerial pay in nonprofits and the board of directors of the nonprofits (i.e., the institution that sets the pay of the top manager). I found that the larger the number of paid board members, the lower the pay of the top executive. Perhaps, if the board is larger, there is less of a need to have a highly paid (able) top manager. Perhaps board size is a substitute for managerial experience or ability.

Gender and Race and Pay in Nonprofits

Steinberg and Jacobs (1994) noted that it is interesting that although such a large fraction of the nonprofit sector is populated by women, very little of the research focuses on them. They argued that "the low level of wages paid in this sector is, in no small part, a function not only of the devaluation of women's work in the sector but also the result of the devaluation of the nonprofit sector because it is heavily populated by women" (p. 90). This section aims to review some of the papers that have touched on issues of gender in nonprofits, especially in regards to pay. It focuses both on women in the sector generally and on female executives and trustees in particular.

Preston (1990) examined why women are more likely employed in the nonprofit sector. Note that Johnston and Rudney (1987) showed that although women are much more likely than men to be in the nonprofit sector, few women are among the well-educated and many are in adminis-trative support jobs. They ask whether women prefer the job characteristics or the wage structure in nonprofits. Preston (1990) used the 1977 quality-of-employment survey and only examined full-time, white-collar workers. She found that women are much more likely than men to join the nonprofit sector, even controlling for occupation. She also found that, on average, those in nonprofits earn much less than those in for-profit organizations, but argued that because there is a smaller gender wage gap in nonprof-its, women may be relatively better off there. Controlling for this "expected wage differential," Preston (1990) concluded that women are no more likely than men to join the nonprofit sector. Preston (1994) noted that between 1973 and 1991, women in the nonprofit sector earned roughly the same as men within occupations, but that they were found in much different occupations.

Preston (1994) found that although women have reached a significant level of equality in the nonprofit sector, nonwhites have not. She wrote that "[w]ithin the nonprofit sector, black women had significantly lower levels of education, significantly lower wages, and a less prestigious occu-pational distribution than white women. In addition, the gaps in earnings and achievement increased between 1969 and 1991" (p. 71).

Very little is known about female executives, both in the for-profit and nonprofit sectors. There are some exceptions. Marianne Bertrand and I (Bertrand and Hallock, 2001) studied the gender wage gap for top executives of large U.S. firms. Over the period we examined (1992–1997), we found that women tripled their presence among the top five managers of large firms, and that although there was a large raw pay gap between men and women, a sizeable part of this was accounted for by measurable characteristics. Bartlett and Miller (1985) discussed female executives and networking. There has been some growth in the percentage of women at the top of large U.S. firms, but there has recently been a significant rise in the fraction of women who serve in higher-level positions in state agencies and nonprofits. Steinberg and Jacobs (1994) noted that "women appear to be having a relatively easier time moving into positions of leadership in nonprofit organizations than in for-profit organizations" (p. 95). For example, Bullard and Wright (1993) reported that although women only accounted for 2 percent of agency heads in state governments in 1964, they accounted for 18 percent in 1988. However, these women seemed to be concentrated in particular types of agencies. They also reported that women in these agencies only earned about 80 percent of what their male counterparts earned. However, there was no discussion of the characteristics (e.g., education, experience) of the men and women in the sample. Also, Guy (1993) compared men and women in public management and found that women were much less likely to be in decision-making positions, but that they were making progress in that regard. For example, in 1910, only 10 percent of the people in the federal GS grade workforce were women. In 1987, this number jumped to 48 percent. In addition, Abzug, DiMaggio, Gray, Useem, and Kang (1994) reported on a case study of a small set of "elite" nonprofits in Cleveland and Boston. They examined the Cleveland Museum of Art, Cleveland University Hospital, Cleveland United Way, Boston Museum of Fine Arts, Massachusetts General Hospital, and Boston United Way in 1925, 1955, and 1985 and reported that female presence on boards of directors of these organizations increased significantly over time.

Preston (1994) noted that although the male-female wage differential in nonprofits generally is small, for managerial workers (as measured in broad managerial categories by the Current Population Survey) it can be as high as 20 percent. In 1999 (Hallock, 1999a), I studied whether there is a gender wage gap at the very top of nonprofits using data on 606 top managers collected from the Council of Better Business Bureaus Annual Charity Index (various years) for the 1990–1994 period. I found that 19 percent of the managers were women, which is a much higher fraction than for large firms. Also, in the raw data, women earned about 21 percent less than men. However, women were found to lead much different kinds of organizations measured by industry or organization size (as measured by assets, income, or revenue). Once simple characteristics are accounted for, the gender wage gap disappears. Note that Oster (1996) also found little evidence of a gender pay gap at the top of nonprofits once other covariates were controlled. I (Hallock, 1999a) also found evidence consistent with the fact that the relationship between pay and performance for executives in nonprofits differs by gender. In the sample, there was evidence of no relationship between pay and performance for men, and a negative one for women.

Nonprofits and International Pay

Although there is surprisingly little research on nonprofits in the United States, there is almost none in other countries. A few of the exceptions that do mention the nonprofit world in general or compensation in nonprofits in particular in other countries are described here. One problem is that comparing "nonprofits" is very difficult across countries. For example, in Germany, there is no perfect translation of the English word "nonprofit."

The closest case is "Organisation Ohne Erwerbscharakter," which translates to "organizations with no profit motive or commercial character" (Anheier, 1993, p. 186). James (1990) also described these problems of comparability. She explained that what are known as nonprofits in the United States can be known as NGOs, private voluntary organizations (PVOs), or community associations in other countries. She also explained that tax breaks to non-profits do not often exist in other countries, although the nondistribution constraint holds universally. Knapp and Kendall (1993) reported that there is very little data on the voluntary sector in the United Kingdom and, there-fore, little is known about it. Salamon and Anheier (1992b) considered the NTEE as a way of classifying nonprofits across countries. They discovered that it is not particularly useful for international comparisons and, there-fore, developed the International Classification of Nonprofit Organizations (ICNPO) which has twelve major groups and twenty-four subgroups. This is a far smaller number of groups than in the NTEE described earlier.

Borzaga (1993) described the Italian nonprofit sector with a very broad overview, including some facts on employment levels, but nothing specif-ically on compensation. Anheier (1993) provided a review of employment and earnings in West German nonprofits. He reported that women hold two-thirds of the jobs in the nonprofit economy and only one-third of the jobs in the entire economy. In the United States, women are also much more highly represented in nonprofits. Anheier (1993) also reported that changes in Germany toward a more service-oriented economy (as in the United States) are helping the nonprofit economy expand because nonprofit jobs are heavily centered in the service sector.

Rose-Ackerman (1996) reported many statistics (from Salamon and Anheier, 1996) by country on the composition of the nonprofit sector by industry. For example, she reported on nonprofit employment as a per-cent of all employment. Salamon and Anheier (1996) also reported the Organisation for Economic Co-operation and Development (OECD) data suggesting value added by the nonprofit sector as a percentage of gross domestic product (GDP) by country, and reported the following statistics: the United States 3.8 percent, Germany 2.3 percent, Sweden 1.4 percent, Austria 0.7 percent, France 0.3 percent, and Portugal 0.2 percent. These data are suggestive at best, especially given the earlier discussion of the dif-ficulties in defining the nonprofit sector. Salamon and Anheier (1996) also studied many other countries including Italy, Japan, the United Kingdom, Hungary, Brazil, Egypt, Ghana, India, and Thailand.

PART IV

WHAT YOU CAN DO TO MAKE MORE AND
CONCLUDING COMMENTS

FOURTEEN

What You Can Do Now to Make More
Now and Later

Remember back in Chapter 3 that we considered what people earn and started a discussion about why. Some of the things that are related to pay are measurable and some are not. Some are also changeable and improved upon and some are not. For example, you can improve your education (this is measurable and improvable) and you can also increase your motivation and organizational ability (but these are hard for economists to measure and even sometimes hard for employers to see or recognize [at least from a resume or a job interview]). This section includes a set of things that one can do to increase his or her wage, salary, and total compensation. Some of it is long term in the sense that it takes a while to earn a high school degree, or a college degree – but we know those with them earn a lot more than those without.

Easy Stuff

I'll start with what I call easy stuff. This includes things like be polite, show up on time, work hard[1], be nice, be kind, don't be a jerk, think before you act, get along with your coworkers, and so forth. Of course, this is "low-hanging fruit." But many managers and people who set compensation levels do not have a lot of training in how to deal with compensation, especially in smaller organizations. This problem is exacerbated by the fact that many workers are similar and do similar jobs. Why not do the easy stuff and get that out of the way? Then you can work on the more difficult things, discussed later in the chapter.

I would also add to this list "don't say anything to anyone at work that you wouldn't want to say to everyone," at least not until you really know whomever you want to tell.

Ask

I know many people who complain about their compensation, but they don't do much about it. One thing that some recommend is to negotiate your compensation before you start. Subject to the potential formal constraints on your organization's compensation system, there is often quite a bit of leeway in how starting pay is set. So why not ask? This is not to suggest that you should be pushy or aggressive, but it may not hurt to ask, if you do it in a nice way. I was recently asked to do some work for a (wealthy) nonprofit organization. It wasn't really clear whether they would pay me for the work or not, and I was going to do it either way. It was interesting work and I wanted to try to be helpful. The person on the other end of the line said that they might be able to pay me but he wasn't sure. I told him something like, "I am happy to do this and will do it for nothing but I would obviously prefer if you sent me some money too." And he did.

I also participated on the other side of a compensation negotiation with a nonprofit. I did some consulting work for a large nonprofit organization. They were being sued over a financial issue, and an expert witness on the other side cited some of my published research, so they hired me to analyze what he had to say. We agreed on an hourly wage and I did the work. After the project was done, they asked me if I would give them a "discount" because they were a nonprofit. I am not so good at negotiating but I told them that (a) we had already negotiated the wage in advance, and (b) if I were interested in donating some fraction of my fee to a nonprofit, it would more likely be the local food relief organization and not their particular organization.

There is a lot of research on negotiation (not just over wages but over anything). When I was at the University of Illinois, I had a colleague, who taught negotiations, who encouraged students to try to get discounts on simple household items at local stores, like toothbrushes – and they did!

But if you are lucky enough to negotiate a relatively high salary (relative to the "typical" salary for your broadly defined skill set), you should also be prepared to keep in mind some of the lessons from Part II on how firms set and structure pay. If your organization is one of the type that has a formalized pay system with pay grades or ranges and you are relatively "high" in the group, then you may experience some relatively slower pay growth in the future – there can be instances where organizations "catch up."

In terms of strict advice for negotiation, many of the issues mentioned in this book can be useful, but I will mention a few here that are more specifically tied to explicit negotiation (see Pinkley and Northcraft [2000] for a broad review of negotiating salary). Among the suggestions of Pinkley and Northcraft (2000) and others is to ask questions, prepare a counter offer, maintain professionalism while negotiating, and be firm but flexible. I think the firm-but-flexible part is very important. Never give an ultimatum to an employer unless you are willing to act on it.

There is also mounting evidence that men are "better" at negotiating than women. That is to say, men experience more success from negotiating than women. Stuhlmacher and Walters (1999) found evidence that men negotiated significantly better outcomes than women in a "study of studies" where they considered the works of many previous authors. They also considered whether men (or women) had better success when negotiating against someone of the same or opposite gender. In the end, none of these kinds of issues had any influence on the fact that men seemed to negotiate better outcomes than women. One study (Barron, 2003) suggests that men and women have different beliefs about requesting higher salaries. As a result, men request higher salaries, and there is evidence that they then get them. Babcock and Laschever (2003) provide an interesting account about why "women don't ask."

Do Your Homework

If you are negotiating over a new offer or considering your current compensation, make sure you do your homework. It is much easier to make progress in terms of increasing your compensation if you know something about each of the following. First, it might be valuable to know something about what other people in a similar position in your organization are making. Second, it might be helpful to know what others in your organization in different jobs are earning. Third, it might be helpful to know something about the compensation structure in your job-type and similar ones in other organizations in your area and elsewhere. It is very difficult to make any progress if you don't know what others are making. Use this book to help understand your organization's pay system. And then use some of the tips elsewhere in this book to gain information on what others earn.

Be Part of the Solution

My father used to tell me to be "part of the solution, not part of the problem." This is just one of the ways he worked on me and my brother while we were growing up. There is obviously something to it when thinking about compensation. Be useful and engaged in your work. If you are not doing something useful to your organization's mission (be it making profits, helping people, reducing poverty, or teaching kids to read), why should they pay you more? But before you go to your employer and ask for more money (see the section on negotiation), you should be sure that *you* are convinced about your contribution to the organization and should be able to communicate that to your employer.

Fisher (2006) suggests strategies for getting a raise that are related to the "be part of the solution" hypothesis of my father. She suggests helping others do better and fulfill their potential ("especially your boss"), find something that is a problem and try to fix it (be part of the solution), and start something new. This is a great way to show your value to an organization. What do you do to make the place better?

Contacts

There is evidence that having contacts helps people get jobs. And more jobs (or job offers) can mean higher earnings. Also, it isn't too expensive to rely on friends, relatives, or neighbors to help you out in trying to find a new job (or a job you prefer). Note that relatives and friends not only have an incentive to help you (their relative or friend), but they also (often) want to help their employer. Relatives and friends help reduce uncertainty (Loury, 2006) for the employer and you. They reduce uncertainty for the employer because the new employee (you) is being recommended by someone on the inside. And that person on the inside doesn't want to recommend someone they don't think will work out. These relatives and friends also reduce uncertainty for you; they don't want to attract you to an employer where you would not be comfortable or fit well. In fact, some employers offer bonuses to workers who recommend new employees who are hired. The employers often have some period of delay before the bonus is paid out. For example, the employer may wait to make sure the new employee is still working with the employer for, say, six months before the bonus is paid out. Otherwise, one employee could recommend a friend who is hired, work one day, and quit, and they could split the bonus.

It is interesting to note that there is evidence of quite a bit of heterogeneity in the effect of friends and relatives on getting a good job, by country. Recent work by Pellizzai (2010), using data from Europe, suggests that the compensation differences from finding a job through friends or relatives is higher in countries that have more intermediaries in the labor market. Other, related work by Antoninis (2006) shows that people have higher wages if referred by someone who has specific knowledge of their productivity. However, these effects were not seen in unskilled jobs.

Switch Employers

Many suggest that a great way to get a raise is to change organizations. Moving is costly and it makes sense that one would have to be paid more to move. At the same time, many organizations are lax and let their pay programs slip or lag, so looking for a new job in a new organization can lead you to renegotiate and earn more as a new person in an organization. One example from a famous case study of Safelite Glass (the windshield installation company discussed earlier) was called "Buck and a Truck." The idea in the industry was that things were so competitive that windshield installers were easily swayed from leaving one company and joining the other for the promise of $1 more per hour and the chance to drive a company truck home at night (Lazear, 1998).

There is some other research on this. One example from psychologists (Brett and Stroh, 1997) suggests that while there is a pay premium for switching jobs, that this is only true for men but not for women. In another study (Drehcr and Cox, 2000) – this time of MBA graduates only – the benefits of job change only accrued to white men.

An interesting paper by Hultin and Szulkin (1999) suggests that one might want to consider choosing your boss. Choosing a boss is not easy. The point is that the gender match between supervisor and subordinate is related to pay. In a study of Swedish workers, the authors found that women who work in establishments where there are relatively more male managers earn less than similarly qualified women with more women as supervisors.

Get a Face-lift or Plastic Surgery?

There is a lot of evidence that "beautiful" people make more than people who are not so "beautiful." In an interesting paper, Hamermesh and Biddle (1994) found that "plain-looking" people earn less than "average-looking" people, who in turn earn less than "good-looking" people. The penalty and the premium (relative to average) are both on the order of 5–10 percent. They find this for both men and women. The authors find that there is some evidence that better-looking people match to occupations where their beauty may be more productive. Still, they find that the effect of the penalty for plainness and the bonus for beauty appears to be the case across occupations. They argue that this is likely to imply what labor economists call "employer" discrimination (rather than, say, "customer" discrimination). Employer discrimination is just as it sounds. Customer discrimination is when customers discriminate against workers. But it wouldn't make sense for this to be customer discrimination because the "bonus" or "penalty" is present for both workers who work in front of customers and for workers who do not interact with customers. In later work, however, Hamermesh and Biddle (1998) studied a group of lawyers, all of whom graduated from the same law school. They found that beauty was more lucrative for the self-employed young lawyers than those who worked as employees. This, in fact, would suggest that it is the clients (customers) that have a preference for beauty. See Hamermesh (2011) for more detail.

There are other theories for why more attractive people earn more, which can go all the way back to kindergarten. If a child is good-looking, it may be the case that teachers are more likely to engage with them and help them. This may lead to either (1) more time with the teacher that could increase the student's human capital, or (2) increased motivation on the part of the student in response to early positive feedback from the teacher, or both.

Some think that the "beauty" effect can be partly related to confidence (Mobius and Rosenblat, 2006). They argue that more "attractive" workers are more confident and confidence increases wages. For a set level of confidence, attractive workers may be incorrectly viewed as better workers by employers.

By the way, I suppose one could make an "economic argument" about actually having plastic surgery or a face-lift in order to raise earnings (some entertainers do exactly this), but I certainly don't advocate it. The way to make the argument would be to consider all the up-front costs including the dollar costs, the pain and recovery time from surgery, and so on. Then one can make a calculation about the extra earnings and extra benefits into the future that one would have owing to his or her extra "beauty." To make this argument, one would have to (1) believe that there is a causal link between beauty and earnings and (2) appropriately make the calculations of the costs (including the nonmonetary costs). Given my appearance, I am sure plastic surgeons could have a field day if I ever walked into their offices; but I won't.

Drink?

Can drinking increase your earnings? There is actually some academic literature on this. For example, Peters and Stringham (2006) suggest that drinkers of alcohol earn on the order of 10–14 percent more than nondrinkers. They further find that those who go to bars at least once per month earn an extra 7–10 percent more. Obviously we need to be careful with findings like these because of the "causality" issue discussed elsewhere in this book. Note that these are adjusted correlations and may not be causal effects. The second finding, concerning those who go to bars at least one per month, is interesting and could mean a variety of things. First, could those who go to bars to drink have higher earnings in the first place (they can afford to go to bars)? This may imply that it is not the drinking that increases earnings but that higher-earning people go to those places to drink. Second, it could imply that work is actually being done during the time in the bar. Third, it could be that bars are among the places one can become a better "networker" or hone certain social skills that could also be valuable in the workplace. Fourth, extroversion may lead people both to go to places where there are many other people (e.g., bars) and to higher earnings because extroversion may be valuable in some jobs. In any event, when you read in the newspaper something like "people who eat lobster have higher earnings," I would suggest that you not interpret this as meaning that eating lobster *increases* earnings; rather that people with high earnings are more likely to eat lobster. Be skeptical when you read the newspaper.

Two Jobs are Better Than One

One of my mentors, frequently said, "Two jobs are better than one." He did not mean that one should actually have two jobs simultaneously (although, obviously, he would not disagree that working more hours would increase one's earnings). What he meant was that two job *offers* are better than one. In one sense, this is just another way to say that one earns more when he or she moves jobs, or that negotiation can work. But it is also the internal issue of having job offers. In academic jobs in particular, but in other jobs too, many employers keep wages relatively low until prompted by an outside offer. So some faculty work away within their universities and suffer a penalty for staying. In fact, an interesting study by Ransom (1993) showed that, controlling for other characteristics of faculty (including age, department, etc.), faculty with higher levels of seniority earned *less*, on average. They were, in essence, penalized for not leaving.

Perhaps the mentor I mentioned has been paid less than he would have been had he taken offers to leave over the years. But he loves his job. In fact, he once told me, "I'd do this for free, but that would be stupid."

Be Flexible

Being flexible can't hurt when trying to earn a higher salary. Flexibility can manifest itself in considering taking on additional tasks at work, to asking to move to a higher-paying position (and taking on the additional work), to moving locations. As is clear from earlier discussions, people in different locations earn different levels of compensation. Of course, as was discussed previously, locations that have higher-paying jobs often also have higher costs of housing and living in general. But note that flexibility isn't free. Some people have much higher costs of moving than others. A single person with an offer to move to a different location has much lower costs of doing so than a married person with a family, who may have to consider a spouse's job, children's schooling, and the like.

Talk to People

Talking to people can be beneficial for higher earnings for a variety of reasons. I'll name just two. First, it might be valuable to talk with people who are doing a job you would like to do next. Learning more about the job, what it entails, what is needed to do it successfully and happily is clearly important. Second, talking to people – or networking – is a fine way to increase and maintain contacts with others. You may never know when an old or new contact may be useful for hiring you elsewhere. This cannot be bad for your earnings.

Be Patient

Job search is costly. If one takes the first job he or she is offered, then the candidate may be missing unknown opportunities around the corner that may either be a better match or have higher earnings. The concept of a "reservation wage" is the lowest wage for which an employee is willing to work. DellaVigna and Passerman (2005) suggest that workers who are impatient search for jobs with less intensity and have lower reservation wages.

Although it is called a reservation wage, I would argue that we should call it reservation compensation, meaning all parts of the compensation, including those we have discussed such as benefits and nonmonetary rewards associated with the work and the workplace. Workers who can be more patient may have the chance to garner more job offers and then choose the one with a higher reservation compensation. Of course, that is easier said than done.

Earning more is typically not a bad thing. If you feel guilty about earning more, you can always give the extra money to charity. But finding ways to earn more is not particularly easy. Clearly formal schooling is among the very best things one can do to increase his or her earnings. But that is a long-term issue and is obviously expensive in terms of your time and money (but don't forget the nonmonetary rewards of schooling too). And there are some other things you can do to increase earnings. To reiterate, these include "easy" things like being polite, showing up on time, working hard, being nice, being kind, avoiding being a jerk, thinking before you act, and trying to get along with your coworkers. There are other things you can do too, of course. These include asking or negotiating, doing your homework, taking advantage of your contacts, switching employers, and being flexible. This isn't all easy. But if it were easy for everyone, there would be no point in doing it.

FIFTEEN

Concluding Thoughts on Pay

This book is about why people earn what they earn and how you can make more. But just as we discussed that wages and salaries are just a part of compensation, remember that your pay is just a part of your job and your job is just a part of your life. I don't think the goal should be to make as much money as possible. Rather, we should strive to do good things and be happy. If, on the margin, you can do some things to make more money along the way – great!

As I noted at the beginning of this book, designing pay plans is not rocket science. But it isn't easy either. In fact, I think it is part science and part art. It is also part economics, part law, part organizational behavior, part industrial relations, part accounting, part finance, part sociology, and part psychology. There are no specific rules that will help organizations get it exactly right. But there are important principles. The fact that there are no simple rules is not obvious to many people until they really think about it. Different firms, even in the same industry, may have drastically different compensation programs and systems and that may actually be the right outcome. Organizations design their optimal business strategy and then compensation strategy for what is best for them.

My hope is that this book is valuable for compensation practitioners, business leaders, and anyone who gets paid to work. In fact, it is important for employees to understand *how* their organizations pay. If organizations can't properly articulate how they pay, this results in an incredibly bad situation. Workers will be frustrated and workers and firms will be earning less than they would under a system where compensation systems were appropriately designed and understood.

Most people don't really understand how much they themselves earn, especially given the difficulty in valuing certain benefits and the problems organizations have in communicating pay to their employees. Worse yet, most people have very little idea what everyone else makes. This book has tried to shed light on both of these issues. First, an overarching point in the book is that *total compensation* matters much more than income from wages and salary. Employees should educate themselves about how they are paid and organizations should educate workers about how their employees are paid. Second, there is increasing evidence that workers are confused and frustrated by what *others* earn (Card, Mas, Moretti, and Saez, 2010). This is interesting given that many workers have trouble truly understanding what they earn, not to mention what others earn.

My hope is that this book will help employees and organizations on both of the aforementioned counts. Part I of the book described wages, wage distributions, and wage inequality. The aim was to show what wage and salary income is relative to the rest of workers. This part went on to describe who makes what and what the characteristics are of workers who earn more (and less).

The second part of the book described how organizations set pay structure and why. This is the central description of how most large companies (and other organizations) set up pay systems for their workers. This included a discussion of business and compensation strategy, job analysis and job evaluation, making internal comparisons and a discussion of why they are so tricky, the outside market, and collecting the right comparison data. This is somewhat "technical" in that it explores the nitty-gritty of pay systems. On the other hand, it is important that organizations get this right. It is equally important that workers understand how organizations do this. From an organizational point of view, there is not a lot of sense in having a formal pay system and then not telling the workers about it. At the same time, it is important for workers to understand the pay system so that they can begin to figure out what they can do to make more.

The third part of the book described why how people are paid can mean as much as how much they are paid. Chapter 8 was a discussion of how executives, athletes, and other superstars are paid. It is not entirely clear why these folks get so much attention. In part, the data are publicly available so it is easy to study these people. On the other hand, many like to hear about what those at the extreme high end of the pay scale earn. This chapter also discussed why some people earn so much more than the rest of us and why that has changed over time.

The rest of Part III discussed how organizations evaluate performance, instances where incentive pay works (and instances where it does not), and the importance of the "mix" of pay (e.g., salary, benefits, piece rates, etc.). It also discussed the complicated issue of international compensation, including a chapter on compensation in nonprofit organizations. This included a discussion of similarities and differences between paying employees in for-profit and nonprofit organizations.

In addition to these parts that show the reader how and why organizations concentrated on how and what to pay, the reader can also find throughout the book and in Chapter 14 some tips on how to make more. These parts described a host of ways to work toward making more including, among others, asking questions, negotiating, using contacts, training, being flexible, searching for new work, and switching employers.

This book was a ton of fun to write, and I hope it was a little bit of fun to read. I also hope that it taught you something about how and why organizations pay the way they pay and also something about what you can do now to make more.

Notes

Two

1. These calculations are based on the Merged Outgoing Rotation Group (MORG) Files of the Current Population Survey (CPS) complied by the National Bureau of Economic Research (NBER) in Cambridge, Massachusetts.
2. The fact that 5% of women who report earnings report less than the minimum wage could stem from a variety of reasons. These include tipped occupations (that can be paid less than the minimum wage), in which workers may not include tips, as well as reporting errors.
3. Only wages of less than $100 per hour are included in the figure. Very few people report wages higher than $100 per hour.
4. Of course there are literally an infinite number of possible measures of inequality similar to each of these.
5. Part of the changes may be because of the change in the sample. As noted earlier, there are three samples of data covering the years 1979–1991, 1992–2006, and 2007–2009.
6. Technically it is the median CEO pay in the sample divided by 2000 (40 hours per week times 50 weeks per year) and divided by the 5th percentile hourly wage.
7. The pay for workers only includes wage and salary income and not benefits. Benefits are discussed in more detail in Chapter 11.
8. See Cameron and Taber (2004) for related work. They do not find evidence that borrowing constraints generate inefficiencies in the market for schooling.

Three

1. See, for example, Blau, Ferber and Winkler (2010).
2. Formally, I used data from the Merged Outgoing Rotation Group (MORG) files of the Current Population Survey (CPS) from the National Bureau of Economic Research (NBER). The estimates come from an ordinary least squares regression on the natural logarithm of the hourly wage (as defined in Chapter 2), on gender, race (white, black, and "other"), age (and its square), schooling (less than high school, high school, some college, college, more than college), a union coverage indicator variable, 21 industry controls, 22 occupation controls, and 50 state indicators.

3. Again, see Blau, Ferber and Winkler (2010) and the associated references for more on these issues.
4. See Card (1999, 2001) for excellent discussions.
5. Also see Card (1999, 2001) for excellent discussions of the rate of return to schooling.
6. These calculations "control[s] for differences among areas in occupational composition, establishment and occupational characteristics, and the fact that data are collected at different times during the year" (U.S. Department of Labor UDSL: 09–0843, 2010).
7. O*NET occupation code 25–2021; see http://online.onetcenter.org/link/summary/25–2021.00

Four

1. Note that different employees may value the same type of compensation differently. As an example, whereas Sam may place a high value on being the employee of the month, Steve may not.
2. To find out more about Employer Costs of Employee Compensation, visit http://www.bls.gov/news.release/ecec.tn.htm
3. I am obviously ignoring taxes entirely in this example. Even taking taxes into account, with these numbers you'd still make the same choice.
4. Of course, there are other potential breakdowns, but only these two are displayed as examples.
5. At the same time, I think it is important for employees to think about how they value their own forms of compensation. More on this later.

Five

1. See Fields (2009) for a discussion of "bottom-line" management.
2. The Association was originally called The American Compensation Association. I received two small research grants from the American Compensation Association early in my career. I was previously a member of the Executive Compensation Advisory Board of WorldatWork, the Board of Directors of WorldatWork and am currently on the Board of the WorldatWork Society of Certified Professionals.
3. In fact, with the help of some excellent research assistants, I have created a database of each faculty member's annual salary at Illinois from 1911 through 1965, and we are working our way forward.

Six

1. From a more technical point of view, there are varying "levels" of occupations. For example, many social scientists, in empirical work, refer to one-digit (very broad categories), two-digit (more narrow), three-digit (even more narrow), down to four-digit (extremely narrow) occupation codes. There are several occupations classification systems.
2. http://online.onetcenter.org
3. This is one area where the standard systems have a bit of a problem. The compensable factors are supposed to be those that lead to higher levels of output and productivity.

The working conditions example, which is used all over the practical literature, is an example where worse working conditions (higher degree) don't lead to better output but should lead to higher pay as a result of compensating differentials.

4. I first saw this example used in the compensation literature in Milkovich and Newman (2008).

5. http://www.biblegateway.com/passage/?search=Matthew+20%3A1–16&version=NIV, Matthew 20: 1–16.

Seven

1. I would actually recommend that the organization consider several sets of data and run the kinds of analysis that are about to be discussed. This is especially true if the organization isn't completely sure which data (e.g., regions) to include. This way the analysis can be run multiple ways and results compared.

2. This is just an illustrative example. In a real example, there could be much more data.

3. Many organizations actually really do it this way. But I am not sure why. There is no reason why we need to have linearity here. A curved line could make things much more interesting. For illustration, however, I am keeping things as a straight line because it is easier to explain.

4. In fact, it is an "ordinary least squares regression line." This just means that it is the line for which the sum of all of the squared differences between each point and the line is the smallest. It is one version of a line of best fit, but not the only one. It is, however, extremely common.

Eight

1. This section draws on Hallock and Torok (2010) and Florin, Hallock, and Webber (2010). The former provides a great deal of detail on executive compensation for 2009 for the "top five" executives for 2,444 publicly traded companies, including analysis by industry. The latter is an overview of the executive pay and performance literature, including a statistical discussion of why finding the link between pay and performance for CEOs is so difficult.

2. In fact, the numbers reported for stock option compensation in the summary compensation table of the proxy statement are accounting-based numbers, and it is recommended that one use data from the options summary tables (later in the proxy statement) for a clearer view of the value of actual compensation earned in a given year. The subject of how to value stock options for executives and other employees is an interesting issue for debate. I do not focus on it in this chapter. The interested reader can find discussion of this in Lambert, Larcker, and Verrecchia (1991), Hall and Murphy (2002), and Hallock and Olson (2010).

3. Recall that it would not be wise to use this information on stock options for compensation value purposes. The numbers reported in the fourth column of the proxy statement for stock options are for accounting purposes. For compensation purposes, it is much better to use data from the stock options grants table in the proxy statement.

4. As noted earlier, this is not precisely the right number to consider the compensation paid to executives in options. Valuing employee stock options is difficult. See

Lambert, Larcker, and Verrechia (1991), Hall and Murphy (2002), and Hallock and Olson (2007, 2009, 2010) for a more detailed discussion.

5. Hallock and Olson (2010) provide a much more comprehensive description of data sources for research on executive compensation and employee stock options.

6. Substantially more detail than provided in this section can be found in Hallock and Torok (2010). This section is based on that work and closely follows Florin, Hallock, and Webber (2010).

7. The layoff data were collected from newspaper accounts in the *Wall Street Journal*. More details can be found in Hallock (1998).

8. These data were collected at a time prior to 2006, when firms were required to disclose CEO pay in a systematic and clear format (as discussed earlier), but not as formally as they do today.

9. More technically, I performed ordinary-least-squares fixed-effect regressions, controlling for years and individual-specific firm fixed effects.

10. In this last instance, this 5% estimated pay gap is not statistically different from zero. That is to say, we cannot actually rule out that once we control for all of the characteristics we have that the "no layoff" and "layoff" groups of CEOs are paid the same amount in total compensation.

11. In fact, the scale is in logarithms, so the increase in executive pay is truly extraordinary.

12. In the parlance of economists, the CEOs are paid higher than their marginal revenue product.

13. This is based, in part, on Florin, Hallock, and Webber (2010).

14. For those readers who might be more statistically minded, Murphy (1985) essentially went from estimating simple cross-sectional ordinary-least-squares models to models that include individual firm's "fixed effects." This means that he could estimate the relationship between pay and performance *within* firms, which is clearly the preferred method to think about these models and statistical relationships.

15. One other reason for the dramatic increase in the use of options could have been because of the accounting treatment of the options. Until recently, most standard employee options did not have to count as an expense on the company balance sheet.

16. See Hallock, Madallozo, and Reck (2010) and Florin, Hallock, and Webber (2010) for more detail on the methodological issues in executive compensation.

17. For more details, see "Avoiding Executive Compensation Disasters: The Worldat-Work Executive Rewards Questionary in Action," webinar, WorldatWork. Also see Brossman and Weis (2005).

18. See Brossman and Weiss (2005) for more details.

19. The complete report, "The Conference Board Task Force on Executive Compensation," is available at http://www.conference-board.org/pdf_free/execompensation 2009.pdf

Nine

1. I worked at the Kelly farms in Hadley, Massachusetts, during the early to mid-1980s when I was in junior high school and early high school. The farm was owned by two couples (two brothers married two sisters. One couple had eight kids, the other couple had twelve). We typically worked from 8:00 A.M. to 5:00 P.M. with one hour

for lunch, six days a week. That's forty-eight hours per week; the rest of the time during those summers I played Wiffle Ball.

2. When teaching in Italy in 2009 in an executive graduate program, I *did* meet a former cherry picker who had subsequently moved on to being a human resource executive in a large European firm.

3. Nice for lobsters but not for cucumbers.

4. Prior to writing these words, I never really thought about this carefully before, but that turns out to be 2.38 pounds per minute, per person. I am not sure the Kellys were computing such numbers at the time.

5. Lazear (2000) is a technical academic paper. Hall, Madigan, and Lazear (2000) is a more practical and traditional case study.

6. The last section of this chapter offers a discussion of some work that is extremely suspicious of this assumption.

7. A rebound is when a player gains possession of the ball after someone else (from either team) has taken a shot and missed.

8. See Hall and Madigan (2000) for a nice case of performance evaluation and forced distribution.

9. Also see Hackman and Oldham (1976).

Ten

1. The numbers here are approximate so as to not identify the company in question.

2. After making adjustments for stock splits, the price went to $600. In essence, the price went up by less, but he was given extra shares under the original terms.

3. Technically, the variance is the variance per period of the continuously compounded rate of return on the stock, and the risk-free rate is the continuously compounded risk-free rate.

4. We now have data on twenty-four additional companies and are working to estimate similar models for them.

5. See Hallock and Olson (2007, 2010) for more details.

Eleven

1. Originally quoted in Oyer (2008).

2. Rosen (2000) agreed, saying, "Individual consumers are in the best position to make the most informed choices on their own behalf. Delegating or contracting it to others is bound to lead to misallocations in most cases."

3. See Hallock and Olson (2009) for more detail.

Twelve

1. See Martocchio and Pandey (2008) for a discussion of benefits around the world. Benefits are not directly addressed in this chapter.

2. Variable-rate mortgages may make great sense in some circumstances. But I personally need to know what I owe and when.

3. Segalla, Rouzies, Besson, and Weitz (2006) discuss cultural factors that influence sales compensation decisions of managers.

4. Lowe, Milliman, DeCieri, and Dowling (2000) asked whether seniority entered into pay decisions. Of the ten countries/regions where they did surveys (Australia, Canada, China, Indonesia, Japan, Korea, Latin America, Mexico, Taiwan, and the United States), those with the highest scores for the importance of seniority were Taiwan, Japan, Indonesia, and Korea (page 56).

5. Lowe, Milliman, DeCieri, and Dowling (2000) found that companies in China, Indonesia, and Taiwan were most likely to pay based on group or organization performance (among a set of companies from the countries/regions of Australia, Canada, China, Indonesia, Japan, Korea, Latin America, Mexico, Taiwan, and the United States).

6. Bloom and Milkovich (1998) discuss cultural differences within regions or countries, such as the case of major cultural differences between Shanghai, Beijing, and Hong Kong.

7. Herod (2008) notes that it is incredibly difficult to get good survey data on international compensation in general for a variety of reasons, including that the same job title may mean different things in different countries.

8. According to the Towers Perrin (2005) report, the data "mainly reflect long-term incentive practices among locally headquartered companies, rather than non-local multinationals" (p. 18). The long-term incentives include stock option plans, restricted stock, performance shares, and performance cash plans.

9. The Web site http://aoprals.state.gov/Web920/allowance.asp?menu_id=95 is a useful starting point. Details from this section come directly from that site.

10. From the Department of State Web site, referencing Department of State Standardized Regulation 222.

11. From the Department of State Web site, referencing Department of State Standardized Regulation 513.

12. From the Department of State Web site, referencing Department of State Standardized Regulation 131.

13. From the Department of State Web site, referencing Department of State Standardized Regulation 652.

Thirteen

1. This chapter is based, in part, on an updated version of Hallock (2000). Emerald Publishing has granted permission to reprint that material here.

2. For interesting reviews of the nonprofit sector generally and related literature, see Hamermesh (1975), Clarkson and Martin (1980), Clotfelter (1985), Rose-Ackerman (1986), Weisbrod (1986), and Powell (1987).

3. This discussion is based heavily on Stevenson, Pollak, and Lampkin (1997). See also Bowen, Nygren, Turner and Duffey (1994) for a careful description of the nonprofit sector.

4. See, for example, Fama and Jensen (1983a, 1983b). In a discussion of agency problems and residual claims in general, Fama and Jensen argue that it isn't donations of organizations alone that lead to the presence of nonprofits, but that the nondistribution constraint is crucial. James and Rose-Ackerman (1986) also provide a careful explanation of theories of nonprofit formation.

5. In a brief review of altruism in economics, Simon (1993) argues that economists should go beyond economic motives and include altruism in their theories.

6. Rawls, Ulrich, and Nelson (1975) described data from two samples of MBA students from Valderbilt University. They suggest that respondents who look for jobs in the nonprofit sector have different personality, behavioral, and value characteristics.

7. Feldstein (1971) called this "philanthropic wage setting" (p. 69) in the hospital industry. He stated that "there is a variety of evidence that suggests that hospitals were paying higher wages than necessary" (p. 69).

8. See Hackman and Oldham (1976) for a discussion of autonomy and skill variety and their effects on work performance in the context of organizational behavior.

9. Hendricks (1977) provides a related example where those in regulated industries might enjoy job amenities and therefore settle for lower wages. The paper aims to focus on the effect of regulation on labor of a given level of quality. He finds that given a fixed level of quality, earnings in regulated industries are lower than in other industries, for the sample considered.

10. See, for example, Werner and Gemeinhardt (1995) who cite a 1998 IRS ruling that allows nonprofits to use pay for performance.

11. Rocco (1991) notes that "recent studies" have found that 25% of nonprofits offer incentive pay.

12. See Steinberg (1990b) for a discussion of this last point.

13. This is computed here as income divided by the product of usual hours per week last year and weeks worked last year. Note that these are full-time, full-year workers from the 2000 U.S. Census of Population.

14. Part of the new law states that pay levels may not be "excessive" but it is not clear what is meant by "excessive" (Nonprofits Ask, 1995).

15. In a study by William Mercer Inc. of seventy-two foundations and trade associations, 58% said they offered incentive and deferred pay, 61% started incentive plans within the last five years, but 30% said they "resist" incentives because it may be inconsistent with their status as exempt entities (Nonprofit Executives, 1995).

16. Note that Oster (1996) stated that although there is a pay to performance link, it is partially constrained because nonprofit boards may feel pressure to not pay managers too much. See Joskow, Rose, and Shepard (1993) and Joskow, Rose, and Wolfram (1996) for studies of the effects of constraints on firms and CEO pay.

Fourteen

1. There is a growing and interesting body of work related to personality psychology and economics. For example, Heckman (2011) notes that "conscientiousness is the most predictive [personality] trait across outcomes such as educational attainment, grades, job performance across a range of occupational choices, longevity and criminality" (p. 7).

References

Abelson, Reed, 1998, "Nonprofit Work Gets Profitable," *New York Times*, March 29, WR3.

Abzug, Rikki, DiMaggio, Paul, Gray, Bradford H., Useem, Michael, & Kang, Chul Hee, 1994, "Change in the Structure and Composition of Non-Profit Boards of Trustees: Cases from Boston and Cleveland, 1925–1985," *Voluntas*, 4, 271–300.

Adams, John S., 1965, "Inequity in Social Exchange," *Advances in Experimental Social Psychology*, 62, 335–343.

Anderson, Sarah, & Cavanagh, John, 1994, *Workers Lose, CEOs Win*, Washington, DC: Institute for Policy Studies.

Anheier, Helmut, 1993, "Employment and Earnings in the West German Nonprofit Sector: Structure and Trends 1970–1987," in A. Ben-Ner & B. Gui (Eds.), *The Nonprofit Sector in a Mixed Economy* (pp. 183–202). Ann Arbor: University of Michigan Press.

Antle, R., & Smith, A., 1986, "An Empirical Investigation of the Relative Performance Evaluation of Corporate Executives," *Journal of Accounting Research*, 24(1), 1–39.

Antoninis, Manos, 2006, "The Wage Effects from the Use of Personal Contacts as Hiring Channels," *Journal of Economic Behavior and Organization*, 59(1), 133–146.

Arias, Omar, Hallock, Kevin F., & Sosa, Walter, 2001, "Individual Heterogeneity in the Returns to Schooling Using Twins Data," *Empirical Economics*, 26(1), 7–40.

Arrow, Kenneth J., 1963, "Uncertainty and the Welfare Economics of Medical Care," *American Economic Review*, 53(5), 946–973.

Ashenfelter, Orley, & Krueger, Alan B., 1994, "Estimates of the Economic Returns to Schooling from a New Sample of Twins," *The American Economic Review*, 84(5), 1157–1173.

Babcock, Linda, & Laschever, Sara, 2003, *Women Don't Ask*, Princeton Universiyt Press.

Bailey, Sally B., & Risher, Howard, 1996, "If the Shoe Fits: Not-for-Profits Try Out New Compensation Plans," *Compensation & Benefits Review*, May'Jene, 28, 47–57.

Baker, George P., 1992, "Incentive Contracts and Performance Measurement," *Journal of Political Economy*, 100(3), 598–614.

Barron, L.A., 2003, "Ask and You Shall Receive? Gender Differences in Negotiators' Beliefs about Requests for a Higher Salary," *Human Relations*, 56960, 635–662.

Bartlett, Robin L., & Miller, Timothy I., 1985, "Executive Compensation: Female Executives and Networking," *The American Economic Review*, 75(2), 266–270.

Bearle, Adolf & Means, Gardiner, 1932, *The Modern Corporation and Private Property*, New York: Transaction Publishers.

Bebchuk, Lucian, & Fried, Jesse, 2004, *Pay without Performance: The Unfulfilled Promise of Executive Compensation*, Cambridge, MA: Harvard University Press.

Bebchuk, Lucian A., & Fried, Jesse M., 2006, "Pay without Performance: Overview of the Issues," *Academy of Management Perspectives*, February, 20(1), 5–24.

Becker, Gary S., 1964, *Human Capital: A Theoretical and Empirical Analysis with Special Reference to Education* (also 1975 and 1993), Chicago: The University of Chicago Press.

Becker, Gary, & Tomes, Nigel, 1979, "An Equilibrium Theory of the Distribution of Income and Intergenerational Mobility," *Journal of Political Economy*, 87, 1153–1189.

Becker, Gary, & Tomes, Nigel, 1986, "Human Capital and the Rise and Fall of Families," *Journal of Labor Economics*, 4, S1–S39.

Bertrand, Marianne, & Hallock, Kevin F., 2001, "The Gender Gap in Top Corporate Jobs," *Industrial and Labor Relations Review*, 55(1), 3–21.

Bertrand, Marianne, Hallock, Kevin F., & Arnould, Richard, 2005, "Does Managed Care Change the Management of Nonprofit Hospitals? Evidence from the Executive Labor Market," *Industrial and Labor Relations Review*, 58(3), .

Bilodeau, Mark, & Slivinski, Al, 1996, "Toilet Cleaning and Department Chairing: Volunteering a Public Service," *Journal of Public Economics*, 59, 299–308.

Black, Fisher, & Scholes, Myron, 1973, "The Pricing of Options and Corporate Liabilities," *Journal of Political Economy*, May–June, 81(3), 637–654.

Blau, Francine D., Ferber, Marianne A., & Winkler, Anne E., 2010, *Economics of Women, Men, and Work*, 6th edition, Upper Saddle River, NJ: Prentice Hall.

Bloom, Matthew C., & Milkovich, George T., 1997, "Rethinking International Compensation: From Expatriate and National Cultures to Strategic Flexibility," Cornell University Center for Advanced Human Resource Studies (CAHRS) Working Paper #97–24.

Bloom, Matthew, & Milkovich, George T., 1998, "A SHRM Perspective on International Compensation and Reward Systems," Cornell University Center for Advanced Human Resource Studies (CAHRS) Working Paper #98–11.

Bloom, Matthew, Milkovich, George T., & Mitra, Atul, 2000, "Toward a Model of International Compensation and Rewards: Learning from How Managers Respond to Variations in Local Host Contexts," Cornell University Center for Advanced Human Resource Studies (CAHRS) Working paper #00–14.

Borjas, George J., 1996, *Labor Economics*, New York: McGraw-Hill.

Borzaga, Carlo, 1993, "The Italian Nonprofit Sector: An Overview of an Undervalued Reality," in A. Ben-Ner & B. Gui (Eds.), *The Nonprofit Sector in a Mixed Economy* (pp. 205–219). Ann Arbor: University of Michigan Press.

Bowen, William G., 1994, *Inside the Boardroom*, New York: John Wiley & Sons.

Bowen, William G., Nygren, Thomas I., Turner, Sarah E., & Duffy, Elizabeth A., 1994, *The Charitable Nonprofits: An Analysis of Institutional Dynamics and Characteristics*, San Francisco: Jossey-Bass.

Boyer, George R., 1998, "The Influence of London on Local Labor Markets in Southern England, 1830–1914," *Social Science History*, 22(3), 257–285.

Brett, J.M., and Stroh, L.K., 1997, "Jumping Ship: Who Benefits from an External Labor Market Career Strategy?" *Journal of Applied Psychology*, 82, 331–341.

Brossman, Mark E. & Weiss, Gregory S., 2005, "Shareholder Activism and Executive Compensation," *Benefits and Compensation Digest*, 17, 40–44.

Bullard, Angela M., & Wright, Deil S., 1993, "Circumventing the Glass Ceiling: Women Executives in American State Governments," *Public Administration Review*, 53(3), 189–202.

Burbridge, Lynn C., 1994, "The Occupational Structure of Nonprofit Industries: Implications for Women," in T. Odendahl & M. O'Neill (Eds.), *Women and Power in the Nonprofit Sector* (pp. 121–154). San Francisco: Jossey-Bass.

Cameron, Stephen, & Taber, Christopher, 2004, "Estimation of Educational Borrowing Constraints Using Returns to Schooling," *Journal of Political Economy*, 112(1), 132–182.

Card, David, 1999, "The Causal Effect of Education on Earnings," in Orley Ashenfelter, & David Card (Eds.), *Handbook of Labor Economics* Volume 3A. Amsterdam: Elsevier, 1801–1863.

Card, David, 2001, "Estimating the Return to Schooling: Progress on Some Persistent Econometric Problems," *Econometrica*, 69, 1127–1160.

Card, David, Mas, Alexandre, Moretti, Enrico, & Saez, Emmanuel, 2010, "Inequality at Work: The Effect of Peer Salaries on Job Satisfaction," NBER Working Paper No. 16396.

Case, John, 2001, "When Salaries Aren't Secret," *Harvard Business Review*, 79(5), 37–49.

Casey, C., 1996, "Many CEOs Earn Opulent Salaries," *Sunday Republican*, December 22, B1–5.

Casteuble, Tracy, 1997, "What Today's Association Executives Earn," *Association Management*, April, 49(4), 53–61.

Clarkson, Kenneth W., 1972, "Some Implications of Property Rights in Hospital Management," *Journal of Law and Economics*, 15(2), 363–384.

Clarkson, Kenneth W., & Martin, Donald L. (Eds.), 1980, "The Economics of Nonproprietary Organizations," *Research in Law and Economics*, Supplement 1, JAI Press.

Cleaverly, W.O., and Mullen, R.P., 1982, "Management Incentives System and Economic Performance in Health Care Organizations," *Health Care Management Review*, Winter, 7–14.

Clotfelter, Charles T., 1985, *Federal Tax Policy and Charitable Giving*, Chicago: University of Chicago Press.

Coughlin, Anne T., & Schmidt, Ronald M., 1985, "Executive Compensation, Management Turnover, and Firm Performance," *Journal of Accounting and Economics*, 7, 43–66.

Council of Better Business Bureaus, undated, *CBBB Standards for Charitable Solicitations*.

Cui, Rui (Susie), 2006, "International Compensation: The Importance of Acting Globally," *WorldatWork Journal*, Fourth Quarter, 15(4), 18–23.

DellaVigna, Stefano, & Passerman, M. Daniel, 2005, "Job Search and Impatience," *Journal of Labor Economics*, 23(3), 527–588.

Dreher, G.F., & Cox, Jr., T.H., 2000, "Labor Market Mobility and Cash Compensation: The Moderating Effects of Race and Gender," *Academy of Management Journal*, 43, 890–900.

Easley, David, & Maureen O'Hara, 1983, "The Economic Role of the Nonprofit Sector," *The Bell Journal of Economics*, 14(2), 531–538.

Easley, David, & Maureen O'Hara, 1986, "Optimal Nonprofit Firms," in Susan Rose-Ackerman (Ed.), *The Economics of Nonprofit Institutions: Studies in Structure and Policy* (pp. 85–93). Oxford: Oxford University Press.

Emory, Meade, Swenson, James B., Lerner, Herbert, & Fuller, James, 1992, "IRS Okays Percentage Management Plan for Exempt Entity," *Journal of Taxation*, 76(6), 379–380.

Fama, Eugene F., & Jensen, Michael C., 1983a, "Separation of Ownership and Control," *Journal of Labor and Economics*, 36, 301–325.

Fama, Eugene F., & Jensen, Michael C., 1983b, "Agency Problems and Residual Claims," *Journal of Labor and Economics*, 36, 327–349.

Feldstein, Martin S., 1971, *The Rising Cost of Healthcare*, Washington, DC: Information Resources Press.

Fields, Gary S., 2009, *Bottom-Line Management*, Berlin: Springer Verlag.

Fisher, Anne, 2006, "3 Smart Ways to Get a Raise," CNN Money, http://money.cnn.com/2006/09/11/news/economy/raise.fortune/index.htm

Florin, Beth, Hallock, Kevin F., and Webber, Douglas A., 2010, "Executive Pay and Firm Performance: Methodological Considerations and Future Directions," *Research in Personnel and Human Resources Management*, Emerald Group.

Frank, Robert, 1996, "What Price the Moral High Ground?" *Southern Economic Journal*, 63(1), 1–17.

Freeman, Richard, 1975, "Demand for Labor in a Nonprofit Market: University Faculty," in Daniel Hamermesh (Ed.), *Labor in the Public and Nonprofit Sectors* (pp. 85–129). Princeton, NJ: Princeton University Press.

Freeman, Richard, & Katz, Lawrence (Eds.), 1994, *Differences and Changes in Wage Structures*, Chicago: University of Chicago Press for the National Bureau of Economic Research (NBER).

Gabaix, Xavier, & Landier, Augustin, 2008, "Why Has CEO Pay Increased So Much?" *Quarterly Journal of Economics*, 123, 49–100.

Gerhart, Barry, 2000, "Compensation Strategy and Organization Performance," in Sara L. Rynes, & Barry Gerhart (Eds.), *Compensation in Organizations*. San Francisco: Jossey-Bass, 151–194.

Gerhart, Barry, 2008, "Compensation and National Culture", in Luis Gomez-Mejia, & Steve Werner (Eds.), *Global Compensation: Foundations and Perspectives*. London: Routledge, 141–157.

Gerhart, Barry, & Rynes, Sara L., 2003, *Compensation: Theory, Evidence and Strategic Implications*, Thousand Oaks, CA: Sage.

Gibbons, Robert, & Murphy, Kevin J., 1990, "Relative Performance Evaluation for Chief Executive Officers," *Industrial and Labor Relations Review*, 43(3), 30s–51s.

Glaeser, Edward L., & Shleifer, Andrei A., 1998, *Not-for-Profit Entrepreneurs*. Cambridge, MA: NBER Working Paper 6810.

Goddeeris, John H., 1988, "Compensating Differentials and Self-Selection: An Application to Lawyers," *Journal of Political Economy*, 96(2), 411–428.

Gomez-Mejia, Luis, & Welbourne, Theresa, 1991, "Compensation Strategies in a Global Context," *Human Resource Planning*, 14(1), 29–41.

Gronbjerg, Kristen A., 1994, "Using NTEE to Classify Nonprofit Organizations: An Assessment of Human Service and Regional Applications," *Voluntas*, 5(3), 301–328.

Guy, Mary E., 1993, "Three Steps Forward, Two Steps Backward: The Status of Women's Integration into Public Management," *Public Administration Review*, 53(4), 285–292.

Hackman, J. Richard, & Oldham, Greg R., 1976, "Motivation through the Design of Work: Test of a Theory," *Organizational Behavior and Human Performance*, 16, 250–279.

Hall, Brian, & Liebman, Jeffrey, 1998, "Are CEOs Really Paid Like Bureaucrats?" *Quarterly Journal of Economics*, 113(3), 653–692.

Hall, Brian, & Madigan, Carleen, 2000, "Compensation and Performance Evaluation at Arrow Electronics," Harvard Business School Case Study 9–800–290.

Hall, Brian, Madigan, Carleen, and Lazear, Edward, 2000, "Performance Pay at Safelite Auto Glass (A)," Harvard Business School Case Study, 800291-PDF-ENG.

Hall, Brian J., & Murphy, Kevin J., 2002, "Stock Options for Undiversified Executives," *Journal of Accounting and Economics*, February, 33(1), 3–42.

Hall, Brian J., & Murphy, Kevin J., 2003, "The Trouble with Stock Options," *Journal of Economic Perspectives*, 17, 49–70.

Hallock, Kevin F., 1995, "Seniority and Monopsony in the Academic Labor Market: Comment," *The American Economic Review*, 85(3), 654–657.

Hallock, Kevin F., 1997, "Reciprocally Interlocking Boards of Directors and Executive Compensation," *Journal of Financial and Quantitative Analysis*, 32(3), 331–344.

Hallock, Kevin F., 1998, "Layoffs, Top Executive Pay, and Firm Performance," *The American Economic Review*, 88(4), 711–723.

Hallock, Kevin F., 1999a, "Gender Compensation Differences among Executives in Nonprofits," Working Paper.

Hallock, Kevin F., 1999b, "Dual Agency: Corporate Boards with Reciprocally Interlocking Relationships," in Jennifer Carpenter, & David Yermack (Eds.), *Executive Compensation and Shareholder Value; Theory and Evidence* (pp. 55–75). Norwell, MA: Kluwer.

Hallock, Kevin F., 2000, "Compensation in Nonprofit Organizations," *Research in Personnel and Human Resources Management*, 19, 243–294.

Hallock, Kevin F., 2002, "Managerial Pay and Governance in American Nonprofits," *Industrial Relations*, 41(3), 377–406.

Hallock, Kevin F., 2004, "Managerial Pay in Nonprofit and For-Profit Organizations," in Sarah Smith-Orr, & Ron Riggio (Eds.), *Improving Leadership in Nonprofit Organizations* (pp. 76–101). San Francisco: Jossey-Bass.

Hallock, Kevin F., 2009, "Layoffs and the Fraying of the Implicit Employment Contract," *Journal of Economic Perspectives*, 23(4), 69–93.

Hallock, Kevin F., Hendricks, Wallace, & Broadbent, Emer, 1998, "Discrimination by Gender and Disability Status: Do Worker Perceptions Match Statistical Measures?" *Southern Economic Journal*, 65(2), 245–263.

Hallock, Kevin F., Lubotsky, Darren, & Webber, Douglas, , "The Night Shift," in preparation.

Hallock, Kevin F., Madalozzo, Regina, & Reck, Clayton, 2010, "CEO Pay for Performance Heterogeneity: Examples Using Quantile Regression," *Financial Review*, 45(1), 1–19.

Hallock, Kevin F., & Olson, Craig A., 2007, "The Value of Stock Options to Non-Executive Employees," Working Paper, Cornell University and University of Illinois at Urbana-Champaign.

Hallock, Kevin F., & Olson, Craig A., 2009, "Employees' Choice of Method of Pay," Working Paper, Cornell University and University of Illinois at Urbana-Champaign.

Hallock, Kevin F., & Olson, Craig A., 2010, "New Data for Answering Old Questions Regarding Employee Stock Options," in Katharine G. Abraham, James R. Spletzer, & Michael Harper (Eds.), *Labor and the New Economy*. Washington, DC: National Bureau of Economic Research, 149–186.

Hallock, Kevin F., & Oyer, Paul, 1999, "The Timeliness of Performance Information in Determining Executive Compensation," *Journal of Corporate Finance*, 5(4), 303–321.

Hallock, Kevin F., & Torok, Judit, 2010, *Top Executive Compensation in 2009*. New York: The Conference Board.

Hallock, Kevin F., & Torok, Judit, 2011, *Top Executive Compensation in 2010*. New York: The Conference Board.

Hamermesh, Daniel S. (Ed.), 1975, *Labor in the Public and Nonprofit Sectors*. Princeton, NJ: Princeton University Press.

Hamermesh, Daniel, 2011, *Beauty Pays: Why Attractive People are More Successful*, Princeton NJ: Princeton University Press.

Hamermesh, Daniel, & Biddle, Jeffrey, 1994, "Beauty in the Labor Market," *The American Economic Review*, 5, 1174–1194.

Hamermesh, Daniel, & Biddle, Jeffrey, 1998, "Beauty, Productivity and Discrimination: Lawyers, Looks and Lucre," *Journal of Labor Economics*, 16(1), 172–201.

Hamner, W. Clay, 1975, "How to Ruin Motivation with Pay," *Compensation Review*, 7, 17–27.

Handy, Feminda, & Katz, Eliakim, 1998, "The Wage Differential Between Nonprofit Institutions and Corporations: Getting More by Paying Less?" *Journal of Comparative Economics*, 26, 246–261.

Hansmann, Henry B., 1980, "The Role of Nonprofit Enterprise," *The Yale Law Journal*, 89, 835–898.

Hansmann, Henry B., 1996, *The Organization of Enterprise*, Cambridge, MA: Harvard University Press.

Harvey, Robert J., 1991, "Job Analysis," in M.D. Dunnette, & L. Hough (Eds.), *Handbook of Industrial and Organizational Psychology*, Volume 2 (pp. 71–163), Palo Alto, CA: Consulting Psychologists Press.

Heckman, James J., 1978, "Dummy Endogenous Variables in a Simultaneous Equations System," *Econometrica*, 46, 931–959.

Heckman, James J., 2011, "Integrating Personality Psychology into Economics," National Bureau of Economic Research Working Paper 17378, Cambridge MA.

Henderson, Richard I., 1984, *Performance Appraisal*, 2nd edition, Reston, VA: Reston Publishing.

Henderson, Richard I., 2006, *Compensation Management in a Knowledge-Based World*, 10th edition, New York: Pearson Prentice Hall.

Hendricks, Wallace, 1977, "Regulation and Labor Earnings," *The Bell Journal of Economics*, 8(2), 483–496.

Herman, R.D., 1994, *The Jossey-Bass Handbook of Nonprofit Leadership and Management*, San Francisco: Jossey-Bass.

Herod, Roger, 2008, *Global Compensation and Benefits: Developing Policies for Local Nationals*, Alexandria, VA: Society for Human Resource Management.

Herzberg, Frederick, Mausner, B., and Snyderman, B.B., 1956, *The Motivation to Work*, London: Wiley.

Herzlinger, Regina E., 1994, "Effective Oversight: A Guide for Nonprofit Directors," *Harvard Business Review*, 72(4), 52–60.

Hodgkinson, Virginia A., 1990, "Mapping the Nonprofit Sector in the United States: Implications for Research," *Voluntas*, 12(2), 6–32.

Hodgkinson, Virginia A., & Toppe, Christopher M., 1991, "A New Research and Planning Tool for Managers: The National Taxonomy of Exempt Entities," *Nonprofit Management and Leadership*, 1(4), 403–414.

Hodgkinson, Virginia A., Gorski, Heather A., Noga, Stephen M., & Knauft, E.B., 1995, *Giving and Volunteering in the United States, Volume II*, Washington DC: The Independent Sector.

Hodgkinson, Virginia A., & Weitzman, Murray S. with Noga, Stephen M., Gorski, Heather A., & Kirsch, Arthur D., 1994, *Giving and Volunteering in the United States*. Washington, DC: The Independent Sector.

Hofstede, G., 1980, *Culture's Consequences: International Differences in Work-Related Values*, Newbury Park, CA: Sage.

Hultin, Mia, & Ryszard, Szulkin, 1999, "Wages and Unequal Access to Organizational Power: An Empirical Test of Gender Discrimination," *Administrative Science Quarterly*, 44, 453–472.

"Incentives Enter the Not-for-Profit Pay Picture," 1992, (no author listed), *Compensation and Benefits Review*, March–April, 24, 10–11.

Ito, Takatoshi, & Domian, Dale, 1987, "A Musical Note on the Efficiency Wage Hypothesis: Programming, Wages and Budgets of American Symphony Orchestras," *Economics Letters*, 25, 95–99.

James, Estelle, 1990, "Economic Theories of the Nonprofit Sector: A Comparative Perspective," in H.K. Anheier, & W. Seibel (Eds.), *The Third Sector: Comparative Studies of Nonprofit Organizations* (pp. 219–229). Berlin: Walter de Gruyter.

James, Estelle, & Rose-Ackerman, Susan, 1986, *The Nonprofit Enterprise in Market Economies*, New York: Harwood Academic Press.

Jensen, Michael, C., & Murphy, Kevin J., 1990, "Performance Pay and Top Management Incentives," *Journal of Political Economy*, 98(2), 225–264.

Johnston, Denis, & Rudney, Gabriel, 1987, "Characteristics of Workers in Nonprofit Organizations," *Monthly Labor Review*, 110(7), 28–33.

Joskow, Paul, Rose, Nancy, & Shepherd, Andrea A., 1993, "Regulatory Constraints on CEO Compensation," *Brookings Papers on Economic Activity*, 1, 1–72.

Joskow, Paul, Rose, Nancy, & Wolfram, Catherine, 1996, "Political Constraints on Executive Compensation: Evidence from the Electric Utility Industry," *Rand Journal of Economics*, 27(1), 165–182.

Kanter, Rosabeth M., & Summers, David V., 1987, "Doing Well While Doing Good: Dilemmas of Performance Measurement in Nonprofit Organizations and the Need for a Multiple-Constituency Approach," in W.W. Powell (Ed.), *The Nonprofit Sector: A Research Handbook* (pp. 154–166). New Haven, CT: Yale University Press.

Kay, Ira T., & Van Putten, Scott, 2007, *Myths and Realities of Executive Pay*, Cambridge: Cambridge University Press.

Knapp, Martin, & Kendall, Jeremy, 1993, "Policy Issues for the UK Voluntary Sector in the 1990s," in A. Ben-Ner, & B. Gui (Eds.), *The Nonprofit Sector in a Mixed Economy* (pp. 221–241). Ann Arbor: University of Michigan Press.

Kohn, Alfie, 1993, "Why Incentive Plans Cannot Work," *Harvard Business Review*, 71(5), 54–63.

Kostiuk, Peter F., 1990, "Firm Size and Executive Compensation," *Journal of Human Resources*, 25(1), 90–105.

Krueger, Alan, 1991, "Ownership, Agency, and Wages: An Examination of Franchising in the Fast Food Industry," *Quarterly Journal of Economics*, 106(1), 75–101.

Lambert, Richard A., Larcker, David F., & Verecchia, Robert, 1991, "Portfolio Considerations in Valuing Executive Compensation," *Journal of Accounting Research*, 29, 129–149.

Langer, Steven, 1989, "How Much are Executives in Nonprofit Organizations Paid?" *Nonprofit World*, 7(3), 25–28.

Latham, Gary P., & Wexley, Kenneth N., 1980, *Increasing Productivity through Performance Appraisal*, London: Addison-Wesley.

Lazear, Edward P., 1986, "Salaries versus Piece Rates," *Journal of Business*, 59, 405–431.

Lazear, Edward P., 1996a, *Personnel Economics*, Cambridge MA: MIT Press.

Lazear, Edward P., 1996b. "Performance Pay and Productivity," Working Paper 5672, Cambridge, MA; NBER.

Lazear, Edward P., 1998, *Personnel Economics for Managers*, New York: Wiley.

Lazear, Eward P., 2000, "Performance Pay and Productivity," *The American Economic Review*, 90(5), 1346–1361.

Lazear, Edward P., & Rosen, Sherwin, 1981, "Rank-Order Tournaments as Optimum Labor Contracts," *Journal of Political Economy*, 89(5), 841–864.

Lee, L.F., 1978, "Unions and Wage Rates: A Simultaneous Equations Model with Qualitative and Limited Dependent Variables," *International Economic Review*, 19, 415–433.

Lewellen, Wilbur G., & Huntsman, B., 1970, "Managerial Pay and Corporate Performance," *The American Economic Review*, 60, 710–720.

Lewis, Michael M., 2003, *Moneyball: The Art of Winning an Unfair Game*, New York: W.W. Norton.

Loury, Linda D., 2006, "Some Contacts Are More Equal than Others: Informal Networks, Job Tenure, and Wages," *Journal of Labor Economics*, 24(2), 299–318.

Lowe, Kevin B., Milliman, John, De Cieri, Helen, & Dowling, Peter J., 2000, "International Compensation Practices: A Ten-Country Comparative Analysis," *Human Resource Management*, 41(1), 45–66.

Lubotsky, Darren, 2011, "The Economics of Employee Benefits," in Joseph J. Martocchio (Ed.), *Employee Benefits: A Primer for Human Resource Professionals*, 4th edition. 49–66, New York: Irwin/McGraw Hill.

Main, Brian G.M., O'Reilly, Charles A., & Wade, James, 1993, "Top Executive Pay: Tournament or Teamwork?" *Journal of Labor Economics*, 11(4), 606–628.

Marin, Gregorio Sanchez, 2008, "The Influence of Institutional and Cultural Factors on Compensation Practices Around the World," in Luis R. Gomez-Mejia, & Steve Werner (Eds.), *Global Compensation: Foundations and Perspectives*, 3–17, London: Routledge.

Martin, Robert E., 1988, "Franchising and Risk Management," *American Economic Review*, 78(5), 954–968.

Martocchio, Joseph J., 2001, *Strategic Compensation: A Human Resource Management Approach*, 2nd edition, New York: Prentice Hall.

Martocchio, Joseph J., & Pandey, Niti, 2008, "Employee Benefits Around the World," in Luis Gomez-Mejia, & Steve Werner (Eds.), *Global Compensation: Foundation and Perspectives*. 179–191, London: Routledge.

Maslow, Abraham, 1943, "A Theory of Human Motivation," *Psychological Review*, 50(4), 370–396.

Masson, Robert, 1971, "Executive Motivations, Earnings, and Consequent Equity Performance," *Journal of Political Economy*, 79(6), 1278–1292.

Matthews, James, 2005, "Global Stock Plans: Greater Sensitivity to Local Conditions," *Benefits and Compensation International*, 11, 18–30.

Mazumder, Bhashkar, 2005, "Fortunate Sons: New Estimates of Intergenerational Mobility in the United States Using Social Security Earnings Data," *Review of Economics and Statistics*, 87(2), 235–255.

Menchik, Paul L., & Weisbrod, Burton A., 1987, "Volunteer Labor Supply," *Journal of Public Economics*, 32, 159–183.

Merton, Robert C., 1973, "The Theory of Rational Option Pricing," *Bell Journal of Economics and Management Science*, 4, 141–183.

Milkovich, George T., & Bloom, Matt, 1998, "Rethinking International Compensation," *Compensation and Benefits Review*, 30(1), 15–23.

Milkovich, George T., & Newman, Jerry M., 2008, *Compensation*, 9th edition, New York: McGraw Hill.

Milkovich, George T, Newman, Jerry M, & Gerhart, Barry, 2011, *Compensation*, 10th edition, New York: McGraw-Hill.

Mirvis, Philip H., & Hackett, Edward J., 1983, "Work and Work Force Characteristics in the Nonprofit Sector," *Monthly Labor Review*, 106(4), 3–12.

Mobius, M.M., & Rosenblatt, T.S., 2006, "Why Beauty Matters," *The American Economic Review*, 96(1), 222–235.

Murphy, Kevin J., 1985, "Corporate Performance and Managerial Remuneration: An Empirical Analysis," *Journal of Accounting and Economics*, 7(1–3), 11–42.

Murphy, Kevin J., 1999, "Executive Compensation," In Orley Ashenfelter, & David Card (Eds.), *Handbook of Labor Economics*, volume 3B (pp. 2485–2563). London: Elsevier Science Publishers.

Murphy, Kevin R., & Cleveland, Jeanette N., 1995, *Understanding Performance Appraisal: Social, Organizational and Goal-Based Perspectives*, Thousand Oaks, CA: Sage.

Nicoson, Robert D., 1996, "Growing Pains," *Harvard Business Review*, 74(4), 20–36.

"Nonprofit Executives See More Incentive Pay," 1995 (no author listed) *HRFocus*, November.

"Nonprofits Ask IRS to Clarify New Law," 1997 (no author listed), *Nonprofit World*, May–June, 8.

O'Connell, Brian, 1992, "Salaries in Nonprofit Organizations," *Nonprofit World*, 10(4), 33–34.

Oster, Sharon, 1996, "Nonprofit Organizations and Their Local Affiliates: A Study in Organizational Forms," *Journal of Economic Behavior and Organization*, 30, 83–95.

Oster, Sharon, 1998, "Executive Compensation in the Nonprofit Sector," *Nonprofit Management and Leadership*, 8(3), 207–221.

Oyer, Paul, 2008, "Salary or Benefits?" *Research in Labor Economics*, 28, 429–467.

Oyer, Paul, & Schaefer, Scott, 2008, "Why Do Some Firms Give Stock Options to All Employees? An Empirical Examination of Alternative Theories," *Journal of Financial Economics*, 76, 99–133.

Paul, Alan, 2007, "Expat Life Gets Less Cushy," *The Wall Street Journal*, October 26, W1 and W10.

Pellizzai, Michelle, 2010, "Do Friends and Relatives Really Help in Getting a Good Job?" *Industrial and Labor Relations Review*, 63(3), 494–510.

Permut, Steven E., 1981, "Consumer Perceptions of Nonprofit Enterprise: A Comment on Hansmann," *Yale Law Journal*, 90, 1623–1632.

Peters, Bethany L., & Stringham, Edward, 2006, "No Booze? You May Lose: Why Drinkers Earn More Money Than Nondrinkers," *Journal of Labor Research*, 27(3), 411–421.

Pfeffer, Jeffrey, 1998, "Six Dangerous Myths about Pay," *Harvard Business Review*, 76(3), 109–119.

Picker, David, 2007, "More Than Just a Handshake Deal for Japanese Baseball Players," *New York Times*, April 17, http://www.nytimes.com/2007/4/17/sports/baseball/17japan.html

Pink, Daniel H., 2010, *Drive: The Surprising Truth about What Motivates Us*. New York: Penguin Group.

Pink, George H., & Leatt, Peggy, 1991, "Are Managers Compensated for Hospital Financial Performance?" *Health Care Management Review*, 16(3), 37–45.

Pinkley, Robin, & Northcraft, Gregory B., 2000, *Get Paid What You Are Worth*. New York: St. Martin's Press.

Porter, Michael, 1996, "What Is Strategy?" *Harvard Business Review*, 74(6), 61–78.

Powell, Walter W. (Ed.), 1987, *The Nonprofit Sector: A Research Handbook*, New Haven, CT: Yale University Press.

Preston, Anne P., 1988, "The Effects of Property Rights on Labor Costs of Nonprofit Firms: An Application to the Day Care Industry," *Journal of Industrial Economics*, 36(3), 337–350.

Preston, Anne, 1989, "The Nonprofit Worker in a For-Profit World," *Journal of Labor Economics*, 7, 438–463.

Preston, Anne, 1990, "Women in the White-Collar Nonprofit Sector: The Best Option or the Only Option?" *The Review of Economics and Statistics*, 72(4), 560–568.

Preston, Anne, 1994, "Women in the Nonprofit Labor Market," in T. Odendahl, & M. O'Neil (Eds.), *Women and Power in the Nonprofit Sector* (pp. 39–77). San Francisco: Jossey-Bass.

Prien Erich P., 1977, "The Function of Job Analysis in Content Validation," *Personnel Psychology*, 30(2), 167–174.

Pynes, Joan E., 1997, *Human Resource Management for Public and Nonprofit Organizations*, San Francisco: Jossey-Bass.

Ransom, Michael, 1993, "Seniority and Monopsony in the Academic Labor Market," *The American Economic Review*, 83(1), 221–233.

Rawls, James R., Ullrich, Robert A., & Nelson, Jr., Oscar Tives, 1975, "A Comparison of Managers Entering or Reentering the Profit and Nonprofit Sectors," *Academy of Management Journal*, 18(3), 616–623.

Roberts, David R., 1956. "A General Theory of Executive Compensation Based on Statistically Tested Propositions," *Quarterly Journal of Economics* 70, 270–294.

Rocco, James E., 1991, "Making Incentive Plans Work for Nonprofits," *Nonprofit World*, 9(4), 13–15.

Rose-Ackerman, Susan (Ed.), 1986, *The Economics of Nonprofit Institutions: Studies in Structure and Policy*. New York: Oxford University Press.

Rose-Ackerman, Susan, 1987, "Ideals versus Dollars: Donors, Charity Managers, and Government Grants," *Journal of Political Economy*, 95(4), 810–823.

Rose-Ackerman, Susan, 1996, "Altruism, Nonprofits, and Economic Theory," *Journal of Economic Literature*,34, 710–28.

Rosen, Harvey S., 1988, *Public Finance*, 2nd edition, New York: Irwin.

Rosen, Sherwin, 1974, "Hedonic Prices and Implicit Markets: Product Differentiation in Pure Competition," *Journal of Political Economy*, 82(1), 34–55.

Rosen, Sherwin, 1986, "The Theory of Equalizing Differences," in Orley Ashenfelter, & Richard Layard (Eds.), *Handbook of Labor Economics* (pp. 641–692). New York: North Holland.

Rosen, Sherwin, 1992, "Contracts and the Market for Executives," in Lars Werin, & Hans Wijkander (Eds.), *Contract Economics (pp. 181–211)*. Oxford: Blackwell.

Rosen, Sherwin, 2000, "Does the Composition of Pay Matter?" in William T. Alpert, & Stephen A. Woodbury (Eds.), *Employee Benefits and Labor Markets in Canada and the United States* (pp. 13–30). Kalamazoo MI: W.E. UpJohn Institute for Employment Research.

Salamon, Lester M., & Anheier, Helmut K., 1992a, "In Search of the Nonprofit Sector I: The Question of Definitions," *Voluntas*, 3(2), 125–151.

Salamon, Lester M., & Anheier, Helmut K., 1992b, "In Search of the Nonprofit Sector II: The Problem of Classification," *Voluntas*, 3(3), 267–309.

Salamon, Lester M., & Anheier, Helmut K., 1996, *The Emerging Nonprofit Sector: An Overview*, Manchester: Manchester University Press.

Shackett, Joyce P., & Trapani, John M., 1987, "Earnings Differentials and Market Structure," *Journal of Human Resources*, 12, 518–531.

Schuler, R.S., & N. Rogovsky, 1998, "Understanding Compensation Practice Variation across Firms: The Impact of National Culture," *Journal of International Business Studies*, 29, 159–177.

Seeger, John A., Harlan, Anne, & Kotter, John, 1976, "Megalith Inc. – Hay Associates (A)," Harvard Business School Case Study.

Segalla, Michael, Rouzies, Dominique, Besson, Madeline, & Weitz, Barton, 2006, "A Cross-National Investigation of Incentive Sales Compensation," *International Journal of Research in Marketing*, 23, 419–433.

Simon, Herbert A., 1993, "Altruism and Economics," *American Economic Review*, 83(2), 156–161.

Skinner, B., 1953, *Science and Human Behavior*, New York: MacMillan.

Smither, James W. (Ed.), 1998, *Performance Appraisal: State of the Art and Practice*, San Francisco: Jossey-Bass.

Solon, Gary, 1992, "Intergenerational Income Mobility in the United States," *The American Economic Review*, 82, 393–408.

Steinberg, Richard, 1990a, "Labor Economics and the Nonprofit Sector: A Literature Review," *Nonprofit and Voluntary Sector Quarterly*, 19(2), 151–170.

Steinberg, Richard, 1990b, "Profits and Incentive Compensation in Nonprofit Firms," *Nonprofit Management and Leadership*, 1(2), 137–152.

Steinberg, Ronnie, & Jacobs, Jerry A., 1994, "Pay Equity in Nonprofit Organizations: Making Women's Work Visible," in T. Odendahl, & M. O'Neill (Eds.), *Women and Power in the Nonprofit Sector* (pp. 79–120). San Francisco: Jossey-Bass.

Stevenson, David R., Pollak, Thomas H., & Lampkin, Linda M., 1997, *The Nonprofit Almanac 1997: Profiles of Charitable Organizations*, Washington, DC: The Urban Institute Press.

Stuhlmacher, A.F., & Walters, A.E., 1999, "Gender Differences in Negotiation Outcomes: A Meta-Analysis," *Personnel Psychology*, 52(3), 653–677.

Suutari, Vesa, & Christelle Tornikoski, 2001, "The Challenge of Expatriate Compensation: The Sources of Satisfaction and Dissatisfaction Among Expatriates," *The International Journal of Human Resource Management*, 12(3), 389–404.

Taxpayer Bill of Rights 2, 1996, Public Law 104–168, July 30.

Toh, Soo Min, & DeNisi, Angela S., 2003, "Host Country National Reactions to Expatriate Pay Policies: A Model and Implications," *Academy of Management Journal*, 28(4), 606–621.

Towers Perrin, 2005, *Equity Incentives around the World*, consulting report, 18 pages.

Turner, Sarah E., Nygren, Thomas I., & Bowen, William G., 1992, "The NTEE Classification System: Tests of Reliability in the Field of Higher Education," *Voluntas*, 4(1), 73.

Viscusi, W. Kip, & Moore, Michael J., 1991, "Worker Learning and Compensating Wage Differentials," *Industrial and Labor Relations Review*, 55, 80–96.

Vladeck, Bruce C., 1988, "The Practical Differences in Managing Nonprofits: A Practitioner's Perspective," in M. O'Neil, & D.R. Young (Eds.), *Educating Managers of Nonprofit Organizations* (pp. 71–81). New York: Praeger.

Weisbrod, Burton A., 1983, "Nonprofit and Proprietary Sector Behavior: Wage Differentials among Lawyers," *Journal of Labor Economics*, 1(3), 246–263.

Weisbrod, Burton A., 1986, "Toward a Theory of the Voluntary Nonprofit Sector in a Three-Sector Economy," in S. Rose-Ackerman (Ed.), *The Economics of Nonprofit Institutions* (pp. 21–44). Oxford: Oxford University Press.

Weisbrod, Burton A., 1988, *The Nonprofit Economy*, Cambridge MA: Harvard University Press.

Weisbrod, Burton A., & Schlesinger, M., 1986, "Public, Private, Nonprofit Ownership and the Response to Asymmetric Information: The Case of Nursing Homes," in S. Rose-Ackerman (Ed.), *The Economics of Nonprofit Institutions: Studies in Structure and Policy* (pp. 133–151). Oxford: Oxford University Press.

Werner, Steve, & Gemeinhardt, Gretchen, 1995, "Nonprofit Organizations: What Factors Determine Pay Levels? *Compensation & Benefits Review*, 27(5), 53–60.

World Family Corp. v. Commissioner of the Internal Revenue Service, 1983, 81, TC 958.

Young, Dennis R., 1984, "Performance and Reward in Nonprofit Organizations: Evaluation, Compensation, and Personnel Incentives," PONPO, Working Paper No. 79, and ISPS, Yale University, Working Paper No. 2079.

Young, Dennis R., 1987, "Executive Leadership in Nonprofit Organizations," in W.W. Powell (Ed.), *The Nonprofit Sector: A Research Handbook* (pp. 167–179). New Haven, CT: Yale University Press.

Young, Dennis R., Hollister, R.M., Hodgkinson, V.A. & Associates., 1993, *Governing, Leading, and Managing Nonprofit Organizations: New Insights from Research and Practice*, San Francisco: Jossey-Bass.

Young, Dennis, & Steinberg, Richard, 1995, *Economics for Nonprofit Managers*. New York: Foundation Center.

Zimmerman, David J., 1992, "Regression toward Mediocrity in Economic Stature," *American Economic Review*, 82, 409–429.

Index